CREATED to Praise

Seven Expressions of the Bride

NANCY EXLEY MORGAN

Created To Praise: Seven Expressions of the Bride
Published by Teshuvah Publishing
PO Box 15115
Savannah, GA 31416

Unless otherwise indicated, Scripture quotations are taken from, and follow the format of, *The New King James Version* Copyright 1999, published by Thomas Nelson Publishers.

Cover by Monica Nagy
M&N Marketing Group
Art by Bill Johnson
Editorial Services by Palmalea Pratt

Library of Congress Cataloging-in-Publication Data
Morgan, Nancy E.
Created to Praise/Nancy E. Morgan
ISBN 978-0-9727366-2-6

First Edition

Printed in the United States of America

www.daystararise.com

In *Created to Praise,* Nancy Morgan has created a praiseworthy work that reflects not only her extensive research on the biblical subject of praise but also her life of praise and devotion to the God of Israel.

By analyzing the foundations of praise in the Hebrew language, this book suggests ideas that open for the reader new vistas and possibilities in praise and worship.

For those who are being led by the Holy Spirit to investigate and to act upon the biblical premise of restoring Davidic praise to the body of the Messiah, this work will be very stimulating and helpful.

John D. Garr, Ph.D., Th.D.
Founder & President
Restoration Foundation

Created to Praise will lead you into higher levels of praise, utilizing the seven Hebrew words in Scripture that mean Praise. Each word translated Praise has other meanings that add practical insight to our praises.

The description of each of the seven words is extraordinary, using Scripture to show how the word is used. The author gives an example of the "Praise" word used in scripture and then explains the true meaning to give the reader understanding of the nuances of each word.

Nancy takes you through all seven words, explaining each word in depth and leaving the reader with a greater understanding of the types of praise and the purposes of each type. This is knowledge everyone should have and is indispensable for those who lead praise and worship as well as those who have authority over it.

I urge all believers to catch the spirit of *Created to Praise*, to take this teaching to heart and make praising Him an essential part of every prayer, every gathering, and certainly every service.

William J. Morford
Author, *The Power New Testament: Revealing Jewish Roots*

TABLE OF CONTENTS

DEDICATION

To my daughters and their families:

Kimberly and Chip

Melanie and Roy

My grandchildren:

Alyssa, Mary, Zachary, Austin and Brandon

May each of you fulfill the call and destiny for which

you have been created: to live a life of praise to our God

and honor the One who has redeemed us all ~

Jesus - Y'shua our Messiah!

ACKNOWLEDGMENTS

I would like to first acknowledge my LORD, God and King, Creator of the Universe, for blessing me with His Salvation, for the revelation of His Word and for His Holy Spirit who has so faithfully led me.

I would also like to express my deep gratitude to Susan Bartlett whose friendship, encouragement, and invaluable support allowed me to see this work to completion. Your administrative gifting has helped navigate this project. From my heart, I thank you.

I would like to thank Pam Pratt who spent many hours editing. Your literary skills have helped me to more effectively communicate Biblical and Hebraic concepts. Your gift has helped bring excellence and clarity to this work. May the LORD continue to gift you with the pen of a ready writer.

Thank you, Monica Nagy, for blessing me so freely with your stellar marketing skills and talents. Your gift in graphic arts is beautifully displayed on the cover of this book. May the LORD richly repay you for your time and efforts.

I thank everyone who has offered me words of encouragement, especially those friends who expressed confidence in what the LORD has given me. Without your encouragement, I would not have undertaken this work.

And to all those who have helped in any way, may the LORD bless each one of you with His everlasting joy. He brings His reward with Him.

FOREWORD

Not knowing how to speak or write the Hebrew language, I have used the Hebrew words for praise listed in the Strong's Concordance and not the forms found today in the written and spoken language of Hebrew. I have also used the Strong's Concordance to reference the words from the King James Version of the Bible to Hebrew and Greek Lexicons. Focusing on the definitions from the lexicons, I have taken the liberty to occasionally add the endings –s, -ed and –ing for easier reading. For the purposes of this book, I used praise words when their focus was praise to God and rarely when they expressed praise or blessing from God to man or man to man.

Translation for any word can be problematic. Lists of definitions in Strong's and the Hebrew and Greek lexicons give each translator of Scripture various definition-choices. Since only one word or phrase can be used to translate *praise*, the word-choice is at the discretion of the translator. This is evident when we compare various translations. For this reason, I have attempted to consider all definitions and explore the spectrum of their uses throughout selected Scriptural passages.

Knowing the definitions of the seven Hebrew words for *praise* is only the beginning of understanding Biblical *praise*. In order to fully appreciate the depth and expression of each Hebrew word, we must consider not only the word's definition but also its usage and context in each passage.

I personally have come to see all Scripture as one continuous work. However, for clarity of reference for various readers, I have used the terms Old and New Testaments or Old and New Covenants. In conclusion, although I have done much personal study, this work is essentially a work of the heart.

PREFACE

One evening I received a call bearing startling news that pierced my heart. As soon as the message was delivered, the unnamed caller left me with the dial tone ringing in my ears. In shock and disbelief, I slowly hung up the phone and headed to my living room where I usually pray. I asked the LORD, "What should I do? Should I intercede? War in the Spirit?" As I knelt down by the sofa, my emotions were in turmoil and I began to cry. Then, just as suddenly as the storm came, I heard the still, small voice of the LORD speak to me. He simply said, "You were created for My praise."

The LORD ignored the messenger and the message. He did not direct me to prayer. It was as if He was separating me from this troubling situation. He reminded me of Psalm 102:18. Picking up my Bible, I read, "This shall be written for the generation to come; and the *people who shall be created shall praise the LORD."* In my heart He spoke, "Nancy, You were created for My praise."

What an awesome thought – my life was created for His praise! A little melody began to sing in my heart. I spent the rest of the evening wrapped in the presence of the King. Penning a new song, my search to understand and fulfill this wonderful *call to praise* had just begun.

Created to Praise!

Created to praise You, Created to bless You,
Created to worship You, I bow before Your throne.
Created to love You, Created to serve You,
Created to dwell with You, I'll be Your very own.

For You have created all things for Your pleasure,
You have created all things for Your name,
You have created all things for Your glory,
You have created all things for Your praise!

The earth was in darkness, without form and empty,
Your Spirit was hov'ring, in power and might,
Piercing the silence, Your mighty voice thundered,
Announcing creation's dawn,
"Let there be Light!"

You have created the earth with its treasures,
The mountains, the valleys, the skies and the seas,
The sun and the moon, the star-studded heavens,
Creatures both large and small,
And fruit-bearing seed.

Still, You were lonely, You had no companion,
Your heart longed for someone to stand by Your side,
You searched deep within You, And out of Your Being,
You brought forth Your heart's desire,
"Let's make a bride!"

You set out to create man in Your image,
After Your likeness, to walk in Your ways,
Out of the dust You fashioned and formed him,
You breathed in the breath of life,
Created for Your praise!

But knowing he'd fall, You made a provision,
You sent forth Your Son in the form of a man,
Conformed to His death we are raised in His likeness,
Forever to reign with You,
Fulfilling all Your plan!

You have created all things for Your pleasure,
You have created all things for Your name,
You have created all things for Your glory,
You have created all things for Your praise![*]

PROLOGUE

As I was driving to work one morning the LORD asked me, "Nancy, who wrote Psalm 100?" Maneuvering through traffic I was unable to pick up my Bible and turn to it so I tried to picture the title above the psalm. Is it a psalm of David, or is the psalmist named? As I searched my memory, suddenly the Holy Spirit dropped the answer into my spirit. I said, "LORD, You wrote Psalm 100! You are the Living Word. All Scripture was Spirit-breathed by You including all the psalms!" Then the LORD followed with, "And to whom did I address My psalm?" I recited the first line under my breath, "Make a joyful noise unto the LORD all ye lands..." All the lands, LORD, all the nations! You wrote Psalm 100 to all the nations." He questioned further, "And how long did it take for all the nations to hear the psalm I sang to them?"

I began to process the answer. First, Y'shua*, the Living Word of God, sang His psalm into the ears of an Israeli psalmist, who sang the psalm to the nation of Israel. For many years only the ears of Israel heard the song, except for a few Gentiles who joined themselves to God's people. Then in the fullness of time, Messiah came to earth, renewed the covenant and sent His disciples into all the world to preach the gospel. Centuries later, the printing press was invented. The Bible was printed and eventually distributed to the nations. I said, "LORD, much time has gone by and yet there are still people in every nation that have not heard the song You wrote to them!"

The LORD began to show me the significance of Psalm 100. It is addressed to all peoples and presents the Pathway to His Presence. Not only is Israel invited to enter His gates with thanksgiving and His courts with praise, but all nations are invited to praise and come before Him. I also began to realize that all seven of the Hebrew words for praise found in the Scriptures are contained in this psalm, either directly, by definition or by practice. Our God invites all people everywhere to offer all seven Hebrew expressions of praise to Him.

---

* Y'shua is the Hebrew name for Jesus. It means "Yah (or Yahweh) saves."

The Beginning

In Genesis we are introduced to an Artist who sees "the end from the beginning."[†] This Artist is our God. Witness the events of ages past. Angels gasp as the Master lays down the first strokes of creation. Through the halls of eternity a question rings, "What is this wonder?" Emerging on the canvas of time is a picture of a man and a woman in a garden. The hosts of heaven cry in exclamation, "What is man that You are mindful of Him..?"[1]

Without a word, the Triune Artist continues to paint with colors of unfathomable love and eternal intent. Suddenly His work of art unveils a mystery: the heart of a holy Bridegroom for a holy Bride. Her voice colors the canvas with praise. It is a voice the Bridegroom longs to hear. Her praise is a rainbow of song sung to Him through the ages. She calls to Him, "Come!" This book is about that call.

Testimony in the Garden

In the beginning God created and placed His Bride[‡] in a beautiful garden. Surrounded with pictures and patterns of Himself, the Bridegroom's nature was displayed in glorious array. Day after day the heavens declared His glory and night after night the heavens uttered the message of His love. Each day the sun of creation rose and left its tabernacle of the morning, making its circuit across the heavens. Its journey became a light-filled testimony of the Son-Bridegroom going forth from *His* chambers to the side of His beloved.[2] The daily course of the sun prefigured the testimony of the gospel: like a strong man running a race, the Son would leave His heaven and "for the joy set before Him"[3] win the prize – His Bride.

[†] From the beginning God set all things into motion. Isaiah 46:10 states, "Declaring the end from the beginning, and from ancient times things that are not yet done, saying, 'My counsel shall stand, and I will do all My pleasure.'" We read in Acts 15:18, "Known to God from eternity are all His works."

[‡] The first letter of Genesis is the letter *Bet* meaning tent or house. God begins creation by building a "house" for Himself. In Hebraic thinking the meaning of "building a house" is for a man to take a bride and have children. Mankind, male and female, were created to be His Bride. Each individual must choose whether to receive His love and walk in union with God, our Creator.

Life filled the garden completing the bride's joy. God walked with her in the cool of the evening until sin entered the garden and disrupted their fellowship. Since then, the Son has left heaven and returned. Time and history have witnessed His suffering, death and resurrection. The "Sun of Righteousness"[4] has paid the full price to restore His Bride. As a consequence of this sacrifice, the bride issued from His side and is now preparing herself for the "Marriage Supper of the Lamb."[5]

We have been created to praise!

The story of God and mankind began in a garden and we are promised in Revelation 22 that we will one day be restored to life in His garden.[6] We are living in the days our Lord spoke of as "the times of restoration of all things, which God has spoken by the mouth of all His holy prophets since the world began."[7] Praise, worship, fellowship and communion were perfectly expressed in the garden because sin was not present. Since the first Pentecost[§] recorded in the book of Acts, the indwelling Holy Spirit has been given to the Bride to lead her into Truth and teach her all things concerning our LORD. Y'shua[¶] said, "When He, the Spirit of Truth has come, He will guide you into all Truth; for He will not speak on His own authority, but whatever He hears He will speak; and He will tell you things to come."[8] One of these "things to come" is a deeper revelation of His praise. The psalmist prophesies in Psalm 102:

**"May this be put on record for a future generation;
May a people yet to be created *praise ADONAI* [the LORD]."[9]****

Today, we are that generation. Through the power of the Holy Spirit we have been invited and empowered to praise the LORD.

---

§   Pentecost is the Greek word for the Hebrew *Shavuot*, the Feast of Weeks..

¶   Y'shua is the Hebrew name for Jesus. It means "Yah (Yahweh or God) saves."

**   When we see the word LORD typed in all capital letters (in the King James Version and New King James Version of the Bible), it stands for the Hebrew name of God YHWH, often transliterated as Yahweh, Yahveh, Jehovah or Yehovah and translated as the title *ADONAI* in the Complete Jewish Bible.

When fully expressed, true praise results in higher worship, communion and fellowship with the Creator. As we explore the expansive revelation of *praise*, we will enter a new garden and, as at the beginning, will experience an intimacy that will plumb the breadth, length, height and depth of praise. This praise will build a throne for the "glory of God" to cover the earth "as the waters cover the sea,"[10] for God inhabits the praises of His people.[11]

Kingdom Protocol

In the ancient East there was a prescribed protocol for approaching a King. For example, an ambassador, citizen or supplicant never entered the presence of the King without gifts. Entrance to the throne room was only by invitation. The King would extend his scepter to grant permission for entry. Again, once in the King's presence, those allowed entry could not leave without his express permission, nor could they turn their backs to him when exiting.

The book of Esther is replete with insights into the Eastern court protocol of that day. It is in this book that we find glimpses into God's desires for the gifts of our praise and worship. The pattern and designs illustrated in the Old Covenant offer present-day believers, His Bride, unique and in-depth revelation of "kingdom" praise and worship. The book of Esther is an important key to the discovery of this level of worship.

The story in Esther begins with a maiden chosen by God to be the king's bride. For one year, Esther, along with other beautiful maidens, bathed in myrrh, spices and other oils. Each girl would be considered for the position of queen. Before being presented to the king, each maiden chose the garments she would wear and the gifts she would present to the king. When it was Esther's turn to visit the king, she consulted the King's chamberlain as to what would please him. Upon the chamberlain's advice, she chose garments whose color and style the king favored. The gifts she brought to the king were also at the chamberlain's discretion. Esther did not "lean to her own understanding."[12] It is this spirit of submission and humility that brought Esther Godly wisdom. Who was this chamberlain upon whose counsel Esther leaned? In this story-picture he is the Holy Spirit. How different from Queen Vashti! This distinction of seeking the King's heart above her own separated and exalted Esther in the king's eyes.

Esther operated in a heavenly protocol. She brought to the king a praise that was the result of seeking God's wisdom. Her submission to the chamberlain's counsel, coupled with humility, won her the crown. Her promotion was ultimately from God.

We find another illustration of perfected praise and worship in the book of Luke. It is the story of the woman who offered a precious possession, an alabaster box.[13] Breaking this valuable box, she poured a costly perfume on Jesus' feet. It was an offering of love. Now Jesus' forgiveness and acceptance of her was her most precious possession. The alabaster box was nothing compared to Him. She brought an offering pleasing to her Bridegroom, lavishing her love upon Him in the most exquisite way. Like Esther, she thought *only of Him* and sought only *His* pleasure, not her own.

Oftentimes we bring to our LORD offerings of praise and worship according to our own preferences and perspectives. How often do we seek *His* pleasure? Like buried treasures, the desires of the LORD are hidden within the pages of His scriptures. As the chamberlain in Esther had hidden knowledge of the King's desires, the Word of God, revealed by the Holy Spirit, has hidden in its pages the secrets of the King's pleasure. Beautiful treasures of gold, silver and precious jewels are there for those who are willing to mine His life-giving Word for revelation of Him.[14]

These treasures and precious revelations are clothed in Hebraic garments but again can be found by believers today."†† To those who are willing to rediscover the colors and styles of the Messiah and His world, it is a treasure hunt. For the scriptures say, "You will seek Me and find Me, when you search for Me with all of Your heart."[15]

---

†† A reference to Esther as she sought the King's pleasure. Esther 2:15

Y'shua ~ He is Praise!

To discover the secrets of entering His presence, we must first look into the life of Y'shua. Y'shua was "born to praise." His lineage was from the house of the tribe of Judah whose name means "praised and celebrated."[16] A very noteworthy concept is found in the Hebrew letters for the name *Judah* (transliterated from Hebrew as *Yehudah*). The Hebrew word *Yehudah* is spelled with the letters of God's name Yahweh (YHWH) but with a "D" or *Dalet* inserted. This letter *Dalet* means "door." So from the meaning of its letters, *Yehudah* means "Door to Yahweh." How significant that the tribe of Judah was the "door" of Messiah's entrance to earth. Even more so that He then opened the "door" to heaven for us. And what a wonder that the letters describing the "Door to Yahweh" make up the word defined as "praise."

Additionally, *Yehudah,* the door to Yahweh, comes from the Hebrew word for praise, *yadah.*‡‡ This word means "to throw, cast or shoot our praises with open hand in strength and victory." As we look at the beginnings of the tribe of Judah, we see Leah, Jacob's wife, bringing forth a son whom she named Judah. This son was cast forth by her as "a praise" to her God. As a result of her praise, this son Judah was sent as an arrow into the heart of the enemy. This act of praise pinnacles in Jacob's prophecy to Judah: "Judah, you are the one whom your brothers shall praise (*yadah*); your hand shall be on the neck of your enemies [Your brothers shall extend their open hands to You in praise and Your hands shall bind the neck of Your enemies]; your father's sons shall bow down to you.... The scepter *or* leadership shall not depart from Judah, nor the ruler's staff from between his feet, until *Shiloh* [the Messiah, the Peaceful One] comes to Whom it belongs, and to Him shall be the obedience of the people."[17]

---

‡‡ *Yadah* – pronounced *yah-dah'* – *Yadah* is the Hebrew praise word used for "casting" or "throwing" stones and "shooting" arrows. The very act of giving birth is a type of casting. Birthing is accompanied by energy, force and forward motion. *Yud,* the first Hebrew letter of the word *yadah* which means "hand," is associated with the "revelation of birth." See Chapter Six.

Who is this *Shiloh*? He is the culmination of Leah's birth-praise. He is called Messiah and the Peaceful One. We know His name as Y'shua, the One who was born to praise, and whose life and testimony is praise to our Father.

Y'shua ~ Enters with Praise

Y'shua's earthly life begins with praise. Mary (*Miriam* in Hebrew) extols and praises the God of heaven while Messiah is still in her womb.[18] John the Baptist evidences his praise by leaping for joy in Elizabeth's womb.[19] The angels herald their praise with their song of "Glory to God in the highest and on earth peace, goodwill toward men."[20] The shepherds glorify and praise God as they return to their flocks.[21] The magi praise Him with gifts of gold, frankincense and myrrh. It is not surprising then that the entrance of the One who was "born to praise" is extolled and welcomed with praise. Y'shua, who enters with praise, is now the door through whom **we** enter His kingdom with praise and thanksgiving.

Y'shua ~ Voice of Praise

The Savior was not only born to receive praise, but also is the voice of praise itself. He offers perfect praise to His Father from 'before the foundation of the world"[§§] to the "forever"[¶¶] of Revelation. He is "The Psalmist" and from eternity composed the Psalms to be sung. These Psalms tell of His earthly ministry, His work of salvation, His thoughts and even His feelings. Casting their light on the gospels,

---

§§   John 1:1-3 tells us that the eternal Word was in the beginning, was with God and was God. Ancient Rabbinical teaching confirms that the pre-existent Word created the heavens and the earth. This eternal Living Word revealed Himself to mankind in time. This Word existed as "Praise." We read in Acts 15:18, "Known to God from eternity are all His works." As the Lamb was slain from the foundation of the world and as Y'shua was born in the "fullness of time," so too there was a "fullness of time" for every work, including the inspiration and revelation of each written word. Isaiah 46:9b-10 states that "I am God and there is no other; I am God, and there is none like Me, declaring the end from the beginning, and from ancient times things that are not yet done...."

¶¶   Resurrected saints, voicing the heart of Y'shua, sing praises around the throne of God forever.

the Psalms offer us insights into Y'shua's earthly and spiritual experience. These *Tehillim*^{***} (Psalms) give man the perfect words to express his own thoughts, feelings, confessions and adoration to the Father. This praise is clearly and perfectly articulated by the Holy Spirit.

Who Wrote the Psalms?

As we consider the scriptures, especially the Psalms and the Prophets, let us remember that the written word is the expression of the Living Word, Jesus – Y'shua. Y'shua, the "Revealed Word", is the Psalmist of Psalms speaking to His Father and to men. Through the Holy Spirit "The Word" spoke into the ears of men over time and through history. Faithful men wrote down His Word. Recognizing that Y'shua is the Word, we also see that He is "The Prophet"[22] who prophesies about Himself into the ears of men. The Word (Y'shua) is the well-spring of encouragement, comfort, rebuke and revelation as well as the voice who reveals events to come.

An Example

Sometimes we find the human writer of Scripture was allowed to overhear a conversation between the Father and Son. It is amazing that men of God were privileged to become a part of the dialogue of heaven.

David wrote, "The LORD said to my Lord, 'Sit at My right hand, till I make Your enemies Your footstool.'"[23] Who is speaking to whom here? LORD (typed in all capital letters translates Yahweh or *ADONAI*) is God the Father and Lord (typed with a capital L and followed by lower case letters) is Y'shua, His Son. Both are Lord over David. The Father is speaking to His Son, Y'shua. In other words, "*ADONAI* said to Y'shua, 'Sit at My right hand till I make Your enemies Your footstool.'"

*** *Tehillim* – pronounced *te-hil-lim'* – is the Hebrew word for "Psalms." See Chapter Five.

In Psalm 2 we hear a decree initiated by the Father but enacted into law by the Son. Again, recognizing God the Father as *ADONAI* and Y'shua as the Lord, we can better understand all that was given to Y'shua by the Father (*ADONAI*):

"...I have set my king on My holy hill of Zion."[24]

Y'shua then repeats what *ADONAI* has said to Him, establishing what the Father had already decreed:

"I will declare the decree: The LORD (*ADONAI*) said to me, 'You are My son; today I have begotten You. Ask of Me, and I will give You the nations for Your inheritance; and the ends of the earth for Your possession. You shall break them with a rod of iron; You shall dash them to pieces like a potter's vessel.'"[25]

Only Y'shua can fit this description, certainly not any man.

As we glimpse into Psalm 110 and Psalm 2, what does *ADONAI* give Y'shua? The following is a list of the Father's gifting to the Son:

1. Lordship over the believer
2. Authority over His enemies
3. Kingship on Mount Zion
4. Sonship to the Father
5. Inheritor of the nations
6. Possessor of the world
7. Victor over the ungodly

These heavenly conversations in Psalm 110 and Psalm 2 bring revelation of the Father's will and the Son's right to decree and inherit.

Praise ~ Its Origins

To better understand praise we need to look at the origins of the word. This is best done by referencing the original language from which the word *praise* comes. In our English language this word often loses its depth and dimension. This is a result of difficulties in translation and the evolution of words themselves over time. By re-introducing the original language and translating the appropriate word for praise into Hebrew, we discover that there are seven different Hebrew words for the one English word *praise*. The Hebrew words for praise can be variously translated from English to Hebrew in seven different forms: *hallel, shabach, tehillah, todah, yadah, barak* and *zamar*. For some it may be a surprise to learn that all of these words not only express inward adoration but also specific physical expressions of joy and praise. Whether in Hebrew or English, however, the heart attitude of the worshiper is central.

In these last days God is gifting us with greater insights into His Word. These insights allow us to more freely worship Him in Spirit and in Truth. As we explore the different meanings for praise, we will discover hidden treasures that will bring a greater reverence and revelation of our God.

As the Holy Spirit translates this revelation of praise into understanding, we can "show forth the praises of Him who has called (us) out of darkness and into His marvelous light."[26] The Greek word for "show forth" here is *exaggello* (pronounced *ex-ang-el'-lo*).[27] This word comes from the word "exit" and the word "angel" which means messenger or message. Its definition is to publish, celebrate and allow the message of praise to exit forth out of our beings. Praise dwells within us in the person of the Holy Spirit and needs the cooperation of our will and the vehicle of our voice to express praise to the Father and the Son. With the breath of the Holy Spirit, we breathe out the praises of God!

"Let everything that has breath praise (hallel) the LORD!"[28]

NOTES

1   Psalm 8:4
2   Psalm 19:1-6
3   Hebrews 12:2
4   Malachi 4:2
5   Revelation 19:7
6   Revelation 22:1,2,14
7   Acts 3:21
8   John 16:13
9   Psalm 102:18 CJB
10 Isaiah 11:9; Habakkuk 2:14; Habakkuk 3:3b
11 Psalm 22:3 (KJV)
12 Proverbs 3:5
13 Luke 7:37-38 (KJV)
14 Job 28:1-6, 12-13, 20-21, 23, 27-28
15 Jeremiah 29:13
16 James Strong, S.T.D., L.L.D., *Strong's Exhaustive Concordance of the Bible* (Madison, N.J.: James Strong, 1973), *Hebrew Dictionary of the Old Testament: Judah, #3063, p.47* from *yadah #3034,* p. 47.
17 Genesis 49:8,10 (Amplified Bible); also see Numbers 24:17 and Psalm 60:7
18 Luke 1:46-55
19 Luke 1:44
20 Luke 2:13-14
21 Luke 2:20
22 Deuteronomy 18:15-19; See John 6:14, Acts 3:22-23 and Acts 7:37
23 Psalm 110:1
24 Psalm 2:6
25 Psalm 2:7-9
26 I Peter 2:9 (KJV)
27 Strong, *Greek Dictionary of the New Testament: exaggello*, #1804, p. 29.
28 Psalm 150:6 – The praise word *hallel* is the subject of the next chapter.

Hallel

Rainbow of Praise

The first of the seven words we will consider is *hallel* (pronounced *hah-lal'*). Like the *Shekinah*,* *hallel's* very essence is the shining forth of light and color. Just as bright white light contains all the colors of the rainbow, so *hallel* contains within its meaning the expressions and manifestations of all the other words for praise, including its own. How fitting this is, since the first act of creation after the heavens and earth was the release of light. Rays streaming into water droplets or prisms divide into seven primary colors and form the arc of the rainbow.† The book of Revelation describes an emerald rainbow encircling the throne of God.[1] Seen from above, the rainbow is a complete circle and like *hallel* displays seven distinct colors. Since the number seven in scripture denotes perfection and completion, we can see that the seven Hebrew words for praise altogether form the complete expression of praise offered in the full light of His Truth.

Hallel is the most frequently used word translated **praise** in the Bible. The first chronological usage of the word *hallel*‡ is found in Psalms 113-118. According to the Jewish sages, these psalms were sung as early as Israel's Exodus from Egypt. Verse 1 of Psalm 113 begins:

"Praise the LORD§ (*Halleluyah*),¶
Praise (*Hallel*), O servants of the LORD
Praise *(Hallel)* the name of the LORD.[2]

---

*   *Shekinah* is the Hebrew word meaning "dwelling," and is associated with the continual, abiding, manifest glory of God.

†   The rainbow has seven primary colors: Red, Orange, Yellow, Green, Blue, Indigo and Violet (ROYGBIV).

‡   *Hallel* is also sometimes transliterated as "*Halal*."

§   When LORD is spelled with all capital letters in the King James Version and New King James Version, it translates the holy name of God. Called the Tetragrammaton, it is formed with the four Hebrew letters *Yud, Heh, Vav, Heh (YHVH or YHWH)* and is sometimes translated Jehovah, Yehovah, Yahweh or Yahveh. The Complete Jewish Bible translates this name as *ADONAI*, a title meaning "LORD."

¶   Literally, **Hallel** (praise) **u** (you) **Yah** (God) or "You praise God," an instruction to give *Hallel* to God.

Hallel is offered:

> In public worship
> As protocol before the king
> As praise before the army
> At the Tabernacle of David
> At the Temple of the LORD
> At the Feasts of the LORD
> As the marriage song at weddings

It is an exuberant and joyous word. Filled with celebration, it calls for total abandonment of self in praise and worship. *Hallel* is ascension. It is praise that translates us into higher dimensions of His glory.

Hallel ~ The Definition

The following adjectives describe the Hebrew word *hallel*: "to be clear – originally of sound, but usually of color; to shine; to make a show; to boast; to be clamorously foolish; to rave; to celebrate; commend; glory; give light; be mad; feign self mad; be mad against; rage; give in marriage; sing praise; be worthy of praise; renowned."[3]

Further enlightenment is gained from the Hebrew Lexicon: "shine, to begin to shine, flash forth light, boast, be boastful, make one's boast, boastful ones, boasters, praise, to be praised, worthy of praise, praised, shout, shout for joy, shouting acclamations to, cry aloud, break through or out (in a cry), rejoice, marriage song, implore, commended, celebrated, renowned, glory, make into a fool, make fool of, mad, act madly or like a madman."[4]

Hallel is the highest expression of praise and a necessary foundational revelation to our worshiping the LORD in Spirit and in Truth. *Hallel*, united with a grasp of the accomplished work of Messiah, produces a demonstrative outpouring of praise. This celebratory praise looks back on our deliverance as a completed work and hails the author and finisher of that work, the King of kings and Lord of lords. *Hallel* begins in our innermost being and radiates outward through our entire person to our LORD! Igniting the candle of our soul, it bursts into fiery flames of love and praise to our Creator. It cannot and will not be contained. It must go forth and manifest itself in the highest magnitude of exaltation of the God of glory.

Hallel ~ The World's Party!

Picture a large sports arena during a big event. The crowds are cheering, waving, shouting, whistling, sounding noisemakers, ringing bells, shouting into megaphones, holding up banners, loudly declaring their loyalty and encouraging their favorite team. Marching bands are dressed in colorful array while playing bright and lively music. Accompanied by booming drums and clanging cymbals, the band parades in measured steps through intricate formations. The crowd responds with thunderous applause and cheers. At the same time, a kaleidoscope of shouting cheerleaders, baton-twirling majorettes, spectacular light shows and exploding fireworks surround the event. Dancing balloons and showers of confetti complete the show. This pageantry, along with brilliant displays of light and color, are a perfect example of the world's version of *hallel*. Should not our *hallel* before the LORD far exceed the world's *hallel* at a sports event? We are praising the King of kings and Lord of lords. He is worthy of all our praise!

Hallel ~ The Father's Party!

We see a beautiful picture of *hallel* in the story of the prodigal's return to his Father.[5] Just imagine the scene. The servants are hustling and bustling with the commands of their master to prepare for a great celebration of the son's return. I can just hear them whispering to each other, "He's finally come home! Can you believe it? The master wants to throw a grand party! We must prepare the fatted calf and decorate the halls. Our Lord has asked for the royal robe and the signet ring. I'll call the minstrels. We'll sing and dance with great joy. Quickly now, send a courier to invite the guests from all around. You get the wine from the cellar. The son who was lost is now found. We'll all join in the great feast!" Since we are a part of heaven on earth, should we not join the party? Let's *hallel!*

Hallel ~ **Heaven's Party!**

Our Father throws the Party of parties for His children. To the returning remnant of Israel the LORD says, "The LORD your God is in your midst, The Mighty One, He will save; He will rejoice[6] over you with gladness,[7] He will quiet you with His love, He will joy[8] (spin around and around) over you with singing."[9] Our Father delights so much in our turning and returning to Him that He extends His gracious forgiveness and throws a great celebration! He Himself sings and dances *hallel* over us. I cannot even imagine His pure joy and delight over His children who were once lost, but who now have returned home. The scripture tells us "...there will be more joy in heaven over one sinner who turns to God from his sins than over ninety-nine righteous people who have no need to repent."[10] The angels rejoice as each name is recorded in the Book of Life. *Hallel!*

The world's *hallel* is not to be compared to the *hallel* manifested by heaven and the Father. It focuses on the earthly and temporal which fade and pass away. In contrast, the display of the believers' *hallel* to God is the testimony of a sold-out people who express their love and devotion to Him with their whole beings. Its revelation and demonstration extol Him. Its expression spotlights His wondrous works and mighty saving power. *Hallel* to the LORD has no end. We will *hallel* the eternal God and His everlasting life and power throughout eternity.

Who, When, Where, How and Why to *Hallel*[**]

Who receives *hallel* in scripture? The honor of *hallel* is given to **the LORD, His holy name,** and **His Word.** It praises **the King, the LORD who dwells in Zion, the Holy One of Israel** and **the beauty of His holiness.**

** For Scripture references see the *Hallel* Concordance in the "Created to Praise Study Guide."

Not only is *hallel* given to the **King of kings**, but it is also extended to those who bear the fruit of the Holy Spirit. The husband in Proverbs 31, a type of Messiah, gives *hallel* to his **godly wife** as she manifests the character and nature of God and demonstrates the King's virtue in her life. *Hallel* is also given by the daughters of Jerusalem to the **Shulamite Bride** in the Song of Solomon. The Shepherd-King Bridegroom extols His bride's beauty and devotion and counts her worthy of the praise (*hallel*) of the daughters of Jerusalem, the queens and the concubines. So, too, our Bridegroom, Y'shua, counts us, **His Bride**, worthy of *hallel* when we display His nature and character.

Who gives *hallel*? Through all the psalms He has inspired, **Y'shua** *hallel*-s[tt] the Father. In and through these psalms He instructs the **soul of every believer**, every child of God, to give *hallel* to the LORD. As we read the psalms and put ourselves in the place of the psalmist, making the words our own, we offer our LORD the utmost *hallel*. We boast of Him. We glory in His presence. We declare the wonders of His person and proclaim His mighty works from the beginning of time into eternity. Taking our place in the symphony of praise, we join all creatures and all creation in *hallel* to our King. In searching the pages of Scripture I found the following list of those the LORD has chosen to bring *hallel*:

The psalmists
Everyone who swears by Him
The poor and needy
Those who dwell in God's house
The servants of the LORD
The generation to come
A people yet to be created
The people of His inheritance
Israel
All the descendants of Israel
All the people

[tt] I have used the endings –s, -ed and –ing to facilitate the flow in English. These are not Hebrew forms. Also I have used the root forms of the Hebrew words for praise which are not the forms used in Modern Hebrew.

All the Gentiles
All the nations
Zion
All creation
Everything that has breath
The heavens
The earth
The seas
Everything that moves in the seas
The great sea creatures
All the depths
The angels
All His hosts
The heaven of heavens
The sun and moon and stars of light
The waters above the heavens
The Levites before the Ark of the LORD
All the assembly
Those who fear the LORD
Those who seek the LORD
Descendants of Jacob
The offspring of Israel
All the living

"The living, the living – they shall thank and *hallel* You...."[11] No person, no creature and no work of creation are excluded. All are called to *hallel* the Maker and Creator of the universe!

Nothing of the flesh or the world is worthy to receive *hallel*. Thus says the LORD, "Let not the wise man glory (*hallel*) in his wisdom, Let not the mighty man glory (*hallel*) in his might, nor let the rich man glory (*hallel*) in his riches."[12] **Neither man nor his works outside of God are worthy of any praise**.

When is *hallel* given? The Psalmist declares: "From the rising of the sun to its going down, the LORD's name is to be *hallel*-ed![13] "Every day will I bless you, and I will *hallel* Your name forever and ever."[14] "While I live I will *hallel* the LORD; I will sing praises to my

God while I have my being."[15] At the Temple Levites were posted "…
to stand every morning to thank and *hallel* the LORD and likewise
at evening."[16] In Psalm 119 we read, "Seven times a day I *hallel*
You because of Your righteous judgments."[17] This is the Psalmist's
response to the treasure of God's Word as revealed to his heart.

Moslems bow and pray to their god five times a day. How much
more should we honor our God, meditate upon His Word and
praise His goodness? **From sun-up to sun-down, every day, forever
and ever, while we live and have our being, every morning and
every evening, seven times a day and continually** we should *hallel*
the LORD, our God. At the Tabernacle of David and the Temple of
Solomon thanksgiving and *hallel* were offered by the Levites **watch
by watch,** or **"twenty-four seven."**

Where is *hallel* given? As stated before, *hallel* is especially
appropriate **in public**. It means to shine forth, make a show, boast,
be clamorously foolish, rave and celebrate in a loud, noisy manner.
This *hallel* is a picture-message the LORD wants us to see and receive.
He invites us to join heaven in its everlasting praise-a-thon. This is a
message for the eyes, ears and heart of His people. Walking in the full
understanding of this type of praise, *hallel*, gives testimony to who
God is and what He has done, both individually and corporately.
The Hebraic understanding of praise is to be expressed in all the
earth and in heaven. Scripture[‡‡] specifically records *hallel* offered in
these places:

> Among the multitude
> Among many people
> Among the nations
> In the gates of the Temple
> In the gates of *ADONAI'S* camp
> In the midst of the assembly
> In the city of our God
> In the company of the elders
> In and from the heavens

[‡‡] For references see the *Hallel* Concordance in the "Created to Praise Study
Guide."

In the heights
In His sanctuary
In His mighty firmament
In the earth
From the earth to the LORD in heaven
At the Tabernacle of David
From the rising to the setting of the sun

How is *hallel* expressed? In each generation God releases unique forms of praise-expressions. Just as His mercy is "new every morning,"[18] so is His creative touch on each generation. This touch is always accompanied by a release of new revelation, power and anointing. This anointing flows with life-giving creativity. Today an outpouring of new songs across the Body of Messiah is evidence of the Master's touch; however, *hallel* is not confined to song only. God's message of praise can also be presented through art, drama and triumphant majestic procession. There are myriad art forms through which God can release creativity – dance, costuming, painting, sculpting and various types of pageantry and light are just a few. More facets of expressive praise are being revealed through time. The spectrum of how God expresses Himself is infinite. Scripture gives us many examples of how to express *hallel*:

With our mouth
With joyful lips
With song
With singing
With dance
With gladness
With voices loud and high
With antiphonal singing
With loud instruments
With the shouting of great shouts
With the words of David & Asaph the seer
From a standing position

David constructed certain musical instruments in order to fulfill the LORD's command to minister *hallel*. In the worship at the Tabernacle of David we have this account: "'...and four thousand praised (*hallel*-ed) the LORD with the *musical instruments*, 'which I made,' said David, 'for giving praise (*hallel*.)'"[19] These instruments were also used at the Temple built by Solomon. At the dedication of this temple we have this account:

> "The priests took their positions, as did the Levites with the LORD's musical instruments, which King David had made for praising the LORD and which were used when he gave thanks, saying, 'His love endures forever.' Opposite the Levites, the priests blew their trumpets, and all the Israelites were standing."[20]

The following instruments are mentioned in conjunction with *hallel* in scripture: the harp, the shofar, the trumpet, the lute, the lyre, the timbrel, tambourines, stringed instruments, loud cymbals and clashing cymbals.

Why is *hallel* offered? The list of God's attributes and wonders is beyond our ability to enumerate. Here are a few reasons to *hallel* drawn from the pages of His Word that have brought forth expressive praise from the heart of His people:

> The LORD is great and worthy.
> His judgments are righteous.
> He lets my soul live.
> His name is pleasant.
> His name alone is exalted.
> His acts are mighty.
> His greatness is excellent.
> His greatness is unsearchable.
>
> His glory is above heaven and earth.
> He has delivered the life of the poor from the hand
>   of evildoers.
> The LORD is good and His mercy is everlasting.
> He has granted good harvest and provision.
> He is good; He is God and He is love.

Salvation and honor and glory and power belong to
the LORD God!
The LORD God omnipotent reigns!

We have this instruction from the LORD Himself, "'But let him who glories (*hallel-s*) glory (*hallel*) in this, that he understands and knows Me, that I Am the LORD, exercising loving-kindness, judgment, and righteousness in the earth. For in these I delight,' says the LORD."[21] Understanding and knowing God is the highest reason to *hallel*.

Hallel ~ Offered by Creation

The sun, moon, stars and celestial bodies radiate *hallel* by their very existence. Created to shine and flash forth light, they exist as continual praise before the Creator. Even the spinning of the earth on its axis is a continual act of rejoicing before the LORD.[§§] *Hallel* is the praise of the angels and the heavenly hosts! It is the praise of all creation, of everything that has breath. It is the loud, boisterous, clamorous, noisy, showy expression of who God is, what He has done, is doing and will yet do. It gives Him glory, crowns Him with praise and fills the earth with His fame.

Hallel ~ As Warfare

David *hallel*-ed in a unique way. He fled from Saul and went to Achish, the king of Gath. When Achish recognized David as King of Israel (even though he had not yet taken the throne), David pretended to be insane and acted like a madman.

> "So he (David) changed his behavior before them, pretended madness (*hallel*-ed) in their hands, scratched on the doors of the gate, and let his saliva fall down on his beard."[22]

---

§§ From the scripture, "Let the earth rejoice" in Psalm 97:1. This Hebrew word for "rejoice' is *giyl* (Strong's Concordance # 1523) and means to "spin around under the influence of any violent emotion; spin around and around like a top."

This behavior was *hallel!* Remember that one of the definitions of *hallel* is to "be mad, feign self mad, be mad against" or, in other words, act crazy. As David acted madly giving *hallel* to God, he was released without a scratch from the snare of the enemy! What a mighty weapon of deliverance! (The unlocking of this word put to rest my concern that David practiced deception here, even though he did not speak.) Now that I understand the root word behind his conduct, I am awed at God's strategies!

Hallel ~ Protocol Before the King

Hallel accompanies the festive ceremony and majestic array at the coronation of the king of Israel. In II Chronicles we find an interesting example:

> "... there was the king standing by his pillar at the entrance (of the temple of the LORD); and the leaders and the trumpeters were by the king. All the people of the land were rejoicing and blowing trumpets, also the singers with musical instruments, and those who led in praise (*hallel*)."[23]

The people of Israel were celebrating their king's ascension to the throne with *hallel!* Recognizing that God teaches us spiritual principles through natural events, we see here a demonstration of kingdom protocol. Let us receive the King of kings with a *hallel* that exalts!

Hallel ~ Before the Army

II Chronicles 20 gives us an example of *hallel* shining forth in the triumphant army of Yahweh Sabbaoth (the LORD of hosts):

> "And when he (Jehoshaphat) had consulted with the people, he appointed those who should sing to the LORD, and who should praise (*hallel*) the beauty of holiness, as they went out before the army and were saying: 'Praise the LORD (Halleluyah), for His mercy

endures forever.' Now when they began to sing and to praise, the LORD set ambushes against the people of Ammon, Moab, and Mount Seir, who had come against Judah; and they were defeated."[24]

Today we can demonstrate Y'shua's victory over Death and the Grave through processional praise. As in Jehoshaphat's day, *hallel* can shine forth through the triumphant army of Messiah. This is the praise that extols the accomplished victory of Y'shua, scatters the enemy and confounds the wise. Imagine being chosen to sing in that choir!

Hallel ~ At the Tabernacle of David

In David's Tabernacle we discover keys pertaining to the ministry of worship. The forty-year ministry at the Tabernacle of David was a prophetic window into kingdom worship. The Ark of the Covenant was placed under a tent made by David. This contrasts with the ministry in the Tabernacle of Moses and the Temple of Solomon, where only the High Priest could enter the Holy of holies once a year. In David's Tabernacle, free access to the Ark was given to both Jews and Gentiles. Unlike the ministry and worship in Moses' Tabernacle and the Temple, David appointed a worship team led by Asaph the seer to minister before the Ark of the LORD day and night. In I Chronicles 16 we read,

> "So David left there (in the Tabernacle of David), before the ark of the covenant of the LORD, Asaph and his brethren, to minister before the ark continually, *as every day's work required.*"[25]

What was every day's work? David outlines a three-fold ministry to be offered before the LORD's Ark: to "bring to remembrance,"¶¶[26] and to thank (*yadah*), and to *hallel [Yahweh] Elohim* of Israel.[27] Continuous *hallel* was to be offered before the LORD day and night, watch by watch.

¶¶ This Hebrew word is variously translated "invoke, record, celebrate (by calling to mind), make petition, and commemorate. (See Endnote #26)

During this incredible window of time, the revelation received was so significant that, in all subsequent revivals in Scripture, the words of David and Asaph the seer were restored as part of the worship. Breathed into this *kairos* time by the Holy Spirit, these psalms prefigured and prophesied the coming kingdom of God and are an important element in decreeing God's reign "on earth as it is in heaven."[28] David received the plans for the Temple as well as the pattern of worship from Yahweh. It was David who set the order of worship and appointed teams of worshipers to minister at his tabernacle. This Davidic worship would carryover to Solomon's Temple.

An astounding prophecy from the book of Amos is quoted in Acts 15:16 confirming the validity of the ministry of *hallel* in the New Covenant:

> "'After this I will return and will rebuild the tabernacle of David, which has fallen down; I will rebuild its ruins, and I will set it up; so that the rest of mankind may seek the LORD, even all the Gentiles who are called by My name, says the LORD, who does all these things.' Known to God from eternity are all His works."[29]

Today *hallel* is being restored. God is releasing His people from the grave clothes of bondage and the traditions of men. He is moving the "kings and priests" of our day into resurrection power and kingdom authority.

At this time we are seeing the restoration of the ministry of the Tabernacle of David in America, Israel and other nations. I personally had the privilege to teach and lead worship on "Prayer Mountain" outside of Kampala, Uganda where this ministry is going forth twenty-four seven. As God's people *hallel*, the praises of God are covering the earth as the waters cover the sea. The result: the enemy is being displaced and the God of Israel exalted above every name that is named. Like a fountain of the deep, the praise of God's people bursts forth, releasing a testimony to God and His works. *Hallel* Y'shua!

Hallel ~ At the Temple

Hallel was offered at the dedication of Solomon's Temple.

> "...it came to pass, when the trumpeters and singers were as one, to make one sound to be heard in praising (*hallel*-ing) and thanking the LORD; and when they lifted up their voice with the trumpets and cymbals and instruments of music, and praised the LORD, saying: 'For He is good; for His mercy endures forever,' that the house, the house of the LORD, was filled with a cloud, so that the priests could not continue ministering because of the cloud; for the glory of the LORD filled the house of God."[30]

Hallel ushers in the GLORY, the *Shekinah* presence of the LORD! "Then Solomon appointed the Levites to praise (*hallel*) and minister (serve) before the priests as the duty of every day required," as a regular part of the ministry at the Temple.[31]

Hallel ~ In Restoration

Later in Israel's history, Hezekiah led a great revival and restored the Temple and its ministry to the nation of Israel.

> "Moreover King Hezekiah and the leaders commanded the Levites to sing praise (*hallel*) to the LORD with the words of David and of Asaph the seer. So they sang praises (*hallel*-s) with gladness, and they bowed their heads and worshiped."[32]

At the rededication of the second temple a great service of *hallel* was held.

> "And they sang **responsively**, praising (*hallel*-ing) and giving thanks to the LORD; 'For He is good, for His mercy endures forever toward Israel.' Then all the people shouted with a great shout, when they praised

(*hallel*-ed) the LORD, because the foundation of the house of the LORD was laid."[33]

The Levites were again set in ministry before the LORD to *hallel* and give thanks by watches.[34] In every revival recorded in the Tanach[***] the Levites were raised up and *hallel* was restored!

Hallel ~ Resurrection Power

The ultimate expression of *hallel* is the resurrection! In the fullness of time the Bride will have been made ready – spirit, soul and body. Then He that is within her, the *Ruach Ha Kodesh* (Holy Spirit), will raise her from the dead to new life and escort her to the throne of her King! She will give herself – her life, will and desires – in total surrender to her Bridegroom. The final expression of this abandonment is portrayed in the power of resurrection as she ascends into the fullness of His presence to attend their wedding. *Hallel* will radiate from the Bride. She will walk in the image of the Bridegroom and will be clothed in His light. Robed in righteousness, she reigns together with Him in the beauty of holiness for all eternity. In the Song of Solomon the Bridegroom-lover extols His beloved. He says,

> "My dove, my perfect one, is the only one, the only one of her mother, the favorite of the one who bore her. The daughters saw her and called her blessed, the queens and the concubines, and they praised (*hallel*-ed) her."[35]

This set-apart Bride-to-be receives *hallel* from those who see her beauty and long to be like her. Her Beloved then cites the praise of those surrounding her as an attribute that draws Him to her. In this context *hallel* is the ultimate reflection of all love, joy and ecstasy that accompanies the wedding of two hearts, making two one. It is the wedding song of love.

[***] *Tanakh* is the Hebrew word for the Old Covenant Scriptures.

The Great *Hallel*

When the *Psalms of Ascent*[†††] (or psalms of *going up* - also referred to as psalms of *aliyah*[‡‡‡]), which are Psalms 120 – 134, are combined with Psalms 135 and 136, they are called the *Great Hallel*. This *Hallel* is made up of Halleluyah Psalms, "halleluyah" meaning "You *hallel* Yah!" or "You give *hallel* to the LORD." It is an instruction to praise. It calls forth the response of *hallel*–praise from God's people. The *Great Hallel* is really the love story of the Bride and her LORD. It portrays the courtship of Y'shua and his Bride from their initial meeting – her cry of distress and subsequent born-again experience – to the consummation of their love celebrated at the wedding supper of the Lamb! It pictures the reconciliation and union of God and man from Genesis to Revelation. The *Great Hallel* is sung at the Feasts of the LORD[§§§] and is our dress rehearsal for His coming and the fulfillment of all things.

The Egyptian *Hallel*

The *Egyptian Hallel* is made up of Psalms 113-118. These psalms, composed long before David lived, recount the history of the children of Israel coming out of Egypt. "The prophets ordained that the six psalms of *Hallel* [literally, *praise*] be recited on each Festival,[¶¶¶] to commemorate times of national deliverance from peril."[36] The

---

[†††] The Hebrew word for ascent is *ma'alah* (pronounced *mah-al-ah'*) and means "a journey to a higher place, a climactic progression." Figuratively it means "arising thoughts." It is #4609 in the Strong's Concordance. For a more in-depth study on these psalms see *Lift Up Your Eyes* Vol. 1 by Nancy E. Morgan.

[‡‡‡] *Aliyah* (going up) is the Hebrew expression for "going up to Jerusalem" for the Feasts of the LORD and also today for the re-gathering of Israelites to the land of Israel.

[§§§] The Feasts of Passover, Pentecost and Tabernacles described in Leviticus 23.

[¶¶¶] **Feast** (Hebrew *moed* – *mo-ade'*) is "an appointment, a fixed time or season, an assembly, a festival." [Strong's #4150]. **Festival** (Hebrew *chag* - *khahg*) is defined as "an appointed assembly, observe a festival, move in a circle, march in a sacred procession, celebrate, dance, be giddy, reel to and fro." [Strong's #2282, 2287]

---

following is a list of significant victories when the *Egyptian Hallel* was sung: by Moses and the nation of Israel "after being saved from the Egyptians at the sea; (by) Joshua, after defeating the kings of Canaan; (by) Deborah and Barak, after defeating Sisera; by Hezekiah, after defeating Sennacherib; (by) Chananyah, Mishael and Azariah**** after being saved from the wicked Nebuchadnezzar; and (by) Mordecai and Esther, after the defeat of the wicked Haman."[37]

"These psalms were singled out as a unit of praise because they contain five fundamental themes of Jewish faith: The Exodus, The Splitting of the Sea, The Giving of the Torah at Sinai, The future (Resurrection) of the dead, and The coming of the Messiah."[38]

How much more appropriate for us to sing the *Hallel* psalms in light of Messiah's total victory over sin, death, Satan, the flesh and the world! What an awesome privilege to have these same words preserved for us that we might join with the saints of all ages in proclaiming them to our Father and the peoples of the earth.

The Egyptian *Hallel* at the Feast of Passover

According to Albert Edersheim in *The Temple: Its Ministry and Services,*

"The singing of the *Hallel* at Passover dates from remote antiquity. The Talmud dwells on its peculiar suitableness for the purpose, since it not only recorded the goodness of God toward Israel, but especially their deliverance from Egypt. Appropriately opening with 'Praise ye Jehovah, ye servants of Jehovah,' the nation of Israel identifies and acknowledges its servant-hood to Jehovah, deliberately underscoring the fact that they were no longer servants of Pharaoh. Hence this *Hallel* is called the Egyptian, or 'the Common,' distinguishing it from the *Great Hallel* (Psalms 120-136)..."[39]

**** Their Babylonian names were Shadrach, Mesheck and Abednego.

Celebrating the victorious and miraculous deeds of the LORD, *Hallel* was sung on the following Feasts: *Pesach* (Passover), *Shavuot* (Pentecost), *Succot* (Tabernacles) and *Hanukkah* (Dedication). The Psalms were sung responsively in a particular way: As the first line of each psalm was read, that line was repeated by the people. The people's response to the other remaining lines was "Hallelujah." An exception to this is found in the reading of Psalm 118. In addition to the first verse, the three lines from verses 25 and 26 were also read and then repeated by the people:

> "Save now, I beseech Thee, O LORD."
> "O LORD, I beseech Thee, send now prosperity."
> "Blessed is he that cometh in the name of the
>   LORD."[40]

Proclaiming God's victory and faithfulness to Yahweh and one another, Y'shua and the disciples sang together the very words we know today as the *Egyptian Hallel*. Part of this *Hallel* (Psalms 113-114) was sung before the *Seder*[††††] meal. The remainder of the *Hallel* (Psalms 115-118) was sung after the meal. Probably Psalms 135 and 136 of the *Great Hallel* were included.

As Y'shua celebrated this meal, He knew what lay before Him. See Him now, His eyes aflame with love, singing *hallel*. Feel His heart race for the "joy set before Him."[41] After singing the last psalm of the *Hallel*, He and His disciples began their walk to the Mount of Olives.[42] Our salvation was secure with Him.

The Key ~ *Hallel* in the New Covenant

Does the Hebrew understanding and expression of the words for *praise* have validity today? How do the seven Hebrew words for praise relate to present-day believers? As I began my research, I looked to see if these seven Hebrew words had Greek counterparts in the New Testament, and if their Hebraic expression was understood or even practiced by the new Messianic community. Searching the

---

†††† *Seder* is Hebrew for "order" or "service." The Passover service is called the Passover Seder.

scriptures, I found that most of the body of Messiah today has a limited concept of Hebraic praise. Through the leading of the Holy Spirit, I discovered that the "key" to finding the Hebrew equivalent to each Greek word for *praise* was to be found in the New Testament quotations of Old Testament passages. The reason the Hebrew-Greek connection is important is that no matter how exacting the writer of the original Greek in his efforts, it is usually impossible to express in one language what another language is saying. Something is most often dropped, missed or left out in the translation from language to language. Additionally, not only is the meaning of the translated word diminished, but the cultural impact of that meaning and its expression can be lost as well.

We find the key to the use of *hallel* in Romans 15:11 of the New Covenant. In this passage of Romans, Paul quotes Psalm 117:1, "Praise (*hallel*) the LORD, all ye nations; and laud Him, all ye peoples." The Greek word used to translate *hallel* in this passage is *aineo* (pronounced *ahee-neh'-o*). The Greek Lexicon defines *aineo* as "to praise, extol."[43] However, when we compare the Old Testament word *hallel* that Paul is quoting and the Greek word *aineo* used by the writer, we find that the Greek word is handicapped and falls short in fully expressing the original meaning of the word *hallel*. Although Greek offers sharp, laser-like definitions, it cannot compare to the expansive deeper definitions and insights offered by the Hebrew language. The Hebrew word in its definition and expanse usually supercedes the Greek word used.

Now using our "key," we'll consider each New Covenant scripture where the Greek *aineo* is found and uncover the expressions of *hallel* hidden there.

New Covenant "*Hallel*-s"

At Y'shua's birth!

Hallel is the praise of the angelic host announcing the birth of Y'shua. "Then suddenly there appeared with the angel an army of the troops of heaven (a heavenly knighthood), praising (*hallel*-ing)

God and saying: 'Glory to God in the highest, and on earth peace among men with whom He is well pleased.'"[44] When this message of *hallel*, "Glory to God in the highest," is offered to the Father, it releases the ministry of Y'shua as Savior and Prince of Peace.

Hallel ~ Response of the Shepherds!

The shepherds *hallel*-ed God in response to the revelation of Messiah to them: "Then the shepherds returned, glorifying and praising (*hallel*-ing) God for all the things that they had heard and seen, as it was told them."[45]

Hallel ~ Given to Y'shua
As He rode through the streets of Jerusalem on the colt!

> "Then, as He was now drawing near the descent of the Mount of Olives, the whole multitude of the disciples began to rejoice and praise (*hallel*) God with a loud voice for all the mighty works they had seen, saying: 'Blessed is the King who comes in the name of the LORD!' Peace in heaven and glory in the highest!"[46]

This passage is a quotation from Psalm 118:26 which is called the "Messianic Greeting." The Messianic Greeting is the phrase that will be used to greet the Messiah. When the multitude cried, "Blessed is He who comes in the name of the LORD," they were consciously hailing Y'shua as their long-awaited Messiah, the King of the Jews!" Y'shua affirmed the usage of this phrase when He said, "You will not see me again until you say, 'Blessed is He who comes in the name of the LORD.'"[47]

Hallel ~ Response of the Disciples to the
Ascension of our LORD!

After witnessing Y'shua's ascension to the Father from the top of the Mount of Olives, the disciples were beside themselves with joy and celebration. "And they worshiped Him, and returned to

Jerusalem with great joy, and were continually in the temple praising (*hallel*-ing) and blessing God. Amen."[48]

Hallel ~ Praise of the Newly Formed Church!

The newly formed "Acts Church" practiced *hallel*. "So continuing daily with one accord in the temple, and breaking bread from house to house, they ate their food with gladness and simplicity of heart, praising (*hallel*-ing) God and having favor with all the people. And the Lord added to the church daily those who were being saved."[49]

Hallel ~ Response to Miraculous Healing!

The lame man at the "Beautiful Gate" of the temple burst forth with *hallel* at his healing. "So he, leaping up, stood and walked and entered the temple with them – walking, leaping and praising (*hallel*-ing) God. And all the people saw him walking and praising (*hallel*-ing) God."[50]

Hallel ~ Praise Called Forth from the Throne!

The very throne of God commands us to praise with our *hallel*-s. The Book of Revelation declares, "Then a voice came from the throne, saying, "Praise (*hallel*) our God, all you His servants and those who fear Him, both small and great!"[51]

Hallel ~ Boasting in God!

Another Old Covenant scripture quoted in the New gives us further insight to the use of *hallel* in the New Covenant. "…As it is written, He who glories (*hallel*-s), let him glory (*hallel*) in the LORD.[52] This is a quotation from Jeremiah 9:24. In this scripture the word glory (*hallel*) is translated with the Greek word *kauchaomai* (pronounced *kow-khah'-om-ahee*) and means "to vaunt, boast, make boast, glory, joy, rejoice."[53] This translation is a clue to other hidden expressions of *hallel* in the New Covenant.

Hallel is given to honor God and His Word (Torah, the expression of the Living Word - Y'shua), yet *hallel* is empty without obedience. "Indeed you are called a Jew, and rest on the law,[‡‡‡‡][54] and make your boast (*hallel*) in God."[55] "You who make your boast (*hallel*) in the law (Torah), do you dishonor God through breaking the law (Torah)?"[56] Disobedience dishonors God. A life not yielded to God negates any honor given though *hallel*.

We bring our *hallel*-s to God *through* Y'shua who has reconciled us to God by His shed blood:

> "For if we were reconciled with God through His Son's death when we were enemies, how much more will we be delivered by His life, now that we are reconciled! And not only will we be delivered in the future, but we are boasting (*hallel*-ing) about God right now, because He has acted through our Lord Y'shua the Messiah, through whom we have already received that reconciliation."[57]

The writer of Romans says we can *hallel* God right now in the present for reconciling and delivering us through Christ's blood! Our salvation is not just future; it is now. We step into eternity at the moment we receive His great salvation!

Paul notes three distinctive marks of those who are spiritually circumcised:[§§§§] (1) Worshiping God in the Spirit, (2) Rejoicing (*hallel*-ing) in Christ Jesus, and (3) Having no confidence (no boasting or *hallel*-ing) in the flesh. Paul in Philippians says it this way, "For we are the circumcision, who worship God in the Spirit, rejoice (*hallel*) in Christ Jesus, and have no confidence (no boasting or *hallel*-ing) in the flesh."[58]

[‡‡‡‡] "Law" is the English word that translates the Hebrew word *Torah* which means "teaching" or "instruction." This passage in Romans 2:23 in *The Power New Testament: Revealing Jewish Roots* reads: "You who boast in Torah, you are dishonoring God by violating the Torah."

[§§§§] Spiritual circumcision brings us into covenant with God through Y'shua's blood.

The *Hallel* of Y'shua

Y'shua is the Sweet Psalmist of psalmists. As the Living Word, He has sung His psalms into the ears of psalmists through the ages, including Moses, David and Asaph as well as many others through the generations. He is still singing to us today. These earthly psalmists have received, sung, played, recorded and expressed Y'shua's psalms since the foundation of the world.

The Son of God and Messiah of the world *hallel*-s His Father throughout eternity. Becoming the Word made flesh was in itself an act of *hallel* to His Father (in the sense of shining and giving forth light). John wrote, "In Him was life, and the life was the light of mankind. The light shines in the darkness, and the darkness has not suppressed it...." "This was the true light, which gives light to everyone entering the world...." "The Word became a human being and lived with us, and we saw His *Sh'khinah*, the *Sh'khinah* of the Father's only Son, full of grace and truth."[59] He was truly "born to praise!"

Hebrews tells us, "But now ... (God) has spoken to us through His Son, to whom He has given ownership of everything and through whom He created the universe. This Son is the *radiance of the Sh'khinah, the very expression of God's essence*, upholding all that exists by His powerful word."[60] When Y'shua left earth and returned to His Father in Resurrection glory, He took off His garment of flesh and revealed the essence of His being – Light! Today and forever He shines forth the glory and *hallel* of the Father's image. He is the essence of *hallel*.

I have heard that at the joining of the egg and sperm in the womb a spark of light flashes. So, too, the seed of Y'shua in us brings light. We are filled with the light of Y'shua's life and, being children of light, are called light-bearers. Y'shua *hallel*-s – shines forth – through us as He indwells us by the Holy Spirit. We become expressions of *hallel* as His light radiates from our innermost beings!

A confirmation of the statement that we are children of light came from the testimony of a warlock, a Satan worshipper, who was converted to belief in Y'shua. He shared that one of the assignments given to the witches and warlocks was to go to hospital nurseries and curse the babies. Interestingly, he said that there were certain babies they could not curse because they were covered in light. It was known to them that these babies were born to believers in Y'shua. Paul in I Corinthians tells us that our children are sanctified or set apart because of our covenant relationship with the LORD.[61]

The book of Hebrews records that Y'shua *hallel*-s His Father in the midst of the congregation. "I (Y'shua) will proclaim Your name (Father) to my brothers; in the midst of the congregation I will sing Your *praise*."[62] This is a direct quote from Psalm 22:22: "I will declare Your name to My brethren; in the midst of the assembly I will praise (*hallel*) You."

In the first verses of Psalm 22 Y'shua describes His agony and sacrifice on the cross. Further on in verse 22 Y'shua prophesied that, after His deliverance on the cross and subsequent resurrection, the day would come when He would declare His Father's name to His brothers and *hallel* His Father from their midst. Even now ~ in His resurrected state ~ Y'shua *hallel*-s the Father in the midst of the congregation! He *hallel*-s His Father in and through the assemblies of those in whom His heart resides! So the Father is *hallel*-ed by Y'shua, His firstborn from the dead, and by us, Y'shua's brothers and sisters. How awesome to realize that as I sing my *hallel*, it is Y'shua singing through me to our Father. I can barely comprehend it. Y'shua *hallel*-s the Father using my voice and I join my heart and agreement to this wonderful praise! Let us always remember that when we praise God, either alone or in the assembly of believers, we are praising with Y'shua and He is praising through us. We are singing with Y'shua and He is singing through us. We are dancing with Y'shua and He is dancing through us. What wonderful love!

Halleluyah ~ Alleluia

The word "Alleluia" was transliterated directly from the Hebrew words *hallel* and *Yah*. It means the same as "Halleluyah," or "Praise you Yah." The great rejoicing in heaven recorded in Revelation 19 resounds with *hallel* as the heavenly choir instructs the saints to "Alleluia," and proclaim His mighty power and works. Antiphonal praise (taken from the practice of singing the ancient Hebrew psalms) is lifted up by the redeemed saints, those redeemed out of the hand of the enemy throughout every generation. We are a part of these redeemed ones.

> "After these things I heard a loud voice of a great multitude in heaven, saying, '*Alleluia* (Halleluyah or You *hallel* Yah)! Salvation and glory and honor and power *belong* to the Lord our God!'"[63]
>
> "And again they said, '*Alleluia* (Halleluyah or You *hallel* Yah)! Her smoke rises up forever and ever!'"[64]
>
> "And the twenty-four elders and the four living creatures fell down and worshiped God who sat on the throne, saying, 'Amen! *Alleluia* (Halleluyah or You *hallel* Yah)!'"[65]
>
> "And I heard, as it were, the voice of a great multitude, as the sound of many waters and as the sound of mighty thunderings, saying, '*Alleluia* (Halleluyah or You *hallel* Yah)! For the Lord God Omnipotent reigns!'"[66]

Hallel ~ The Hebrew Letters

We see an astounding revelation when we look at the Hebrew letters that construct the word *hallel*. Each letter of the Hebrew alphabet presents both a picture and a sound and each has a specific meaning in and of itself. The transliteration of *hallel* into English is spelled *halal*. Consequently only the "H" (*Hey*) and the "L" (*Lamed*) which occurs twice are considered. (Remember in Hebrew, vowels are sounds and not letters and are notated only by jots and tittles.)

Hey means "wind," "roar," "to thunder" and "behold." *Lamed* means "the tongue, goad, teach or learn." According to Dr. Frank Seekins in his book "Hebrew Word Pictures" one may interpret *halal* as, "Behold the tongue of tongues."[67] We can also put it this way, "The tongue of tongues is revealed." This is none other than Y'shua, the Living Word of God, the Tongue of tongues, King of kings, Lord of lords, Psalmist of psalmists and Song of songs! When we consider the meanings of *Hey* as "wind," "breath," "roar" and "to thunder" we may also say, "The Tongue of tongues roars and thunders praise by the breath of God!" Y'shua's voice, like the sound of many waters, resounds the wonderful praises of God through time and eternity. Defining "tongue" as a language, *hallel* is the greatest and highest language of praise, the ineffable Word of God!

Created to *Hallel*

Looking into Psalm 102, we find several clues which help us further understand our role in the expression of *hallel*. The psalmist sings prophetically:

> "But you, *ADONAI,* are enthroned forever; Your renown will endure through all generations. You will arise and take pity on *Tziyon,*¶¶¶¶ for the time has come to have mercy on her; the time determined has come…. The nations will fear the name of *ADONAI* and all the kings on earth Your glory, when *ADONAI* has rebuilt *Tziyon,* and shows Himself in His glory, when He has heeded the plea of the poor and not despised their prayer. May this be put on record for a future generation; may a **people yet to be created** *hallel ADONAI.*"[68]

The psalmist is prophesying of a time in the future, the time when God will have mercy on Zion and rebuild her – the time when Israel will be restored. He is also singing about a generation of the future, the same generation who will live during the time of this restoration.

¶¶¶¶   *Tziyon* is the same as "Zion."

This is the same generation who will see the glory of the LORD. We see this confirmed by the Hebrew word *acharon* (pronounced *akh-ar-one'*)[1] which translates "future." According to the Hebrew lexicon, *acharon* can also be rendered "latter," "last," "the last" or "at the last." As both the meaning of *acharon* and the context confirm, this passage is referring to the "last generation." We are living in that day; we are that generation. The psalmist continues his description of Yahweh's deliverance:

> "For He has looked down from the height of His sanctuary; from heaven *ADONAI* surveys the earth to listen to the sighing of the prisoner, to set free those who are sentenced to death, to proclaim the name of *ADONAI* in *Tziyon* and [to proclaim] His praise *(hallel)* in *Yerushalayim****** when peoples and kingdoms have been gathered together to serve *ADONAI*."[69]

An explosion of *hallel* is coming to believers in our day as the King of kings sets His people free to praise Him in liberty and joyous abandon. *Hallel* is as creative in expression as each new day, each new act of God and each new generation. This creative expression shines forth in dance, art, drama, singing, playing instruments, and many other art forms. Today we have the opportunity to join with the redeemed and shine with His light; make a show of His praise; boast of His glory and goodness; rave, celebrate, and act clamorously foolish or "crazy" in His presence as we abandon ourselves to Him in sacred union.

> *"Holy, Holy, Holy, Lord God Almighty,*
> *Who was and is and is to come!"*[70]
> *"You are worthy, O Lord,*
> *To receive glory and honor and power;*
> *For You created all things,*
> *And by Your will they exist and were created."*[71]

*****   *Yerushalayim* is the Hebrew word for Jerusalem.

Our Father God,

*We thank You for delivering us from intimidation and every evil, fleshly bondage. We accept Your finished work. We look forward to the ultimate fulfillment of **hallel** in resurrection power. May we **hallel** You not only with our voices but also with our hearts and lives. Now we choose to praise You as You have ordained and revealed in Your Word. We make a joyful noise, rave, celebrate and act clamorously foolish, boast of You and make a show of Your awesomeness. We shine with Your light and Your life as You form Your image in us. We honor You and Your plans and purposes for our lives with **hallel**. Prepare us for our wedding!*

Psalm 150

Halleluyah!

***Hallel** God in His holy place!*
***Hallel** Him in the heavenly dome of His power!*
***Hallel** Him for His mighty deeds!*
***Hallel** Him for His surpassing greatness!*

***Hallel** Him with a blast on the shofar!*
***Hallel** Him with lute and lyre!*
***Hallel** Him with tambourines and dancing!*
***Hallel** Him with flutes and strings!*
***Hallel** Him with clanging cymbals!*
***Hallel** Him with loud crashing cymbals!*
*Let everything that has breath **hallel** Adonai!*

Halleluyah!

Hallel to Yahweh

Make a joyful noise,
Sing unto the LORD,
Shout unto the God of Jacob,
Give thanks unto Him,
Bless His holy name,
Enter His courts with praise!

Hallel the LORD of glory,
Hallel the great "I AM,"
Hallel the King of Israel,
Father of Abraham!
Let everything that has breath
Hallel the name of Yahweh,
Let every creature He's made
Lift up their praises to Him!

Make a show, boast,
Celebrate the LORD,
Rave and be clamorously foolish,
Tell of His works,
Glory in His name,
Wave your flags and banners on high!

Hallel with glorious music,
Hallel in symphony,
Hallel our great Creator,
Praise Him in harmony!
Declare His glory to the nations,

Proclaim His victory,
Show His wonders to all people,
Hallel His majesty!

Hallel Him in the depths,
Hallel Him in the heights,
Hallel Him in the midst of the sea,
Hallel Him in the heavens,
Hallel Him in the earth,
Hallel the King of victory!

Hallel Him wherever you are,
Hallel Him wherever you go,
Hallel Him wherever He leads you,
Hallel Him and make a show!
Make a show of His glory,
Make a show of His power,
Make a show of His goodness and love,
In this very hour!

Hallel Him with your heart,
Hallel Him with your soul,
Hallel Him with your mind and your strength!
Hallel Him with your voice,
Hallel Him with your song,
Give yourself in marriage to Him!

Hallel the LORD of glory,
Hallel the great "I AM,"
Hallel the King of Israel,

Father of Abraham!
Let everything that has breath
Hallel the name of Yahweh,
Let every creature He's made
Lift up their praises to Him!

Hallel Him with the drum,
Hallel Him with the harp,
Hallel Him with the strings and the lute,
Hallel Him with the cymbals,
Hallel Him with the dance,
Hallel Him with the trumpet and flute!

Hallel the LORD of glory,
Hallel the great "I AM,"
Hallel the King of Israel,
Father of Abraham!
Let everything that has breath
Hallel the name of Yahweh,
Let every creature He's made
Lift up their praises to Him!

*Lift up **your** praises to Him!*
*Lift up **your** praises to Him!*
*Lift up **your** praises to Him!*†††††

NOTES

1 Revelation 4:3

2 Psalm 113:1

3 James Strong, S.T.D., L.L.D., *Strong's Exhaustive Concordance of the Bible* (Madison, N.J.: James Strong, 1973), *Hebrew and Chaldee Dictionary* #1984, p. 33.

4 Francis Brown, D.D., D.Litt. with the cooperation of S.R. Driver, D.D., Litt.D. and Charles A. Briggs, D.D., D.Litt., *The New Brown-Driver-Briggs-Gesenius Hebrew and English Lexicon* (Peabody, Massachusetts: Hendrickson Publishers, 1979), #1984, p. 237b.

5 Luke 15:11

6 Brown, *The New Brown-Driver-Briggs-Gesenius Hebrew and English Lexicon*, #7797, p. 965a. Rejoice – Hebrew – *suws (soos)* – "exult, rejoice, display joy over."

7 Brown, *The New Brown-Driver-Briggs-Gesenius Hebrew and English Lexicon*, #8057, p. 970b. Gladness – Hebrew – *simchah (sim-khah')* – "joy, gladness, mirth (especially in festivity), gaiety, pleasure."

8 Strong, *Hebrew and Chaldee Dictionary* #1523, p. 27. Joy – Hebrew – *giyl (gheel)* – "to spin round under the influence of any violent emotion."
Brown, *The New Brown-Driver-Briggs-Gesenius Hebrew and English Lexicon*, #1523, p. 162a. "Go round or about, be excited to levity (excessive or unseemly frivolity), rejoice."

9 Zephaniah 3:17

10 Luke 15:7 CJB

11 Isaiah 38:19 Amplified Version

12 Jeremiah 9:23

13 Psalm 113:3

14 Psalm 145:2

15 Psalm 146:2

16 I Chronicles 23:30

17 Psalm 119:164

18 Lamentations 3:23

19 I Chronicles 23:5

20 II Chronicles 7:6 NIV

21 Jeremiah 9:24

22 I Samuel 21:13

23 II Chronicles 23:13

24 II Chronicles 20:21-22

25 I Chronicles 16:37b

26 The rich meanings of the Hebrew word *zakar (zah-kar')*, together with give thanks (*yadah – see Chapter Six*) and praise (*hallel*), give us great insight into the ministry at the Tabernacle of David.
Francis Brown, *The New Brown-Driver-Briggs-Gesenius Hebrew and English Lexicon* #2142, p. 269b-271a. The Hebrew word *zakar (zah-kar')* – "remember,

recall, call to mind as affecting present feeling, thought or action. Remember past experiences or things formerly known. Recall past distress, remember sins to repent of them or to renew and repeat them. Remember the dealings of. Remember persons to their advantage, to make use of them or their acts to their advantage or to their disadvantage, to take vengeance. Remember human obligations. Remember, call him to mind, recall, keep in mind. Remember the words of Moses, the instructions through the prophets, the commandments of God (so as to do them), remember His covenant. Think of or on, call to mind something present or future. Remember a day, to observe, commemorate it. Remember persons, individuals with kindness, granting requests, protecting, delivering. Remember individuals to punish. Remember his servants, people, the afflicted. Remember his land. Remember the distress of his servants, their devotion, their intercession. Remember his own covenant (with them), remember his mercy, remember extenuating circumstances. Remember sins, idolatries. Be brought to remembrance, remembered, thought of. Cause to remember, remind, be remembered, observed, celebrated, observe, celebrate, keep in remembrance. Mention, call upon, boast of, praise, strength, righteousness, loving-kindness, commemorate, praise, record, recorder – a title of public office, make a memorial."

27 I Chronicles 16:4 *The Scriptures*
28 Matthew 6:9-13
29 Acts 15:16-18; Amos 9:12
30 II Chronicles 5:13
31 II Chronicles 8:14 KJV
32 II Chronicles 29:30
33 Ezra 3:11
34 Nehemiah 12:24 KJV
35 Canticles 6:9
36 Nusach Ashkenaz, *The Complete ArtScroll Siddur*, trans. Rabbi Nosson Scherman (Brooklyn, NY: Mesorah Publications ltd., 1988), p. 632.
37 Ibid, p. 632 Quoted from Pesachim, p. 117a.
38 Ibid, p. 632 Quoted from Pesachim, p. 118a.
39 Alfred Edersheim, *The Temple and Its Services* (Grand Rapids, MI: Wm. B. Eerdmans Publishing Company, Reprinted August 1987), p. 225.
40 Ibid, p. 223-224.
41 Hebrews 12:2
42 Matthew 26:30 CJB
43 Joseph Henry Thayer, D.D., *The New Thayer's Greek-English Lexicon of the New Testament* (Peabody, Massachusetts: Hendrickson Publishers, 1981), #134, p. 10b.
44 Luke 2:13, 14 NASB
45 Luke 2:20
46 Luke 19:37, 38
47 Matthew 23:39 NIV
48 Luke 24:52, 53

49   Acts 2:46-47

50   Acts 3:8-9

51   Rev 19:5

52   I Cor 1:31; II Cor 10:17 (quotation of Jeremiah 9:24)

53   *Kauchaomai* (pronounced *kow-khah'-om-ahee*) which means "to vaunt, boast, make boast, glory, joy, rejoice." [Thayer, *The New Thayer's Greek-English Lexicon of the New Testament*, #2744, p.359b.]

54   *The Power New Testament: Revealing Jewish Roots, trans.* William J. Morford Third ed. (Lexington, SC: Rev. William J. Morford, 2003), p. 211.

55   Romans 2:17

56   Romans 2:23

57   Romans 5:10-11 CJB

58   Philippians 3:3

59   John 1:4-5, 9, 14 CJB

60   Hebrews 1:2- 3 CJB

61   I Corinthians 7:14b

62   Hebrews 2:12

63   Rev 19:1

64   Rev 19:3

65   Rev 19:4

66   Rev 19:6

67   Dr. Frank T. Seekins, *Hebrew Word Pictures: How Does the Hebrew Alphabet Reveal Prophetic Truths?* (Phoenix, Arizona: Living Word Pictures, Inc., 1994, 2003), p. 149b.

68   Psalms 102:12-13, 15-18 CJB

69   Psalms 102:19-22 CJB

70   Revelation 4:8b

71   Revelation 4:11

Shabach

Shout to the LORD!

Shabach ~ The Definition

Shabach (pronounced *sha-vakh'*) is the double-edged sword[1] of praise. Its definition is two-fold. First, it means "to address in a loud tone, praise God in a loud tone, laud, triumph, commend, and glory." Secondly, *shabach* is used by God Himself toward His creation. The meaning is "to still, pacify, muzzle, grow calm, still the temper, the waves and the roar of the seas."[2] *Shabach* is a **shout with a message!**[*] We shout our praises to the LORD[†]; shout out His wondrous works to each other, loudly boast of His greatness to the next generation and command the storms to cease. The following is a list of verses that will help us express *shabach*.

Shout out praises to the LORD!

Your loving-kindness is great to us!
Your Truth endures forever![3]
Your loving-kindness is better than life![4]

Your salvation is from everlasting to everlasting!
You alone are worthy of our praises!

The LORD lives! Blessed be my rock!
Let the God of my salvation be exalted.
It is God who avenges me,
And subdues peoples under me.
He delivers me from my enemies.

---

* *Shabach* is a shouted message and to be distinguished from shouts or cries of one word or phrase or nonsense syllables. It is never translated as "shout" in the King James Version.

† When LORD is spelled with all capital letters in the King James Version and New King James Version of the Bible, it translates the holy name of God. Called the Tetragrammaton, it is formed with the four Hebrew letters *Yud, Hey, Vav, Hey (YHWH)* and is sometimes translated Jehovah, Yehovah, Yahweh or Yahveh. The Complete Jewish Bible translates this name as *ADONAI,* a title meaning "Lord."

You also lift me up above those who rise against me;
You have delivered me from the violent man.[5]

"One generation will shabach Your
works to another, and will declare
Your mighty acts."[6]

Shout the LORD's praises to one another!

Oh, clap your hands, all you peoples!
Shout to God with the voice of triumph!
For the LORD Most High is awesome:
He is a great King over all the earth.
He will subdue the peoples under us,
And the nations under our feet.[7]

Shout out God's praises to the next generation!

Great is the LORD, and greatly to be praised
In the city of our God, in His holy mountain...
The city of the great King.[8]

The counsel of the LORD stands forever,
The plans of His heart to all generations.[9]
He remembers His covenant forever,
The word which He commanded, for a thousand generations.[10]

Our God is great!
Our God is good!
His Word is faithful and true!

Now command the winds and the waves!

Peace! Be still![11]

Shabach Him with acclamation after acclamation! Filled with phrases of praise, the Book of Psalms is our praise dictionary. It contains a complete list of every expression of exaltation that God

Himself desires to hear. These Spirit-breathed, eternal proclamations of praise have been and continue to be sung by Y'shua through His eternal word and through His people.

Traditionally, the sons of Israel memorized the *Torah* (the five books of Moses) and the *Haftorah* (the Prophets) for their *Bar Mitzvah* ceremonies. During these ceremonies, young Jewish males recite the Scriptures and are adopted as "sons of the covenant."[‡] No more called children or servants they are accepted into manhood and citizenship. Because of this, every psalmist, prophet and priest as well as every other man of Israel knows the written Scriptures word for word. That is their foundation, their beginning place. What a privilege we have to "hide the [written] Word in our hearts"[§] so that it becomes high praises in *our* mouths and a two-edged sword in *our* hands!

Let us now consider the first definition of *shabach*, our shouts of praise. Y'shua[¶] is our example and our teacher as He demonstrates *shabach*-praise. The psalms are perfect praise, for they are the Son of the Most High God's praises to His Father. His *shabach*-life on this earth teaches this. The praise of Jesus through His life and words are what the Father loves to see and hear from us. Even now, Y'shua continues to minister *shabach* throughout eternity to His Father! He sits "at the right hand of"[**] the Father, and invites us to join Him in forever exalting the LORD our God. True Kingdom praise is earth joined in heaven's expressions of adoration before the throne! "Thy Kingdom come, Thy will be done on earth as it is in heaven" becomes reality. In order for us to understand the dimensions of *shabach*, we need to ask the following questions:

[‡]   In this century in some sects of Judaism, Jewish girls also go through the same ceremony known as *Bat Mitzvah* (daughter of the covenant).

[§]   To "hide the word in the heart" is a Hebrew idiom for "memorize."

[¶]   Y'shua is the Hebrew name of Jesus and means "Yah saves."

[**]   "At the right hand of" is a Hebrew idiom meaning "in the authority of."

Who in scripture *shabach(s)*?[††]
- God
- Psalmists
- All Peoples
- Each Generation – to the next generation
- Jerusalem
- Y'shua
- Daniel
- Nebuchadnezzar
- Disciples – at Y'shua's Triumphal Entry
- Crowds – in Jerusalem
- Children – in the Temple

To Whom/What is *shabach* addressed?
- God
- LORD
- Most High God
- God of our fathers
- King of heaven
- Name of God in all its expressions
- Him who lives forever
- The next generation
- The noisy seas ~ Peace! Be still!
- The raging waves ~ Peace! Be still!
- The winds ~ Peace! Be still!
- The tumult of the peoples ~ Peace! Be still!

What is the message *shabach* declares?
- God's works
- God's mighty acts
- Peace
- Calm to raging storms and seas

When is *shabach* appropriate?
- Forever and ever
- From generation to generation

[††] See *Shabach* Concordance in the "Created to Praise Study Guide" for scripture references.

At the giving of:
- Wisdom
- Might
- Understanding
- Word of knowledge
- Revelation

At the end of:
- Judgment/testing - when reason returns

At the point of:
- Restoration
- Impartation of authority

When:
- Wind/waves of sea arise to bring destruction
- Peoples/nations rise against God & His Anointed

Why is *shabach* expressed?[‡‡]
- God's loving-kindness is better than life.
- His merciful-kindness is great toward us.
- His Truth endures forever.
- He has given us wisdom, might, understanding, revelation and words of knowledge.
- His dominion is an everlasting dominion.
- His kingdom is from generation to generation.
- He acts according to His will in the army of heaven and among the inhabitants of the earth.
- No one can restrain His hand or say to Him, "What have You done?"
- God brings restoration and blessing.
- He grants authority and position.
- All of His works are Truth and His ways just.
- He is able to put down those who walk in pride.
- He has strengthened the bars of our gates.
- He has blessed our children within us.
- He makes peace in our borders.
- He fills us with the finest wheat.

[‡‡] The Scriptures are replete with infinite reasons to offer *shabach*-praise. Listed here are only a few. See the "Created to Praise Study Guide" for a complete list of *shabach* scripture references.

- He sends out His command to the earth.
- His word runs very swiftly.
- He gives snow like wool, He scatters the frost like ashes, He casts out His hail like morsels. Who can stand before His cold? He sends out His word and melts them.
- He causes His wind to blow and the waters to flow.
- He declares His word to Jacob, His statutes and His judgments to Israel.
- Wisdom and might are His.
- He changes the times and the seasons.
- He removes kings and raises up kings.
- He gives wisdom to the wise.
- He gives knowledge to those who have understanding.
- He reveals deep and secret things.
- He knows what is in the darkness.
- Light dwells with Him.
- His signs are great.
- His wonders are mighty.

How is *shabach* to be offered?
- With our lips
- With shouting
- In our psalms of praise

We thank and **shabach** *You, O God of our fathers,*
For You have given us wisdom and might
and have answered our prayers.

The Holy Spirit teaches us and leads us in praise to Y'shua. Y'shua exalts the Father and the Father exalts Y'shua and the Holy Spirit breathes forth the words of each. What union and communion! What perfect praise!

All Nations Will *Shabach* the LORD!

Hallel the LORD, all you Gentiles!
Shabach Him all you peoples,
For His merciful kindness is great toward us;
And the truth of the LORD endures forever.
Hallel the LORD. (Halleluyah!)

Psalm 117

Psalm 117 is one of the six songs in the *Egyptian Hallel* which is composed of Psalms 113-118. Its earthly writer is not recorded, but, according to Jewish sages, it was received by an Israeli psalmist soon after Israel's deliverance from Egypt. This psalm, sung through the centuries at the Feasts of the LORD, continues to be Y'shua's prophetic song.§§ The words of Y'shua, eternal and all-powerful, are heard in the psalms. When we set ourselves to praise, we are privileged to sing with Him. Opening our hearts, minds and mouths, we breathe in the Breath of God and breathe out the wonders of His song, sung in the heart of the Lamb before the foundation of the world. Today the Spirit is searching for those who have ears to hear and hearts to understand the power of the song of Y'shua.

First sung to Israel as God's covenant people, Psalm 117 was not addressed to them. Instead, the first line is directed to all the Gentile nations. The word for nations here is *goy* (pronounced *go'-ee*) and is defined as "a foreign nation, a Gentile, heathen people."[12] Two distinct Hebrew words for praise are used. The word translated "praise" in verses 1 and 2b is the Hebrew *hallel* and the word translated "laud" in verse 2a is *shabach*. Here these verses of Psalm 117 invite the Gentile nations to *hallel* and **shabach** the LORD. It is interesting to note that Psalms 113 – 118 were probably written when Israel exited Egypt. At this point in salvation-history, Gentile nations as a whole did not worship *ADONAI;* neither did they show

---

§§ How can "For His merciful kindness is great toward us" be Y'shua's song, since He was perfect and did not need mercy? Because He not only praised the Father and instructed His people to praise, He also gave us complete expression for our praises. We also know that Y'shua identified with us on the cross as He bore our sin. See Chapter Five-*Tehillim*.

any desire to acknowledge Him. However, through this psalmist and these psalms, Y'shua prophetically commanded the nations (Gentiles) to sing *hallel* and shout *shabach* to the LORD.

Y'shua affirmed His mission, not only to the Jews, but also to the Gentiles. He sang forth the splendor and love of the Father to all of the world from Psalm 117 at His last Passover on earth. Looking beyond the cross He so soon would face, He saw the fulfillment of the words His Father had spoken to Him. Isaiah the prophet penned the words of this heavenly conversation several hundred years earlier.

> "I, the LORD (the Father) have called You (Y'shua) in righteousness; I will take hold of Your hand. I will keep You and make You to be a covenant for the people (Israel), and a light to the Gentiles, to open eyes that are blind, to free captives from prison and to release from the dungeon those who sit in darkness."[13]

In the first part of Isaiah 49:6, Isaiah startlingly states that it is too small a thing for Y'shua to restore Israel only, but the Father's salvation is "to the ends of the earth!"[14]

From the very beginning God had called Y'shua to bring salvation to Israel as well as to the Gentiles. (They were not an afterthought.) And from the beginning He prophesied in the Psalms to the Gentile nations. Because of the salvation purchased on the cross, all nations are called to *shabach* Him for the mercy and loving kindness shown to them. Before the foundation of the world, before the birth of the nation of Israel and all other nations, before the cross, and thousands of years before the Gentiles would have the opportunity to hear His song, Y'shua *shabach*-ed His call to praise! When we remember that sound waves never cease and are always accessible to an appropriate receiver, we are graphically reminded of the astounding power of words! Each time we repeat His message, the message is affirmed and amplified. This is the power of the spoken Word. His Truth, His Word spoken before the foundation of the world, truly endures – sounds forth – forever!

Let us review this again. This psalm, addressed to all Gentile nations and all peoples (including Israel), was sung from heaven by the "Living Word" to an Israeli psalmist on earth who then sang it to the nation of Israel. Together, the nation of Israel sang it for many generations, continuing and amplifying its sound before the Gentile nations ever heard it. In fact, the Gentiles did not hear it until many years later when the resurrected Y'shua commanded His disciples to take the gospel from Jerusalem to Judea and Samaria and to the ends of the earth.[15]

In the book of Romans Paul presented the dilemma so clearly when he asked, "How then, can they (the nations) call on the One they have not believed in? And how can they believe in the One of whom they have not heard? And how can they hear without someone preaching to them? And how can they preach unless they are sent? Then, quoting the words of Isaiah, he exclaimed, "As it is written, 'How beautiful are the feet of them that preach the gospel of peace, and bring glad tidings of good things!'"[16] In another place Isaiah wrote, "I will set a sign among them, and I will send some of those who survive to the nations … that have not heard of My fame or seen My glory. They will proclaim My glory among the nations."[17] Paul continued in Romans 10, "So then faith comes by hearing, and hearing by the Word of God."[18]

Reversing the order of Paul's questions, we can clearly see God's plan to send the gospel forth to the ends of the earth. First, the LORD commissions His messengers to preach the good news of salvation. Then those messengers preach the Word (Messiah) to those to whom they are sent. And to those who confess with their mouths and believe in their hearts the resurrection of Y'shua, salvation comes. It is then no surprise to find that the results of this glorious salvation are *hallel* and **shabach** to Him, and that Psalm 117 is again echoed in Romans 15:11:

"Praise the LORD, all you Gentiles!
Laud (*shabach*) Him, all you peoples!"

Thanks to the singing and teaching in the synagogues and at the Feasts of the LORD! Thanks to the scribes who wrote the scriptures on scrolls! Thanks to the assemblies of believers who chant the psalms! Thanks to all believers everywhere who carry the gospel! Thanks to those who have and are disseminating the Word (Messiah) using the technology of their age! The message of Psalm 117 has been and continues to be broadcast through various forms of media throughout the earth to the glory of Y'shua and for the salvation of all peoples!

Daniel *Shabach*-ed!¶¶

Daniel *shabach*-ed the LORD in Babylon! You may remember the story. King Nebuchadnezzar had a dream that greatly troubled him. He wanted to know the interpretation of his dream. The problem: He could not remember his dream! The king extended gifts, rewards and honor to the one who could reveal the dream and its interpretation. Failure would result in death. The "wise men" of Babylon faced an impossible request.

Enter Daniel. Daniel intercepts the king's henchman on his mission to kill the wise men of Babylon. (That would include Daniel and his companions.) Inquiring about the king's sudden edict, Daniel is able to pacify the captain of the king's guard, and then judiciously makes a request to the king for more time. Returning home to Hananiah, Mishael, and Azariah,*** Daniel and his companions seek the answer from the One "who knows all things."[19] God responds with knowledge and understanding to Daniel in a night vision. The king's dream with its interpretation is given to Daniel with clarity and great import. Daniel's thankful response to God's answer is recorded in his prayer in Daniel 2:20-23. The word *shabach* is used in Daniel's thanksgiving.

'Blessed be the name of God forever and ever. For wisdom and might are His. And He changes the times

---

¶¶ I have added the "-ed, -ing, -s" endings to facilitate the flow of sentences in English. This is not the Hebrew form.

*** Shadrach, Meshach and Abed-Nego are their Babylonian names.

---

and the seasons; He removes kings and raises up kings; He gives wisdom to the wise and knowledge to those who have understanding. He reveals deep and secret things. He knows what is in the darkness, and light dwells with Him. I thank You and *shabach*††† You, O God of my fathers; You have given me wisdom and might, and have now made known to me what we asked of You, For You have made known to us the king's demand.'[20]

Not only did Daniel's intercession produce great revelation and deliverance, but this revelation and deliverance brought great *shabach*. Daniel's first response was to the King of kings. King Nebuchadnezzar received his answer only after Daniel *shabach*-ed **his** King! Oh, that we would all follow Daniel's example.

Nebuchadnezzar *Shabach*-ed the LORD!

This next story is really exciting in light of Psalm 117. Remember that Y'shua sang to the Gentile nations and all peoples inviting them to *hallel* and *shabach* the LORD? We see the first fruit of this invitation manifested in Nebuchadnezzar, King of Babylon. He is the first Gentile recorded who *shabach*-ed the Most High God. Let us see how it happened.

Some time had passed after Daniel's revelation and interpretation of the king's dream. Daniel's three friends went through the fiery furnace and Babylon's famous king once again acknowledged that no other god could deliver like the God of Israel. He even decreed that anyone who spoke against our LORD would be cut in pieces and their houses burned. How like the pattern of our own revelation of God. First, Nebuchadnezzar saw that only El Elyon, the Most High God, could reveal secrets. He believed, at least in his mind, that God was all-knowing. Then he saw that only Daniel's God could deliver. Nebuchadnezzar, however, had not put away the gods of Babylon.

---

††† The Chaldean form of *shabach*. (Strong's Concordance # 7624)

Knowing this, Yahweh determined to bring Nebuchadnezzar to a full understanding of His Lordship.

God gave Nebuchadnezzar a second dream. This time the king did remember the dream but did not understand it. Acknowledging that the Spirit of the Holy God was in Daniel, Nebuchadnezzar asked Daniel to entreat his God for the interpretation of this troubling dream. Daniel prayed, received the interpretation and gave it to the king. You can read the whole story in detail for yourself, but in essence the LORD caused the dream to come to pass and Nebuchadnezzar ended up being driven out of his palace. For seven years he "ate grass like oxen and his body was wet with the dew of heaven until his hair had grown like eagles' feathers and his nails like birds' claws." At the end of this time Nebuchadnezzar said:

> "…I, Nebuchadnezzar, lifted my eyes to heaven, and my understanding returned to me; and I blessed the Most High and *shabach*-ed[‡‡‡] and honored Him who lives forever: for His dominion is an everlasting dominion, and his kingdom is from generation to generation. All the inhabitants of the earth are reputed as nothing; He does according to His will in the army of heaven and among the inhabitants of the earth. No one can restrain His hand or say to Him, 'What have You done?' At the same time my reason returned to me…. I was restored to my kingdom, and excellent majesty was added to me. Now I, Nebuchadnezzar, *shabach* and extol and honor the King of heaven, all of whose works are truth, and His ways just. And those who walk in pride He is able to put down."[21]

This story and Nebuchadnezzar's praise is recorded in the fourth chapter of Daniel as a letter addressed "to all peoples, nations, and languages that dwell in all the earth." Nebuchadnezzar begins,

---

[‡‡‡] The Chaldean form of *shabach*. (Strong's Concordance # 7624)

"Peace be multiplied to you. I thought it good to declare the signs and wonders that the Most High God has worked for me. How great are His signs, and how mighty His wonders! His kingdom is an everlasting kingdom and His dominion is from generation to generation."[22]

Here we have an instance of the gospel going forth to a Gentile king and his resulting SHOUT of praise to the Most High God and to "all peoples, nations and languages that dwell in all the earth." At the revelation of the God of Abraham, Isaac and Jacob, Creator and King of all the earth, loud praises issued from the heart of King Nebuchadnezzar and he *shabach*-ed the LORD, shouting out God's wonderful works to all in his kingdom, to every nation dwelling on the known earth and to the generations to come.

Just think of it! Nebuchadnezzar was the king who ordered the destruction of Jerusalem and Solomon's Temple. His armies ravished the people of Israel, killing some and taking others captive. It is amazing that this same wicked despot is sought after by God for His eternal purposes. (Remember it was Nebuchadnezzar who also stole the sacred vessels from the Temple and stored them in Babylon.) This was a king who had no understanding of Yahweh's holiness or sovereignty. God, however, extended His loving-kindness toward Nebuchadnezzar and demonstrated that He gives grace that is greater and better than life itself!

First, God used Nebuchadnezzar to judge Israel because they had sinned and acted wickedly. Then He set out to save the soul of Nebuchadnezzar and influence a nation and its people. Miraculously, this humbled king accepted the revelation and salvation of the God of Daniel, Hananiah, Mishael, and Azariah. These men of God not only sought the wisdom of their God but believed and obeyed Him. Is there anything too hard for our God? Great and mighty is His name!

Our Souls *Shabach* the LORD!

Psalm 63 reiterates the **reason** for our *shabach*-s stated in Psalm 117:

> "Because Your loving-kindness is better than life, my lips shall **shabach** You. Thus I will bless You while I live; I will lift up my hands in Your name."[23]

Again in this scripture *shabach* is the natural overflow of praise issuing from our souls through our lips. Spontaneously, we lift up our hands in response to the overwhelming love and kindness of the LORD. When we come to the deep realization that knowing, receiving and experiencing His love is better than life itself, joy springs from the depths of our being and becomes a gushing fountain of praise. Shouts of joy!

O LORD, remove every hindrance from
our souls which would prevent us from expressing **shabach** *to You.*

Jerusalem *Shabach*-s the LORD!

Jerusalem is called corporately to *shabach* the LORD. Jerusalem, the city of God, is instructed by Y'shua the psalmist to shout praises to her God.

> "**Shabach** the LORD, O Jerusalem; *Hallel* your God, O Zion. For He has strengthened the bars of your gates; He has blessed your children within you. He makes peace in your borders, and fills you with the finest wheat. He sends out His command to the earth; His word runs very swiftly. He gives snow like wool; He scatters the frost like ashes; He casts out His hail like morsels; Who can stand before His cold? He sends out His word and melts them; He causes His wind to blow, and the waters to flow. He declares His word to Jacob,

His statutes and His judgments to Israel. He has not dealt thus with any nation; and as for His judgments, they have not known them. Praise the LORD!"[24]

For all of your many blessings, for Your power, protection and provision, and most of all for revealing Yourself, Your Word and Your ways to us, we **shabach** *You, O ADONAI! We shout Your praises! "Who is like You, O LORD among the gods? Who is like You, glorious in holiness, fearful in praises,[§§§] doing wonders!"[25] There is no god like You in the heavens or in the earth or under the earth or in the seas! You alone are God and there is no other. Mighty is Your name!*

Each Generation *Shabach*-s the Works of the LORD To the Next Generation!

Each generation is called to teach the next generation about the LORD and to impart the revelation they have received. We have been given the privilege and responsibility by God to prepare our children – not only our own children but as many in the next generation as He allows us to reach – in the ways of *Yahweh*. The Word says to train them up in the way they should go[26] and to teach them as we rise up and lie down, as we come in and go out.[27] We are to prepare them by example, through prayer and through communicating our faith. How effective it would be if a whole generation would take up this call to teach and emulate the ways of the LORD to the next generation.

"One generation will *shabach* Your works to another, and will declare Your mighty acts."[28]

Think about the excitement, the energy and the vitality expressed by shouting. There can be no doubt about what is being communicated, nor can there be any doubt about how important, precious and real the message is to the one who is shouting. Jews all over the world fulfill this scripture every year at each feast. It is at these feasts that they celebrate the acts of God on their behalf. It is also at these feasts

---

§§§   The word for *praises* here is *tehillim* -- our *sung hallel*-s or *psalms*.

that the people acknowledge God's works in their lives and in their history. The feasts are a shout of faith to the next generation.

Intercessory Prayer for *Shabach*!

"Give thanks to the LORD, for He is good!
For His mercy endures forever.
And say,
"Save us, O God of our salvation;
Gather us together,
And deliver us from the Gentiles (the unbelievers),
To give thanks to Your holy name,
To ***shabach*** (shout, triumph, glory) ~
In Your praise (*tehillah* – sung *hallels*, psalms)."[29]

As noted in the underlined portions, the praisers at the Tabernacle of David offered a three-fold request to the LORD: save us; gather us together; and deliver Israel.

Salvation, the assembling together of God's people and deliverance are pre-requisites to corporate *shabach*. These three aspects of God's redemption are the catalyst for God's people to shout His praise! It is the corporate shout of salvation, unity and deliverance.

The Disciples *Shabach*-ed Y'shua!

During the triumphal entry of Y'shua into Jerusalem, the disciples shouted their praises to Him. Luke records:

> "...throwing their robes on the colt, they put Y'shua on it. As He went along, people carpeted the road with their clothing; and the entire band of *talmidim* (disciples) began to sing and praise [***shabach***¶¶¶] God

---

¶¶¶   *Shabach* is, of course, not the word used here. However, the translated word in Greek means "praise God at the top of their voices" (CJB) or "praise God with a loud voice" (NKJV). The incident fits the definition.

at the top of their voices for all the powerful works they had seen:

> 'Blessed is the King who is coming in the
> name of *ADONAI!*' 'Shalom in heaven!'
> and 'Glory in the highest places!'

Some of the Pharisees said to him, 'Rabbi! Reprimand your disciples!' But He answered them, 'I tell you that if they keep quiet (are "muzzled" by the enemy and do not *shabach*), the stones will shout!'"[30]

The Greek word used here for "shout" is very interesting. It is *krazo* (*krad' - zo*) and means "to croak as a raven or scream; to call aloud, shriek, exclaim, entreat, cry out."[31] This expression is even louder and more piercing than *shabach*! Do you get the message of this passage? If **we** do not shout our praises, the stones will shriek and scream their praise to Him Who is worthy. We do not want to miss the opportunity to praise Him. With our hearts we shout His welcome. Let our voices echo our hearts and join those of His disciples. May our *shabach* join theirs and amplify their holy welcome:

> *Blessed is the King who is coming in the name of ADONAI!*
> *Shalom in heaven!*
> *Glory in the highest places!*

Crowds *Shabach*-ed Y'shua!

Again we see *shabach* is the "shouted message in Matthew's account of the triumphal entry. The crowds who carpeted Y'shua's way with their clothing and tree branches shouted:[****]

> 'Hosanna to the Son of David!
> Blessed is he who comes in the name of the LORD!
> Hosanna in the highest!'"[32]

[****]   *Shabach* is, of course, not the word used here. However, the translated word in Greek means "praise God at the top of their voices" (CJB) or "praise God with a loud voice" (NKJV). The incident fits the definition.

Children *Shabach*-ed Y'shua!

Y'shua's triumphal entry into Jerusalem ended **in** the Temple where He drove out the money-changers and healed some who were blind and lame.

> "But when the chief priests and scribes saw the wonderful things He did, and the children **crying out** in the Temple and saying, "Hosanna to the Son of David!" they were indignant and said to Him, "Do You hear what these are saying?" And Jesus said to them, "Yes. Have you never read,
>
>> 'Out of the mouth of babes and nursing infants You have **perfected praise'**?"[33,34]

"Hosanna" is the translation of the two Hebrew words *Yah* and *yasha*[35] *(ya-shah')*. *Yasha* means "to free, defend, deliver, preserve, save" and together these words mean "Yah saves" or "Yah delivers." Addressing Y'shua as "Son of David," the people were crying out "O save us!" and proclaiming Jesus as the Messiah who was able to save and deliver them. This was a public pronouncement of His Messiahship. Note Jesus' response to the Pharisees:

> "Out of the mouth of babes and nursing infants You have **ordained strength**, because of Your enemies, that You may silence the enemy and the avenger."[36]

In quoting this passage the New Testament translators substituted the words "perfected praise"[37] for "ordained strength."[38] What a powerful confirmation of all that *shabach* means! In Psalm 8 the result of this *shabach*-praise coming from the mouths of babies and nursing infants[39] is a strength that stills and silences the enemy and the avenger. This power against the enemy is **perfected praise** in action! Oh, the power of the shouted message: *Shabach!*

Y'shua *Shabach*-s!

The book of Romans tells us that Jesus came to earth with a two-fold mission. First,

> "...Messiah became a servant of the Jewish people in order **to show God's truthfulness** by making good His promises to the Patriarchs, and (He became a servant of the Gentiles) in order **to show (God's) mercy** by causing the Gentiles to glorify (*shabach*) God...."[40]

In other words, He came to prove to the Jews that His Word to their fathers was true and He came to the Gentiles to show God's mercy to them, giving them reason to shout their praises and glorify God. Referring to several Old Covenant passages Paul recalls Y'shua's words:

> "...As it is written in the *Tanakh* (the Old Testament), 'Because of this, I (Messiah, author of the Word) will acknowledge You (God, the Father) among the Gentiles and sing praise to Your name.' And again it says, 'Gentiles, rejoice with His people.' And again, '(*Hallel*) ADONAI, all Gentiles! Let all peoples (*shabach*) Him.'"[41]

This passage tells us that the Messiah Himself will *reveal* the Father to the Gentiles and sing His praises in their midst. Further, He calls the Gentiles to rejoice with the people of Israel and join them in the expressions of *hallel* and **shabach**.

Hallel and **shabach** are the vehicles with which to glorify, bring glory to, and make glorious the praises of our God and Father. These words have similar expression in that they both include shouting and are both expressed with fervor, energy, and strength as they boast in and of the LORD and His works. As in the above passage, they are often recorded together in the same sentence – partners in praise.

God *Shabach*-s!

Another aspect of *shabach* is when *shabach* is used by God Himself toward the earth and its people. This secondary meaning is "to soothe, still, pacify, keep in, muzzle, be free from care, grow calm, still the temper, the waves and the roar of the seas."[42] The psalmist sings to the LORD,

> "You rule the raging of the sea; when its waves rise,
> You *shabach* (soothe, still, calm) them.[43]

And again he addresses God,

> "You who *shabach* the noise of the seas, the noise of
> their waves, and the tumult of the peoples.[44]

God *shabach*-s! Not only does He *shabach* the natural elements of the winds and the storms, but also spiritual winds and storms coming through peoples and nations. "Seas" is often used metaphorically in the scriptures for peoples and nations who are rebelling against God. Psalm 2 begins,

> "Why are the nations in an uproar, the peoples grumbling in vain? The earth's kings are taking positions, leaders conspiring together, against *ADONAI* and His anointed…. He who sits in heaven laughs; *ADONAI* looks at them in derision. Then in His anger He rebukes them, terrifies them in His fury."[45]

God is in control of all things at all times. The nations are but a "drop in a bucket" to Him.[46]

Y'shua *Shabach*-ed the Storm!

Yes, Y'shua *shabach*-ed the storm! The book of Mark records an astounding incident:

"A furious windstorm arose, and the waves broke over the boat, so that it was close to being swamped. But Y'shua was in the stern on a cushion, asleep. They woke him and said to him, 'Rabbi, doesn't it matter to you that we're about to be killed?' He awoke, rebuked the wind and said to the waves, 'Quiet! Be still!††††† The wind subsided, and there was a dead calm. He said to them, 'Why are you afraid? Have you no trust even now?' But they were terrified and asked each other, 'Who can this be, that even the wind and the waves obey Him?'"[47]

Notice that Jesus used two different words to still the storm. He first told it to be still and quiet (Peace!) and then instructed it to hold its peace and stay still and quiet (Be still!)! The words *peace* and *be still* together complete the Hebrew expression of *shabach*. The storm, having no other alternative but to obey, subsided, responding obediently to the "Living Word" of God.[48]

We Can *Shabach*!

Again referring to this same scripture in Mark, Y'shua asked His disciples why they were fearful. Their fear was the result of their lack of trust. He, the One Whose words created the world, was with them in the boat and the storm. They had the power to *shabach* the storm but did not understand the power of *shabach* in their hearts. Instead of speaking to (*shabach*-ing) the storm they succumbed to the storm's power.

The platform for the release of the power of *shabach* is trust in Y'shua and His works. *Shabach* in its fullness is expressed by both Greek words for *peace* and *be still*. When the storms of life assail us, *shabach* will not only quiet the storms but keep them quiet, still and calm. John's gospel emphasizes the importance of trust in the LORD. Trust in Him is the foundation of *shabach*.

†††† Two different Greek words are used here: one for "Peace" and another one for "Be still." See explanation in the reference for Mark 4:39 in end-note #48 at the end of this chapter.

...whoever trusts in Me will also do the works I do! Indeed, he will do greater ones, because I am going to the Father. In fact, whatever you ask for in My name, I will do; so that the Father may be glorified in the Son. If you ask Me for something in My name, I will do it."[49]

Just think of it. To those who trust in Y'shua, to them is the power of *shabach*.

Shabach as the Two-Edged Sword

The perfect example of the two aspects of *shabach* is the two-edged sword of praise. Psalm 149 says,

> "Let the high praises of God be in their mouth, and a two-edged sword in their hand, to execute vengeance on the nations, and punishments on the peoples; to bind their kings with chains, and their nobles with fetters of iron; to execute on them the written judgment...."[50]

One edge of the Sword is shouted praise to the LORD. The LORD is lauded and given glory. This is the first aspect of *shabach*. The other edge of the Sword is the shouted message of the Word of God. This second aspect of *shabach* quiets the enemy. Natural storms are stilled and the enemy's assignments are cancelled. The enemy is quieted and commanded to be still. His evil assignments are nullified. What a weapon of praise! God has given His people power and dominion over creation and over the enemy.

It is important to note that shouting emphasizes the message of the Word and faith to our own ears and hearts as well as the ears and hearts of others. It builds our faith and the faith of those who hear and receive the two-edged sword of *shabach*. It releases the established work and victory of Y'shua from our hearts to the heart of the enemy. What power is in the sword of *shabach*!

Shabach ~ The Hebrew Letters

The word *shabach* is spelled with the Hebrew letters *sheen* (teeth, to destroy), *bet* (house or tent) and *chet* (a fence, a wall, to separate, to protect, to private, to fence off). There are times when the house and what is in it – the family and its possessions or the soul in its body (temple) – need to be protected from the evil without. But there are other times when what is in the house of the righteous – the love, the caring, the praise – needs to be revealed and released. When the fence or wall around the house is destroyed, the sound or shout of *shabach*-praise within can be heard. This bears witness with a beautiful verse in Psalm 118. Verse 15 reads, "Shouts of joy and victory resound in the tents of the righteous."[51] Destroying the fence or wall which makes the house private allows these shouts of joy and victory to be heard well beyond the bounds of the house. This lines up with the verses that tell us to *shabach* our praises to the LORD, to shout out His wondrous works to each other and to loudly boast of His greatness to the next generation. Let the voice of His praise be heard!

What are some of the fences or walls that keep the praises in the house from being heard? There are many things that bind us and hinder the voice of our praise. Sometimes we put up walls: fear of what other people think, fear of rejection or of not performing well, intimidation, timidity, self-consciousness and insecurity. These "fences" keep our souls in prison and quench the voice of our praise. Praise *ADONAI* for His redemption and deliverance from the enemy!

*O Father, be glorified in Y'shua! Let the two-edged sword of the high praises of God be in my mouth. May my **shabach** bind the enemy and cut through fetters of iron. May I shout the judgments of the Word of God over Y'shua's enemies. Strengthen me to always choose to **shabach** the storms and hindrances in my life and those around me – trusting and believing that the victory is already won. May I shout Your works to the next generation and to the generations to come. Let me always triumph, revel and glory in You. Thank You for teaching me the praises in which You delight.*

NOTES

1   Psalm 149:6-9a
2   James Strong, S.T.D., L.L.D., *Strong's Exhaustive Concordance of the Bible* (Madison, N.J.: James Strong, 1973), *Hebrew and Chaldee Dictionary* #7623, p. 111 **and**
    Francis Brown, D.D., D.Litt. with the cooperation of S.R. Driver, D.D., Litt.D. and Charles A. Briggs, D.D., D.Litt., *The New Brown-Driver-Briggs-Gesenius Hebrew and English Lexicon* (Peabody, Massachusetts: Hendrickson Publishers, 1979), #7623, p. 986b.
3   Psalm 117:2 (paraphrased)
4   Psalm 63:3b (paraphrased)
5   Psalm 18:46-48
6   Psalm 145:4
7   Psalm 47:1-3
8   Psalm 48:1,2b
9   Psalm 33:11
10 Psalm 105:8
11 Mark 4:39
12 Strong, *Hebrew and Chaldee Dictionary* #1471, p. 26.
13 Isaiah 42:6-7 NIV
14 Isaiah 49:6
15 Acts 1:8
16 Romans 10:14-15 KJV
17 Isaiah 66:19 NIV
18 Romans 10:17
19 Dan 2:22 (Paraphrased)
20 Daniel 2:20-23
21 Daniel 4:34-37
22 Daniel 4:1-3
23 Psalm 63:3-4
24 Psalm 147:12-20
25 Exodus 15:11
26 Proverbs 22:6
27 Deuteronomy 6:7 (Paraphrased)
28 Psalm 145:4
29 I Chronicles 16:34-35
30 Luke 19:35-40 CJB
31 "Crying out" - *krazo* (pronounced *krad'-zo*) - Strong, *Greek Dictionary of the New Testament*, #2896, p. 43.
32 Matthew 21:9b
33 Matthew 21:15-16
34 The phrase "perfected praise" translates "ordained strength" in Psalm 8:2. The Greek word for "praise" used here is *ainos* (*ah'-ee-nos*) – Praise, laudatory discourse – Joseph Henry Thayer, D.D., *The New Thayer's Greek-English Lexicon*

of the New Testament (Peabody, Massachusetts: Hendrickson Publishers, 1981), #136, p.16a. This Greek word is also used to translate *hallel*. See End Note # 38.

35   The word *Y'shua* comes from two Hebrew words, *Yah* and *yasha (ya-shah')* meaning Yah saves or Yah delivers–Strong's *Hebrew and Chaldee Dictionary*, #3091, p. 48 from #3068, p. 47 and #3467, p. 53. *Yehoshua*, Joshua

36   Psalm 8:2

37   Matthew 21:16 – See End-note #35.

38   Psalm 8:2 – The word translated "strength" comes from the Hebrew word *owz* (pronounced *oze*) from #5810: *strength* in various applications *(force, security, majesty, praise)*: - boldness, loud, might, power, strong. Strong, *Hebrew and Chaldee Dictionary* #5797, p. 86.

39   Psalm 8:2 – Nursing infant - *olal* (pronounced *o-lal'*) – a suckling, babe, young child, infant, little one. Strong, *Hebrew and Chaldee Dictionary*, #5768, p. 86.

40   Romans 15:8-9a CJB

41   Romans 15:9b-11 CJB – Quoting II Samuel:22:50; Psalm 18:50 (49); Deuteronomy 32:43 CJB; Psalm 117:1

42   *Shabach - The New Brown-Driver-Briggs-Gesenius Hebrew and English Lexicon*, #7623, p. 986b; and
     Strong, *Hebrew and Chaldee Dictionary*, #7623, p. 111.

43   Psalm 89:9

44   Psalm 65:7

45   Psalm 2:1-2, 4-5 CJB

46   Isaiah 40:15

47   Mark 4:37-41 CJB

48   Mark 4:39 - "Then He arose and rebuked the wind, and said to the sea, *"Peace"* - *siopao (see-o-pah'-o)* – "silence, muteness, involuntary stillness, or inability to speak, to be dumb, to be calm (as quiet water), hold peace." [Strong, *Greek Dictionary of the New Testament*, #4623, p. 65. This definition in *The New Thayer's Greek-English Lexicon*, #4623, p. 576b is "to be silent, hold one's peace." Used of one who is silent because he is dumb and used for a calm, quiet sea.]
     "Be still." - *phimoo (fee-mo-'-o)* - to muzzle (*shabach*). (In other words: "Be quiet and stay quiet!") [Thayer, *The New Thayer's Greek-English Lexicon*, #5392, p. 655a.]

49   John 14:12-14 CJB

50   Psalm 149:6-9a

51   Psalm 118:15 NIV

Todah

Sacrifice of Praise

Todah ~ The Definition

Todah (pronounced *toh-dah'*) comes from the root word *"yadah'"*and is defined as "an extension of the hands in avowal or adoration."[1] According to the Gesenius Hebrew Lexicon the original meaning of *todah* was described as acknowledging and abandoning sin. It is variously translated as "praise; confess; confession; give thanks; thanksgiving; a thanksgiving choir, procession, line or company; a thank offering and to offer a thank offering."[2] We may summarize *todah*'s meaning as an individual worshiper or a group of worshipers having pure hearts; lifting up clean hands in adoration to God; singing songs of thanksgiving and praise and often marching in procession.

Who receives *todah*?
- The LORD
- The LORD God of Israel
- The LORD God of your fathers
- God

Who gives *todah*?
- The worshiper
- The assembly of Israel
- The priests and the Levites
- Jonah in the belly of the whale (a promise made to God)
- The body of Messiah
- Jerusalem

When is *todah* offered?
- When you have consecrated yourselves to the LORD

---

* The root word from which *todah* is derived is *yadah* which is defined as "to shoot, throw, cast, confess, praise and give thanks." The Gesenius Hebrew Lexicon states that "its meaning is commonly derived, perhaps, from gestures accompanying the act."

- When you come into His presence
- When you enter His gates
- When the LORD comforts Zion
- When the LORD brings back the captivity of Jacob's tents
- With the multitude going up to the Feasts of the LORD
- Continually
- When we repent and return to the LORD

Where is *todah* offered?
- In the House of the LORD
- At the Altar of the LORD
- In restored Zion when she becomes like Eden, the garden of the LORD
- Out of Jacob's restored tents
- In the restored cities of Judah
- In restored Jerusalem
- At the Feasts of the LORD

How is *todah* offered?
- With a willing heart
- As a peace offering
- As confession of sin
- As a sacrifice of praise and thanksgiving
- In purity
- With a life obedient to God's will and separated unto Him
- With gladness
- With singing
- With cymbals, harps and stringed instruments
- In procession
- With choirs
- With the voice of joy
- With the voice of those who make merry
- With the voice of gladness
- With singing and psalms
- With uplifted hands

Why is *todah* offered?
- It magnifies and glorifies God
- The LORD is worthy of all praise
- It pleases and delights the LORD

Todah ~ Hands Lifted to Our Father

Todah expresses the uninhibited simplicity and innocence of childlike devotion. A little child lifts up his hands to his mother or father in love and adoration, communicating by this act his desire to be picked up and lovingly held in his parent's arms. *Todah* is this same trusting and loving expression toward our heavenly Father; however, the Father receives our gesture of love and trust with even more delight than our earthly parents. The LORD says, "…I will not forget you. Behold, I have indelibly imprinted (tattooed) a *picture* of you on the palm of each of My hands."[3] Of course He was speaking of Y'shua on the cross. Can you fathom this? Our picture is forever engraved in the nail prints of Y'shua's hands, the Lamb slain from the foundation of the world. He has redeemed us from the enemy and birthed us into the Kingdom. Having created us in His image and delivered our lives from death, our *Abba*[†] calls us His children. What joy it must give Him to look down from heaven and see our hands lifted toward Him as we take up our cross and follow Him. Truly this is the sacrifice of praise.

Establishing natural families to mirror His own spiritual family was the perfect plan to teach us relationship – father, mother, children, brothers, sisters – in His family. Y'shua said we must be like little children. This was the way of heaven. As we begin to express *todah* to the LORD in our own praise and worship, we can draw from His examples and learn how to offer this gift of *todah* and sacrifice in a way that is delightful to Him. We are created to sing and dance and play in our Father's house. I am amazed at the simplicity of expression which pleases Him.

---

†   *Abba* is the Hebrew word for Father.

Todah ~ Hands Lifted Up in Surrender

Another example which helps us to understand *todah* is that of a defeated army. Hands lifted up in surrender signal the victory to a stronger, conquering host. When we yield our own desires, ambition and pride to God, He in turn is able to release His power, purpose and will into our lives. At the foot of His cross we exchange unrighteousness for His righteousness; sickness for His healing; worry, stress and anxiety for His peace. *Todah* is the praise of surrender and humility, honor and reverence, love and affection. How fitting to come into His presence with hands lifted high (*todah*) in surrender to His Lordship over our lives!

Todah ~ Procession of Praise!

Yahweh‡ loves pomp and pageantry. His feasts and celebrations are replete with festive imagery. As a picture of the kingdom of God, they not only represent what Y'shua has already done, but are shadows of things yet to come. We find an excellent depiction of *todah* in Nehemiah 12. The walls around Jerusalem had been constructed in an astonishing fifty-two days. Nehemiah planned a great celebration to dedicate the completion of this miraculous endeavor to *Yahweh*. Sending out messengers to all the countryside surrounding Jerusalem, Nehemiah summoned all the Levites to participate in this momentous event and to

> "...celebrate the dedication with gladness, with thanksgivings (***todah***), and with singing, cymbals, harps, and lyres."[4] "And the priests and the Levites purified themselves, the people, the gates, and the wall...."[5]

After the Levites made everything ready, Nehemiah appointed two large choirs to offer thanksgiving with *todah*.[6] Ascending the wall with hands lifted high, they walked in procession. One choir led half

---

‡ *Yahweh* is the ineffable name of God made of the four Hebrew letters *Yud, Hey, Vav, Hey* and rendered LORD (spelled with all capital letters) in the King James Version. Also translated Yahveh, Yehovah or Jehovah.

---

of the people on the wall to the right and the other choir led the other half to the left.[7] The priests blew shofars and the musicians played the instruments of David – the cymbals, harps and lyres. Processing around the wall, they all met at the Temple. Then in a great ceremony of praise, everyone stood and sang psalms of *todah*. As the musical instruments played, the sound of trumpeting shofars filled the air. There was great thanksgiving and joy in Israel that day![8]

Picture It!

Visualize this awesome scene: The two *Todah* Choirs[§] are lined up by the wall dressed in their festal robes. With long, loud blasts, the shofars signal the holy procession to begin. There they go! As the musicians play, the choirs sing and lift their hands high, thanking *Yahweh* for His "wall of protection."

With the air resonating from the melodious praise of instruments and song, the two appointed choirs separate and process up the steps to the top of the wall. Moving in opposite directions, each choir is followed by half of the priests in attendance. Following the priests are the Levites with the instruments of David. These Levites go before the leaders of Judah who also march behind the choirs.

Ezra, the Torah-teacher, leads both the Levites and the leaders of Judah. As they process, Ezra's group veers off to the right toward the Dung Gate. As they approach the Fountain Gate, Ezra ascends and leads the celebrants up the steps to the City of David. The wall rises at this point and this great pageant of sight and sound passes above the house of David and marches toward the Eastern Water Gate.

My heart beats with excitement and awe as I watch this holy procession around the restored wall of Jerusalem! The second choir, followed by Nehemiah, turns to the left and marches above the Tower of Furnaces to the Broad Wall, above the Ephraim Gate, then by the gate to the Old City. As they proceed past the Fish Gate, they

---

§   Capitalized in the Complete Jewish Bible.

come to the Tower of Hanan'el and then the Tower of the Hundred. Continuing to walk, they pass the Sheep Gate and then halt at the Prison Gate. Finally the two choirs meet and together enter the Temple singing loud, high praises to *Elohim*.¶ *Antiphonally chanting the beautiful verses of the psalms, they todah Yahweh.* He is the One who enabled them to rebuild the Wall. It is His finished work!

The shouts and rejoicing of men, women and children reverberate in the atmosphere. One can hear the high-sounding blasts of shofars for miles.⁹ Israel's dedication of the wall of salvation is saluted by the high praises of *todah.* As this momentous event in history concludes, the people of God possess for Yahweh the walls of *Yerushalayim! Todah* His name!

Todah ~ Key to the Gates!

Todah is the key to the gates of the Temple. "Enter His gates with *todah!*"¹⁰ The Psalmist instructs us in Psalm 100 to process through His gates and, with uplifted hands, sing songs of thanksgiving. God receives our *todah,* thanksgiving-praise, with clean hands, surrendered lives and pure hearts.

Todah ~ Gift for the King!

Let us come into His presence with *todah.*¹¹** We have been created a kingdom of priests and our ministry to *Elohim* includes gifts of joy, thanksgiving and praise. Humility and a contrite spirit distinguish the offering of these gifts. The words of the psalmists, the voice of Y'shua, continue to echo through time:

> "Let (us) offer sacrifices of **todah** and proclaim His great deeds with songs of joy!"¹²

¶   *Elohim* is the Hebrew name for God.

**   As noted in the introduction, the protocol of a kingdom says that we must never presume to enter the presence of the King without gifts and sacrifices. This is the priestly function. The duties of the Hebrew priests were to offer gifts and sacrifices to *Yahweh* as they entered and ministered before His presence.

"Sing to the LORD with *todah*; sing praises on the harp to our God."[13]

"I will offer a sacrifice of *todah* to You and will call on the name of *ADONAI*."[14]

"I will sacrifice to You with the voice of *todah*; I will pay that which I have vowed. Salvation is of the LORD."[15]

"Your vows are upon me, O God; I will render *todah* to You."[16]

Todah ~ Sacrifice of Thanksgiving!

Remembering that the sacrifice of *todah* is offered with clean hands and pure hearts, Psalm 24 exhorts us to acknowledge and abandon sin.[17]

"Who may ascend the hill of the LORD? Who may stand in His holy place? He who has clean hands and a pure heart...."[18]

Confession is an integral part of *todah*. At the dedication of the wall in Nehemiah, the first preparation was the cleansing and purification of the priests, the Levites, the people, the gates and the wall. This preparation is **key** to the offering of *todah*. King David understood the necessity of confessing sin and coming into the LORD's presence with a righteous heart. He sang,

"I will wash my hands in innocence, so I will go about Your altar, O LORD, that I may proclaim with the voice of *todah*, and tell of all Your wondrous works."[19]

Todah ~ Praise at the Feasts of the LORD

As the worshipers went up or processed into Jerusalem for the festivals of *Pesach* (Passover); *Shavuot* (Pentecost) and *Sukkot* (Tabernacles), they offered *todah*. David fondly remembered these special times in Psalm 42:

"I recall, as my feelings well up within me, how I'd go with the crowd to the house of God, with the voice of joy and *todah* (praise) from the throngs, observing the festival.[20]

Todah ~ Our Freewill Offering!

In the *Tanakh*[††], *todah* – the sacrifice of thanksgiving – was sometimes offered with the peace offerings. However, it was always a **freewill** offering and never required. We know that Y'shua became THE SACRIFICE. He offered Himself as a freewill offering and completely fulfilled all of the required offerings. He is our PEACE in every sense of the word. We now enter the presence of the LORD by the blood of the Lamb and by His holy and perfect sacrifice. But the sacrifice of thanksgiving – *todah* – is still a freewill offering. It is still the key to the gates and a delight to our Father when we voluntarily lift up our sacrifice of thanksgiving to Him. The scriptures exhort and invite us to offer thanksgiving to the One who gave His Son and to the Son who gave His life.

There tends to be a mindset in the body of Messiah that spiritual fulfillment is only in the world to come – heaven. This is a Greek philosophical view that has infiltrated the church. This mindset practically eliminates the need for thanksgiving because we are still waiting, looking and hoping for things in the future for which to be thankful. Hebraic thinking, however, is much more practical and focused on the present. Each act of God, each blessing, each promise is something for which we are to be thankful. Furthermore, faith says that we offer thanksgiving even before the promise for which we are believing is manifested. The more I meditate on *todah*, the more the LORD impresses on me the value of continual thanksgiving in our walk with Him. Thanksgiving ushers us into His presence

---

†† *Tanakh* is the Hebrew acronym for what we call the Old Covenant Scriptures. The "T" stands for the *Torah* (Instruction) or the five books of Moses, the "N" stands for the *Nevi'im* (Prophets) and the "K" stands for the *K'tuvim* (Writings) which includes "Psalms," "Proverbs" and all the other books not part of the *Torah* or the Prophets. (The other letters represent vowel sounds written as "jots and tittles" in Hebrew.) See Luke 24:44.

in the "now" and secures for us those things promised but not yet evident.

How much time do we spend offering our thanksgivings to Him? Think about it. It is the key to His presence as well as the building of our faith. As we remember His faithfulness to us and His manifested deeds, it strengthens our faith! Many of the psalms follow this pattern. The psalmist, who speaks for all of us, often begins his psalm with a cry of distress from the pit of despair and trouble. As the psalm progresses he recounts how God has helped and delivered him and the entire nation of Israel through past struggles. Thankfully, the psalm most often ends victoriously with acclamations of joy and faith because the psalmist has encouraged himself in the LORD and allowed his faith to rise! God's faithfulness in the past builds faith and hope for the future.

Todah ~ Key to Our Deliverance and God's Glory!

Yahweh says,

> "Offer to God thanksgiving (*todah*), and pay your vows to the Most High. Call upon Me in the day of trouble; I will deliver you, and you shall glorify Me."[21] Whoever offers praise (*todah*) glorifies Me.[22]

We offer *todah* to the LORD and He delivers us because we are in right relationship with Him and this brings Him glory. Then we offer *todah* to Him for His deliverance in our life and He is again glorified. This is the cycle of *todah*. *Todah*-thanksgiving repeatedly brings glory to the King!

Todah ~ Restored In Every Revival!

We see *todah* as an essential element of restoration and revival. This was recognized by Hezekiah:

> "Then Hezekiah answered and said, 'Now *that* you have consecrated yourselves to the LORD, come near,

and bring sacrifices and thank offerings (*todah*) into the house of the LORD.'" So the assembly brought in sacrifices and thank offerings (*todah*), and as many as were of a willing heart *brought* burnt offerings."[23]

King Manasseh also understood the power of *todah*::

"And he (Manasseh) repaired the altar of the LORD, and sacrificed on it peace offerings and thank offerings (*todah*) on it, and commanded Judah to serve the LORD God of Israel."[24]

The repeated pattern of the restoration of *todah* in these times of renewal shows us that *todah* is an integral part of worship to be offered to the LORD forever.

Todah ~ Reinstituted In Restored Jerusalem.

In the prophecies of the end-time restoration of Jerusalem we see *todah* again:

"For the LORD shall comfort Zion; He will comfort all her waste places, and He will make her wilderness like Eden, and her desert like the garden of the LORD; joy and gladness shall be found in it, thanksgiving (*todah*), and the voice of melody."[25]

Jeremiah prophesies that in the last days *todah*-praise will be a distinguishing mark of God's restoration to Israel of its lands:

"Thus says the LORD, 'Behold, I will bring back the captivity of Jacob's tents, and have mercy on his dwelling places, and the city shall be built upon its own mound, and the palace shall remain according to its own plan. Then out of them (Jacob's dwelling places ~ Israel) shall proceed thanksgiving (*todah*) and the voice of those who make merry; I will multiply them, and they shall not diminish; I will also glorify them, and they shall not be small.'"[26] "Thus says the LORD, 'Again there shall be heard in this place – of which you say, "It is desolate, without man and without beast" – in the cities of Judah, in the streets of Jerusalem that are desolate, without man and without inhabitant and without beast, 'the voice of joy, and the voice of gladness; the voice of the bridegroom, and the voice of the bride; the voice of those who will say: "Praise the LORD of hosts; for the LORD is good; for his mercy endures forever" – and (the voice) of those who will bring the sacrifice of praise (**todah**) into the house of the LORD. For I will cause the captives of the land to return as at the first,' says the LORD."[27]

Todah ~ Continued In the New Covenant.

The writer of Hebrews encourages New Covenant believers to offer *todah*-praise:

> "Therefore by Him – Y'shua – let us continually offer the <u>sacrifice of praise</u> (***todah***) to God, that is, the fruit of our lips, giving thanks to His name (literally, confessing thanks to His name)."[28]

This word "praise" is translated by the Greek word "*ainesis*" (pronounced *ah'-ee-nes-is*) meaning "praise, the act of praising, a thank offering or sacrifice of praise presented to God for some benefit received."[29] The sacrifice of praise (*todah*) is defined as the "fruit of our lips giving thanks to God." This is the **voice** of *todah*.

Our lips are to be altars for the sacrificial praises to God! We offer them for His use. To speak His words becomes our desire. In the Old Covenant Hosea states it this way:

> "Take words with you, and return to the LORD. Say to Him, 'Take away all iniquity; receive us graciously, for we will offer the sacrifices (literally, fruit) of our lips.'"[30]

"O LORD, take away all iniquity from us.
Receive us graciously – by Your grace and undeserved
favor – and we will offer the sacrifices of our lips
giving thanks to You."

Isaiah lays a foundation for the writer of Hebrews when he quotes the LORD as saying:

> "Peace, peace to him who is far off [both Jew and Gentile], and to him who is near…. I create the fruit of his lips and I will heal him – make his lips blossom anew with speech [in thankful praise]."[31]

From the Old Testament we glimpse Isaiah's revelation and discover that our God is the one who cleanses our lips and releases us to *todah*-praise. Isaiah 6:5-7 says:

> "Woe is me, for I am undone! Because I am a man of unclean lips, and I dwell in the midst of a people of unclean lips, for my eyes have seen the King, the LORD of hosts. Then one of the seraphim flew to me, having in his hand a live coal which he had taken with the tongs from the altar. And he touched my mouth with it, and said: 'Behold, this has touched your lips; your iniquity is taken away, and your sin purged.'"[32]

Through His cleansing we are able to breathe the breath of the Holy Spirit and pour forth praise to the LORD of Glory.

Here I am, LORD. Send me to the harvest fields,
that I may speak Your words and share Your salvation.

The Tabernacle of David Rebuilt

The Tabernacle of David presents a prophetic picture of New Covenant believers in praise! As David worshiped the LORD, he received revelation that the sacrifices which were pleasing to *ADONAI* are not the sacrifices of bulls and goats, but the sacrifices of a contrite heart, joy, thanksgiving and praise! Since the sacrificial system was still in place, this was an astounding revelation. David's worship before the Ark on Mount Zion looked forward to the New Covenant. According to the writer of Hebrews, we – New Covenant believers –

> "**have** come to Mount Zion and to the city of the living God, the heavenly Jerusalem, to an innumerable company of angels, to the general assembly and church of the firstborn who are registered in heaven, to God the Judge of all, to the spirits of just men made perfect, to Jesus the Mediator of the new covenant, and to the blood of sprinkling that speaks better things than that of Abel."[33]

Notice that it does not say **will** come, but **have** come. This is a **present** reality for us. We are called to ascend the holy mountain of God by the Spirit. We make this ascension with clean hands and a pure heart. By this we **now** enter the gates of the heavenly Jerusalem with *todah*. The Tabernacle of David is our pattern. Actually it is the very pattern of heaven's worship revealed to David. God is the same today, yesterday and forever! While our praise and worship is new everyday and ever expanding in expression, heaven's protocol still calls us to enter His presence with thanksgiving and praise.

Todah ~ The Hebrew Letters

Tav, Vav, Dalet and *Hey* are the Hebrew letters that make up *todah*. The first letter *Tav* means "the sign, the covenant." In antiquity it was drawn in the shape of a cross, which we know as the sign of our covenant. The second letter of *todah* is *Vav* which denotes a "hook or nail" and is often used as a conjunction (e.g. "and"). The third letter of *todah* is *Dalet* and when drawn symbolizes a "door." Positioned at the end, *Hey* means "what comes from" and also "breath," often representing the Holy Spirit. *Hey* was originally drawn as a "man with his hands raised" or an "open window."[34] Looking at the letters that make up the word *todah*, we can interpret its deeper message. We may say that the door to salvation is revealed by the cross and the nail. The nail joins heaven and earth. Putting it another way, what comes from the cross and the nail is the open Door to God's presence. *Todah*-praise is praise that springs from the revelation of all that He, The Door of Salvation, did for us. That is why we enter "in" with the sacrifice of praise and thanksgiving. *Todah* makes entrance into Salvation's gates.

> *Father, we offer our lips upon Your altar.*
> *Put your coal to our lips and make them clean. Create*
> *the fruit of our lips to speak thanksgiving and praise. Let*
> *us not utter any word except it come from You. Forgive*
> *us for idle words, words of doubt and unbelief, words*
> *confessing fear, judgment, accusation and unforgiveness.*
> *Forgive us of pride and arrogance and replace these*
> *with humility and gratitude to You. Create the fruit of*
> *thanksgiving* **(todah)** *on our lips and in our hearts. Let*
> *us offer* **todah** *to You as we ascend into Your presence,*
> *and let it be a sweet, fragrant offering. Let the words of our*
> *mouths and the meditation of our hearts be acceptable in*
> *Your sight, O LORD, our strength and our Redeemer.*[35]

I Will Dance

I will dance, I will sing, I will praise the King of kings,
Lai, lai, lai, lai, lai, lai, lai, lai, lai, lai.

I will make a joyful noise unto the LORD my God,
I will come into His presence with singing,
I will shout for joy and bless His holy name,
For He is the Rock of my salvation.

I will dance, I will sing, I will praise the King of kings,
Lai, lai, lai, lai, lai, lai, lai, lai, lai, lai.

I will enter His gates with thanksgiving[‡‡] in my heart,
I will enter His courts with my praises,
I will dance and I will sing in the presence of my King,
For He is the Rock of my salvation.

I will dance, I will sing, I will praise the King of kings,
Lai, lai, lai, lai, lai, lai, lai, lai, lai, lai.

Make a joyful noise to the LORD, all you lands,
Come before His presence with singing,
Shout for joy and bless His holy name,
For He is the Rock of our salvation!

I will dance, I will sing, I will praise the King of kings,
Lai, lai, lai, lai, lai, lai, lai, lai, lai, lai.
Lai, lai, lai, lai, lai, lai, lai, lai, lai, lai.[§§]

[‡‡] *Todah*
[§§] Copyright 2003 Nancy E. Morgan

NOTES

1   James Strong, S.T.D., L.L.D., *Strong's Exhaustive Concordance of the Bible* (Madison, N.J.: James Strong, 1973), *Hebrew and Chaldee Dictionary* #8426, p. 123.

2   Francis Brown, D.D., D.Litt. with the cooperation of S.R. Driver, D.D., Litt.D. and Charles A. Briggs, D.D., D.Litt., *The New Brown-Driver-Briggs-Gesenius Hebrew and English Lexicon* (Peabody, Massachusetts: Hendrickson Publishers, 1979), #8426, p. 392b.

3   Isaiah 49:15b-16a Amplified Version

4   Nehemiah 12:27 Amplified Version

5   Nehemiah 12:30 Amplified Version

6   Nehemiah 12:31

7   Nehemiah 12:38

8   Nehemiah 12:41-42

9   Nehemiah 12:43b

10 Psalm 100:4

11 Psalm 95:2

12 Psalm 107:22 CJB

13 Psalm 147:7

14 Psalm 116:17 CJB

15 Jonah 2:9

16 Psalm 56:12

17 Joshua 7:19; Ezra 10:11

18 Psalm 24:3-4 NIV

19 Psalm 26:6-7

20 Psalm 42:4 CJB

21 Psalm 50:14,15

22 Psalm 50:23

23 II Chronicles 29:31

24 II Chronicles 33:16

25 Isaiah 51:3

26 Jeremiah 30:18-19

27 Jeremiah 33:10,11

28 Hebrews 13:15

29 Strong, *Greek Dictionary of the New Testament*, #133, p.8 **and**
    J. H. Thayer, *The New Thayer's Greek-English Lexicon of the New Testament*, #133, p. 16a.
    (The Greek Lexicon connects this word "*ainesis*" in Hebrews 13:15 with Leviticus 7:11-15: *Todah* – a thank-offering to God for some benefit received.)

30 Hosea 14:2

31 Is 57:19 Amplified Version

32 Is 6:5-7

33 Hebrews 12:22-24

34 Dr. Frank T. Seekins, *Hebrew Word Pictures: How Does the Hebrew Alphabet Reveal Prophetic Truths?* (Phoenix, Arizona: Living Word Pictures, Inc., 1994, 2003), p. 28.
35 Psalm 19:14

Psalm of Praise

Tehillah ~ The Definition

The next Hebrew word for praise we will consider is **tehillah** (pronounced *teh-hil-lah'*). *Tehillah* is translated into Greek as *psalmos* and into English as psalm. The plural for *tehillah* is *tehillim* and in the Hebrew Scriptures the Book of Psalms is called *"Tehillim."* The word *tehillah* offers golden nuggets of wisdom and rich treasures of revelation. This beautiful word, I believe, will continue to be illuminated throughout eternity. Let us begin our search with its definition. As with the other words for praise, this one is variously used as a noun and a verb. According to the Hebrew Lexicon *tehillah* is defined as "the shouting of a sacred formula; praise, adoration, thanksgiving; song of praise; the act of general, public, praise; praise-song; qualities, deeds, etc. of or demanding praise; renown, fame, glory; psalm."[1] Derived from the root word *"hallel,"* *tehillah* becomes our "sung *hallel.*"

Tehillah ~ The Hebrew Letters

The first Hebrew letter in this word is *Tav,* meaning "sign," "mark" or "covenant." It was originally drawn in the shape of a cross. The second and last letter is *Hey.* Interestingly the meaning of *Hey* varies with its position. At the beginning of a word it means "behold." However, when it is placed in the middle of a word it means to "reveal the heart or the core of" and at the end of a word means "what comes from." *Hey* also means "wind" or "breath." The third and fourth letters are *Lamed,* meaning goad or tongue. *Tehillah* comes from the root word *hallel* and contains the word *hallel* in the center of its construction. So we can conclude that *tehillah,* our song of praise, is defined as what comes from our covenant relationship with the Tongue of tongues, Y'shua Ha Mashiach. Not only do these songs reveal the heart of the Tongue of tongues, they also reveal our hearts when joined to His. Sung by the breath of His Holy Spirit they are our "sung *hallels.*"

Vessels of *Tehillah!*

Regarding this praise word Isaiah heard the LORD* make a powerful statement. In chapter 43 he quotes Yahweh as saying, "This people that I have **formed** for Myself shall **declare** My *tehillah*."[2] The two key words here are "formed" and "declare." **Formed**[3] in the Hebrew means "to press, squeeze, mold into a form, fashion, form, frame, potter and purpose." **Declare**[4] is "to inscribe, write, count, account, recount, number, speak, talk, tell out and show forth." Inserting these meanings into the context of our LORD's statement, we may amplify it this way: We are being molded, fashioned and formed **by** our heavenly Potter **for** Himself **into** a vessel that will declare, proclaim, publish and show forth His *tehillah!*

Just think of it. For His own pleasure the LORD created all things and for His pleasure they continue to exist![5] We are part of that creation! Earlier we learned that we have been *created*[6] (created, chosen, selected) to be instruments of His "*hallel*." Now we learn that once He creates us, Yahweh fashions and molds us into vessels of *tehillah*. As He continues to fill us with His love and presence, we begin to overflow with the perfume of His praise. In exuberance and delight we have boldness to proclaim it openly. His purpose for our very existence is to sing forth our praise to **Him** and make **His** *tehillah* – His psalms or "sung *hallels*" – glorious![7]

Further confirmation of our call to praise is found in Psalm 51. David psalmed: "O LORD, open my lips and my mouth shall **show forth** Your *tehillah*."[8] In this psalm David's voice of praise has been silenced because of the pain of his sin with Bathsheba and its consequences. Overcome with sorrow, heaviness, guilt and remorse, he cries to God in repentance and accepts Yahweh's loving forgiveness and mercy. David knows that only God can open his

---

* When LORD is spelled with all capital letters in the King James Version and New King James Version, it translates the holy name of God. Called the Tetragrammaton, it is formed with the four Hebrew letters *Yud, Heh, Vav, Heh* (*YHVH or YHWH*) and is sometimes translated Jehovah, Yehovah, Yahweh or Yahveh. The Complete Jewish Bible translates this name as *ADONAI*, a title meaning "LORD."

mouth and restore his joy and praise. What a challenge David brings to the LORD. He beseeches Him to open his lips so that the LORD will see that his mouth is so full of praise that, when it is opened, the full measure of *tehillah* dwelling there will burst forth in jubilant expression of thanksgiving to Him! This *tehillah*-praise, a work of the Holy Spirit, sings David's newest testimony of Yahweh's gracious mercy in restoring the contrite heart.

In Psalm 34 David vows:

> "I will bless the LORD at all times; **His [*tehillah*] shall continually *be* in my mouth**. My soul shall make its boast (*hallel*) in the LORD; **the humble shall hear *of it*** and be glad."⁹

Let us pause for a moment and take a little test. If Yahweh opens your mouth right now, will He find it filled with *tehillah*?

Tehillah ~ Song of the Bride

Remember that *hallel* means "giving ourselves in marriage" and *tehillah* is our "sung *hallel*." It stands to reason then that *tehillah* is our love song, the wedding song of the Bride to her holy Bridegroom. Can you see that *praise* is not a ministry or calling appointed just for a chosen few? Absolutely not! It is the pre-eminent ministry for all of God's creation! Our *first* calling is to minister PRAISE to our Creator and then to publicly declare His honor and majesty! He delights in us as we enumerate one by one His awesome characteristics and works which are all worthy of the highest praise. We are created to praise! May I challenge you to make a list of all the names, attributes and works of God you can find in the Scriptures? This will expand your "Praise Vocabulary." Then use all of these words and phrases of praise as you celebrate the Maker of heaven and earth with the *tehillah* that only He deserves. Begin with a few at a time and as you find more accolades add to the list. Our God is worthy of all praise!

Tehillim ~ The Psalms

Now let us take a closer look at the word *tehillah*. As we know, the Greek word *psalmos* is transliterated into English as *psalm*. We can learn volumes about *tehillah* from the people of the Book, the children of Israel, who have remarkable insight into the Psalms. After all, they received these Spirit-breathed songs from the LORD and have sung them for generations. In *The Artscroll Tehillim* we read these fascinating words:

> "For nearly three thousand years, every situation in a Jew's life has been reflected in the chapters of *Tehillim*. This was the book of which Hashem [Hebrew for "The Name," referring to the LORD] said to King David, 'One day of your songs and praises is more precious to Me than the thousands of offerings that will be offered by your son Solomon.' In illness and in strife, in triumph and in success, the Jew turns to his Book of Psalms and lets David become the harp upon which his own emotions sing or weep."[10]

Still today all who call on the name of the LORD can find the same comfort, strength, encouragement and instruction for every facet of life in the songs recorded by the psalmists of Israel.

Tehillim ~ Our Praise Manual

Tehillah is central to the worship of Yahweh. Y'shua's psalms were conceived before time, spoken into time and yet transcend time. They include prophecies concerning individuals and nations – some already fulfilled and others yet to be fulfilled. They sing His own praise to the Father, His instructions to believers on how to praise and His commands to us to offer the praise in which He and His Father delight. The psalms also contain the expressions of Y'shua's own soul's travail as He walked on earth in perfect union with the Father, experiencing every temptation known to man, yet perfect and victorious in all things. A "man of sorrows and acquainted with grief,"[11] Jesus our high priest is able to "empathize with all our weaknesses."[12] He who knew no sin became sin for us.[13] Taking the curse and punishment for our sin upon Himself, He totally identified with us in experiencing everything that we experience. His soul's expressions in the psalms give us utterance for all that we encounter and endure as we take up our cross and follow Him. He experienced the curse and punishment for our sins so that we can experience His blessed forgiveness and death-conquering resurrection! **Every situation we face and every emotion we feel are powerfully articulated in *Tehillim*.**

As already stated, *hallel* encompasses the expression of all seven Hebrew words for praise as light contains the colors of the rainbow.[†] On the other hand, the Book of *Tehillim* (Psalms) is our "Praise Manual" or "Praise Dictionary" and contains instructions concerning the expression of *Tehillah* as well as the other six Hebrew words for praise: *Hallel, Shabach, Todah, Yadah, Barak and Zamar.*

Who Receives *Tehillah*?[‡]

The praise and adoration given through *tehillah* is a sacred praise offered to God which includes various manifestations of His name, His titles and His works. In Isaiah 42 God affirms that He is jealous over His *tehillah* and that it belongs to Him and Him alone. He declares, "I AM the LORD; that is My name. I will not give My glory to another or My *tehillah* to idols."[14]

Who Gives *Tehillah*?

Numerous instances of the offering of *tehillah* to God are contained in the Word. **Levites, psalmists, prophets, the congregation of Israel, the praisers before Jehoshaphat's army, the righteous, the upright, the sheep of His pasture and collectively all the saints of God** are called to be vessels of praise. The command to bring *tehillah* to the God of Israel is given to **all nations, Gentile kings** and the abundance of the **sea.** (The word *sea* is symbolic for "nations.")

† See the chapter on "*Hallel*."
‡ See the *Tehillah* Concordance in the "Created To Praise Study Guide" for references.

Isaiah prophesied that three specific nations – **Midian, Ephah and Sheba** – will one day proclaim the *tehillim* of Yahweh as they bring gifts of camels, gold and incense to the people of restored Israel.[15] It is encouraging to note here that these are three of the many nations that God promised Abraham: "As for Me, behold, My covenant is with you, and you shall be a father of many nations."[16] Midian was Abraham's son by his concubine Keturah after Sarah's death. A nation was born of him. According to *Unger's Bible Dictionary* Midian was called the "Judah of the Arabians." How appropriate that Midian should bring his "*tehillah*-praise" to Yahweh in light of the fact that the name Judah means "praise." Midian's territory was located on the coast of the Gulf of Aqaba.[17] Ephah was Midian's son, Abraham's grandson. A city was named after him in the land of Midian and was located on the east shore of the Dead Sea. Later accounts name Ephah as a separate nation located opposite the extremity of the Sinaitic Peninsula.[18] Sheba was also Abraham's grandson by another son of Keturah. This nation "may have been situated in either present-day Ethiopia or present-day Yemen."[19]

Who Qualifies to Offer *Tehillah?*

In Psalm 106 Y'shua sings these questions, "Who can utter the mighty acts of the LORD? Who can declare all His *tehillah?*[20] Immediately He chants the answer: "Blessed are **those who keep justice**, and **he who does righteousness at all times!**"[21] We see that only those who walk justly and live righteously qualify. Only **those with clean hands, pure hearts and lives laid down** can ascend the hill of the LORD to minister at His footstool and receive blessing and righteousness from Him.[22] Only they can proclaim His mighty acts and declare all His *tehillah*, His songs of praise!

LORD, I ask that You cleanse, purify and qualify us to sing Your psalms and bring You praise!

When Do We Offer Our *Tehillah?*

Our *tehillah* is to reside **continually** in our mouths,[23] to be brought with us **when we come into His courts** and offered all

day long. Our Creator and His works are to be the theme of our song. *Tehillah* is to increase more and more in quantity, quality and intensity and **be offered forever and eternally – from now through eternity, as long as I live** and **while I have my being**. It is to be our spontaneous response to believing His Word and will be recounted **from generation to generation**.

As Paul and Silas sang *tehillim* **at the midnight hour**, so we too can follow their example. Using this mighty weapon of praise in every time of trouble, we can see the same miraculous deliverance and salvation in our lives and the lives of those around us. Again, **whenever New Covenant believers come together**, we are instructed by the Lord through Paul that every one of us should bring a *psalm*, a doctrine, a tongue, a revelation and an interpretation.[24] His *tehillah* **endures forever!**[25]

Where Is *Tehillah* to Be Found?

Our **mouths** should be filled with our sung *hallels*. **From the ends of the earth** we will sing forth our new and ever flowing songs of *tehillah*. They will reach **to the ends of the earth, filling the earth** with the glorious accolades of God and His works. God's people will give glory to the LORD and declare His *tehillah* **in the coastlands**. We who are raised from death to life can now move on to proclaim *tehillah* **in the gates of the Daughter of Zion**.[26]§ Processing through the **Gate of *Tehillah***, the awesome praises of God will fill the **courts of His Temple**. These *tehillah* praise songs will pour forth from the great congregation of saints entering His holy presence. *Tehillah* will be declared **in Zion and in Jerusalem** and sung **among the peoples and the nations**. *Tehillah* praise waits for God **in Zion**.[27] Isaiah prophesied that *tehillim* will spring forth along with righteousness **before the nations**.[28] Psalm 149 instructs us to "let the high *tehillim* be **in our mouths** and the two-edged sword in our hands, executing vengeance on the nations, punishments on the peoples, binding their kings with chains and their nobles with fetters of iron."[29] The writer of Ephesians instructs us to make melody **in our hearts** and **speak**

§   Hebrews 12:22a states that we (believers in Y'shua) have already "come to Mount Zion, to the city of the living God, the heavenly Jerusalem…."

to ourselves and one another in psalms and hymns and spiritual songs, thus teaching, admonishing and encouraging one another in the Lord.[30] This honor have **all** His saints. Hallelujah! *Hallel* the LORD."[31]

Y'shua prophesies in Psalm 22, "I will proclaim Your name to My brethren; **in the midst of the assembly** I will praise You."[32] Finally, we read in the Book of Revelation that the redeemed of the Lord sing a new song of *tehillah* (a sung *hallel*) **before the throne, the four living creatures and the elders!**[33]

Why Bring *Tehillah*?

The "whys" of *tehillah* are far too numerous to count. Since God is not only the subject of our *tehillah* but *He is* our *Tehillah,* the reasons are as infinite as His Being. The reasons and themes of our *tehillim* are **His attributes and awesome works of love and power. The Lord is King over all the earth and He has done great and awesome things for us; He has preserved our lives and kept our feet from slipping; He has bestowed great goodness on us and on the house of Israel. He blesses us according to His mercies and the multitude of His loving-kindnesses.**[34] **It is beautiful, good, pleasant and fitting to offer our psalms of praise to the LORD**[35] for **His name is pleasant.**[36] Messiah gives *tehillah* to the Father **so that the Gentiles (all nations) will glorify God.**[37] We sing the Word of the LORD **to teach, admonish and encourage others.**[38] Praises are due the LORD **because He has called us out of darkness and into His marvelous light.**[39] We chant our proclamations of **God's redemption and His deliverance.** Joining the host of heaven we sing, 'You are worthy to take the scroll, and to open its seals; **for You were slain, and have redeemed us to God by Your blood out of every tribe and tongue and people and nation, and have made us kings and priests to our God; and we shall reign on the earth.'**[40] We sing *tehillah* to **express our joy**[41] **in the LORD and His salvation.** We could go on and on filling every book with reasons to *tehillah* and yet eternity will not be long enough to express them all.

How Do We Bring Our *Tehillah?*

By offering *tehillah* **with understanding,** we fulfill Yahweh's mandate to worship Him **in Spirit and in Truth.** The psalmist cries, "Open my lips and **my mouth shall show forth** Your Tehillah."[42] **With my lips** I will utter *tehillah* and **with my tongue** I will speak it. **With my mouth and my voice** I will sing *tehillah* to Him. Sing His praise **with triumph, shouting and loud voices.** We are called to *shabach* – **triumph in, shout forth and address in a loud tone** – the *tehillah* of God. "Save us, O LORD our God, and gather us from among the Gentiles, to *give thanks* unto thy holy name, to *triumph (shabach)* in thy *tehillah*.[43] Yes, we are called to **show forth and display** our *tehillah* before the world, declaring His works, proclaiming His salvation, delighting in His goodness and boasting in His faithfulness. Scripture commands us to **let the voice and sound of His *tehillah* be heard** and to **make His *tehillah* glorious** – full of glory and honor and skillful presentation. Praise Him **with musical instruments,** and accompany *tehillim* **with the harp,**¶ **the ten stringed harp,**** **the lute, the timbrel, the drums and all musical instruments.**

Tehillah ~ Healing and Salvation

Giving *tehillah* to the LORD sets us in position to receive healing and salvation. The prophet Jeremiah sang to Yahweh, "Heal me, O LORD, and I shall be healed; Save me, and I shall be saved, **for You are my *Tehillah*.**"[44] Because he had made God his "Praise," Jeremiah expected healing and salvation to be extended to him. He coupled this praise with his faith, acknowledging God's power to make him whole. We can paraphrase it this way, 'If **You** heal me, I **will** be healed and if **You** save me, I **will** be saved, because **You are my praise.**' Only our LORD has this power and He **is** willing to extend it to us.

¶ Hebrew – *nevel*
** Hebrew – *kinnor*

Tehillah brings forth much fruit. As a result of our giving *tehillah* to the LORD, many will be touched and drawn to God. David sings, "My mouth shall speak the *tehillah* of the LORD, and **all flesh shall bless His holy name forever and ever.**"[45] Singing out his testimony, David *tehillah*-s his deliverance out of the miry pit, his being set upon the rock and the establishing of his new walk. David affirms the victory of his *tehillah* in Psalm 40 when he declares "**many will see and fear and will trust in the LORD.**"[46] *Tehillah* proclaims the LORD's salvation, bringing in a great harvest of souls!

Tehillah ~ Weapon of Warfare

Tehillah praise led Israel's hosts into battle. Obeying the instruction of the LORD, King Jehoshaphat placed the singers **in front** of God's army. In II Chronicles 20 we read: "As they began to sing and *tehillah*, [Yahweh] set ambushes against the men of Ammon and Moab and Mount Seir who were invading Judah, and they were defeated."[47] God honored their obedience to first praise "the beauty of His holiness, His Name and His mercy." They praised in the most adverse circumstances and Yahweh fought the battle. Praise proceeds victory!

Let us look at three verses in Psalm 149:

> "*Hallel* the LORD. Sing to the LORD a new song, *and* His *tehillah* in the assembly of saints."[48] "Let them *hallel* His name with the dance; Let them sing *tehillim* to Him with the timbrel and harp."[49] "Let the ***high praise*** of God be in their mouth, and a two-edged sword in their hand."[50]

Here we see instructions for *tehillah* praise to be lifted to the LORD in the congregation of His people, accompanied by timbrel and harp. The Father enjoins us to let or allow the high *tehillim* of God be in our mouths along with the two-edged sword in our hands in order

> "to execute vengeance on the nations, and punishments on the peoples, to bind their kings with chains and

their nobles with fetters of iron; to execute on them the written judgment – this **honor** have all His saints. *Hallel* the LORD."[51]

The descriptive Hebrew word translated "high" means "uplifting, arising, extolling, praise.[52]" We can amplify verse six this way:

Let the arising, uplifting, extolling, high praise of God be in our mouths and a two-edged sword in our hands, a sword of praise and judgment that both looses the captives and binds the enemy powers.

In summary, when we voice the high praises of God from our mouth, we are allowing the praises of Y'shua to arise from the depths of our soul. This "high praise" fills the atmosphere exalting and enthroning Yahweh. These melodious words which are sung by the Ruach Ha Kodesh are resident in His body which we are. Yielding in obedience to the Psalmist's commands, this praise is transformed by His power into the two-edged sword that both delivers captives from the enemy's grasp and binds that enemy in chains and fetters.

Tehillah releases power to open prison doors and brings testimonies of deliverance that lead to salvation. Remember the story of Paul and Silas in prison? At the midnight hour they testified their love and trust in the Lord through *tehillah*. This "public praise" created an atmosphere of divine deliverance. The power of God's response shook foundations. (Is there a prison in your life whose foundations need to shake and break through the power of *tehillah*?) The prison doors swung open and chains fell off. The results of Paul and Silas' *tehillah* were not only salvation but joy! The prisoners then and now are set free! *Tehillah!*

When we understand the cycle of praise as taught by the Word, we will discover the "wheel within the wheel." In Him, praise brings victory and victory births love. Love's response is praise!

According to Psalm 148 our *tehillah* is a horn, which not only trumpets military might and authority, but strength and power. It was from the ram's horn that the anointing oil flowed. Today it is the same. The anointing flows from Messiah through His people, His horn. By *tehillah* the LORD exalts His strength and his warfare through the praises of His body.

> "And He has exalted the horn of His people, the *tehillah* of all His saints – of the children of Israel, a people near to Him. *Hallel* the LORD![53]

This same *tehillah* is a shield that protects us from judgment and keeps us through all the processes of refining:

> "For My name's sake I will defer My anger, and for My *tehillah* I will restrain it from you, so that I do not cut you off. Behold, I have refined you, but not as silver; I have tested you in the furnace of affliction. For My own sake, for My own sake, I will do it; for how should My *name* be profaned? And I will not give My glory to another."[54]

Tehillah ~ A New Song

The psalmist declares:

> "Oh, sing to the LORD a **new song**! Sing to the LORD, all the earth. Sing to the LORD, bless His name; proclaim the good news of His salvation from day to day. Declare His glory among the nations, His wonders among all people."[55]

When Y'shua sang, "Sing to the LORD a **new** song, *and* His *tehillah* from the ends of the earth,"[56] He was speaking to each of us as we read and sing His psalms. The understood subject here is "You." (You) sing to Yahweh a new song, His *tehillah* from the ends of the earth."[57] All who read, hear, or sing the words of Y'shua are instructed to personalize the psalms – to identify with and become the psalmist – and bring their *tehillah* to the LORD.

In singing a new *tehillah*, we release the creative work of the Holy Spirit. These new phrases and creative praises celebrate the mighty works of God. This celebration becomes a catalyst for new and fresh discoveries. For the worshiper, the new psalms of *tehillah* can be the door to new heights of creativity and open undiscovered horizons in their lives.

Through the continual "springing up" of *tehillah* to Him, we are not only given new songs but fresh insights. The word for "new" in Hebrew means "to renew, rebuild, repair or refresh."[58] Our song of praise should always be sung in the freshness of newness, in the spontaneity of new revelation and first love, whether it is a song we've just received from the Holy Spirit, whether the song is already known to us or whether the song has just been introduced to us.

Personal Discovery

In my own personal walk there were times I had to lay down my music and songwriting for a period of time in order to break the old patterns of melody, rhythm and harmony. This time of silent waiting allowed Y'shua to again breathe His new song of life-giving power into my spirit. As a trained pianist in classical music, I was glued to the written page. In order to break through into the limitless wonders of the liberty of the Spirit, I would sit down at the piano and ask the LORD to play using my fingers. Beginning awkwardly, I would "play with the keys," trying new sounds and combinations, scales, chords and arpeggios. I would praise, pray and worship the LORD as I allowed my hands and fingers to span the length of the keyboard. There were times when the music was discordant and disjointed but in persevering, I experienced the release of new songs and sounds.

Another example of creative *tehillah* is in nature itself. Our God as Creator expresses His renown and glory (*tehillah*) in our natural world. Spinning on its axis, the earth is a continual offering of praise.

The psalmist sings, "Yahweh shall reign. The earth **rejoices**[tt]."[59] We see the *tehillah* of creation in the changing seasons of nature. We view an earth that is a canvas of light and shadow. The heaven above us is a moving kaleidoscope. The sun shines brightly and then is intermittently hidden by rain-filled clouds, sleet and snows. Our days are punctuated with red-gold dawns and splendor-colored sunsets. We watch as tides flow in and out forming new edges of our seascapes. Nature's beauty is an endless testament to His limitless art and design. The *tehillah* of nature is new everyday.

As in His natural creation, so our lives move through seasons of spiritual growth. Our understanding of God, ourselves and the world around us is constantly changing. Through valleys of sorrow and weeping, through the joys of sudden revelation and mountain-top epiphanies, through times of rock-bed faith and trials that shake, our God's creative hand and blessings move through *tehillah* praise in our lives. Paul encourages us:

> "...put on the new self, which is continually being renewed in fuller and fuller knowledge, closer and closer to the image of its Creator.... Let the Word of the Messiah, in all its richness, live in you, as you teach and counsel each other in all wisdom, and as you sing psalms (*tehillim*), hymns and spiritual songs [new spirit-breathed songs of *tehillim*] with gratitude to God in your hearts."[60]

Today science tells us that our DNA[##] is a song, unique to each individual. The LORD's breath upon our lives is evidenced in this new song. This holy and personal touch by our Creator becomes a part of God's creative symphony when we receive His life in us.

[tt] The Hebrew word for "rejoice" is *giyl* (Strong's #1523) and means"to spin round (under the influence of any violent emotion), be glad, joy, be joyful, rejoice." The Hebrew lexicon further defines it as "go round or about, be excited to levity, rejoice."

[##] For more information, type "DNA is a song" into your search engine and be astounded!

Years ago, as I played a new melody, a sister in the LORD had a vision. She described a beautiful rose bud with its petals tightly curled together. As she watched, the bud grew larger and the petals gradually opened. As if in slow motion, the colors began to reveal themselves in an ever-widening palette of hues. The sweet fragrance of this blossoming filled the air. Finally the rose displayed itself in its full glory: its bloom a grand, radiant testimony to its Creator.

Our life's song is an unfolding rose. It begins at our new birth as a simple but beautiful melody and develops over the passing of time. As we walk in light and Truth, our life becomes a composition of melody, rhythm and harmony. Its lyrics express our purpose and our unique placement in the body of Messiah. As we are changed and transformed, our lives display, like the rose, ever-deepening facets of color and expression. As each member of Y'shua's body manifests his song, the symphony of the Creative LORD crescendos and celebrates *tehillah*.

> "Oh, sing to the LORD a new song! For He has done marvelous things; His right hand and His holy arm have gained Him the victory."[61]
> "He put a new song in my mouth, a song of *tehillah* to our God. Many will look on in awe and put their trust in the *ADONAI*."[62]
> "Sing to the LORD a new song, *and* His *tehillah* from the ends of the earth...."[63]

This is the reason our mouths should be continually filled with new songs of joy and praise, testimony, salvation and deliverance. Despite the flux of constant creative change in our lives, there is stability and steady predictability in Him. Our God is a God we can trust and whose love is constant. He is the same yesterday, today and forever. Sing a new song! *Tehillah!*

Tehillah ~ Sung by Y'shua

The Psalmist of psalmists, Y'shua Ha Mashiach,[§§] sings *tehillah* to the Father and to believers throughout the ages. As the author of the inspired written Word and thus the composer of all the psalms, Y'shua sang all the psalms and other songs recorded in the Bible into the ears of earthly psalmists and prophets who then rehearsed them to the congregation of Israel and recorded them in the Scriptures.

In Y'shua's Psalms we discover many amazing prophetic truths. For instance, in Psalm 108 Y'shua sings to His Father: "I will praise You, O LORD, **among the peoples**, and I will sing *tehillim* to You **among the nations**."[64] We know that Y'shua came in the flesh only to the lost sheep of the house of Israel. How, then, and when, could He fulfill this vow to sing praise to the Father among the peoples and among the nations? Psalm 22 gives us the clue:

> "I will declare Your name to My brethren; in the midst of the assembly I will [*hallel*] You.
>
> You who fear the LORD, [*hallel*] Him! All you descendants of Jacob, glorify (*hallel*) Him, and fear Him, all you offspring of Israel!
>
> For He has not despised nor abhorred the affliction of the afflicted; nor has He hidden His face from Him; But when He cried to Him He heard.[65]
>
> From You (Father) comes the theme of my *tehillah* in the great assembly; before those who fear You I will fulfill My vows."[66]

Here we see an astounding prophecy of future praise promised by Y'shua to His Father. In verse 22 He sings, "I will declare Your name to My brethren; in the midst of the assembly I will *hallel* You. He continues in verse 25, "From You (Father) comes the theme of my

---

[§§] Hebrew for "Jesus the Christ."

tehillah – (the subject of my song) – in the great assembly; before those who fear you I **will** (future tense) fulfill My vows."

What are His vows? After singing of the sufferings He would endure on the cross in the preceding verses of Psalm 22, Y'shua prophesied that He would bring *hallel* and *tehillah* to the Father **after** His resurrection! In verse 21 of this psalm He cried to the Father for salvation from the power of the enemy. Acknowledging the Father's answer of deliverance, Jesus vowed to proclaim the name of the Father to His brethren and to praise Him in the midst of the congregation and before all those who fear God after He was raised from the dead! What a declaration of faith! But how would He do this? Through the vessels of His indwelt believers on the earth! Using our mouths and voices, Y'shua praises the Father from the midst of our beings! What a thought! We are **His instruments** of praise. In other words, before He endured the cross Jesus prophesied that after He was resurrected He would testify of His Father's deliverance of Him and all mankind on the cross. In front of those who fear and revere the Father, He – Messiah – would fulfill His vows of obedience and praise throughout eternity – in the midst of the congregation, from His dwelling place in the hearts of His people!

Remember that Y'shua told the Father, "From You comes the theme of My *tehillah* in the great assembly?" The subject of Y'shua's song is praise to the Father for the miracle of His own resurrection and the accomplishment of the redemption of mankind on the cross! A powerful confirmation of this is recorded in the book of Hebrews. Chapter two quotes Psalm 22:22 and attributes the words to Y'shua:

> "For it was fitting for Him, for whom are all things and by whom are all things, **in bringing many sons to glory**, to make the captain of their salvation (Y'shua) perfect through sufferings. For both He who sanctifies and those who are being sanctified are all of one (of the same origin – the same Father), for which reason He (Y'shua) is not ashamed to call them brethren, saying: 'I *will* declare Your name to My brethren; in the midst

of the assembly I *will* sing praise (sing *hallel, tehillah*) to You.'" And (saying) again: 'I will put My trust in Him (Y'shua trusting the Father).' And (saying) again: 'Here I am, and the children God has given Me.'"[67]

A Word to Worship Leaders ~ Today's Fulfillment!

Several years ago, I was leading worship in a church service. We had ascended in praise to the throne room of God and were basking in His presence when in my spirit I heard the words, "Here I am, and the children You have given me." It seemed I, as the psalmist, was presenting the congregation to the LORD and backing out of the way for Him to continue to move. However, now as I study Psalm 22, I see the fuller picture of what was happening. In His resurrected state, and from His place of dwelling in my spirit, Y'shua had psalmed to the Father using my vessel. Then, at the point of reaching the Father's presence, He presented the congregation, including me, to the Father, fulfilling the prophetic vow He had made in Psalm 22 before the foundation of the world! "Here I AM and the children You have given Me." God is faithful to fulfill His Word!

Tehillah ~ Sung by Y'shua's Disciples

We find the disciples singing *tehillah* in their daily practice of Temple worship. They sang the Psalms of Ascent¶¶ as they went up to the Temple for the feasts of the LORD; they sang the Psalms of *Hallel* during every Passover (*Pesach*) *Seder* (*Seder* means order of service) and at the feasts of Pentecost (*Shavuot*), Tabernacles (*Succot*) and *Hanukkah*. On Shabbat they sang Psalm 92 as well as the Songs of Moses found in Exodus 15 and Deuteronomy 32. It is noted in the book of Acts that, after His resurrection, Y'shua's disciples sang *tehillim* to the LORD as they went to the temple daily and broke bread from house to house:

¶¶ The Hebrew word for "ascent" is *ma'alah* (pronounced *mah-al-ah'*) and means "a journey to a higher place, a climactic progression." Figuratively it means "arising thoughts." It is #4609 in the Strong's Concordance. For a closer look at these psalms see *Lift Up Your Eyes* Vol. 1 by Nancy E. Morgan.

"Continuing faithfully and with singleness of purpose to meet in the Temple courts daily, and breaking bread in their several homes, they shared their food in joy and simplicity of heart, praising God and having the respect of all the people. And day after day the Lord kept adding to them those who were being saved."[68]

Tehillah ~ Instructions to New Covenant Believers

Peter instructs New Covenant believers to offer *tehillah*:

"But ye *are* a chosen generation, a royal priesthood, a holy nation, a [people of His own], that ye should show forth the *praises*[69] of Him who hath called you out of darkness into His marvelous light."[70]

This reference uses language similar to many Old Covenant passages. Isaiah recorded: "This people have I formed for Myself; they shall **show forth** My *tehillah*."[71] Also from Psalm 73: "So we, Your people, and the sheep of Your pasture, will give You thanks forever; we will **show forth** Your *tehillah* to all generations."[72] The term "show forth" here in I Peter stems from the Greek word *exegello* from which we derive our English word "exit." We have been chosen as a special, holy nation of royal priests to allow the praises of our indwelling Messiah to exit out of us, sounding forth in splendorous display for all to see and hear, proclaiming our deliverance from darkness into His marvelous light! This is the vocal picture of resurrection. As our Lord prophesied, proclaimed and praised the Father for His own resurrection, so let us! Can you imagine the power and majesty in His thundering voice as He commanded the heavenly gates to open before Him? "Lift up your heads, O you gates! And be lifted up, you everlasting doors! And the King of glory shall come in."[73] Just as Y'shua's *tehillah* prophesied and proclaimed His victorious resurrection, so can we. Through *tehillah* we can praise Him for His resurrection power in our lives and "at that Day."[74]

Paul gave believers the protocol for their meetings. He said, "When you come together, every one of you has a <u>psalm</u> (*psalmos–tehillah*), a doctrine, a tongue, a revelation, an interpretation."

The writer of Ephesians instructs us,

> "Don't get drunk with wine, because it makes you lose control. Instead, keep on being filled with the Spirit – sing **psalms** [the *tehillim* recorded in scripture], **hymns** [great hymns written by God's people through the ages] and **spiritual songs** [new, Spirit-breathed songs – new psalms or *tehillim*] to each other; sing to the Lord and **make music** [singing *tehillim* accompanied by musical instruments] in your heart to Him...."[75]

These verses reveal that by continually singing *tehillim* we will continue to be filled with the Holy Spirit. As we let our hearts become instruments to accompany our songs of praise, they will bubble up, overflow and spill over into testimony and encouragement to those around us. The letter to the believers at Colosse (the Colossians) adds:

> "Let the Word of the Messiah, in all its richness, live in you, as you teach and counsel each other in all wisdom , and as you sing **<u>psalms</u>, <u>hymns</u>** and **<u>spiritual songs</u>,** with gratitude to God in your hearts."[76]

We sing to the LORD, and we sing to one another. With our song we give thanks and also teach and counsel one another in the wisdom of the Word of Y'shua. The words of our songs should reflect the Word of God. The book of James teaches us that our joy is to be expressed by psalming. "Is any merry? Let him sing psalms (*tehillim*)."[77]

Is there any doubt that we of this present generation of believers are called to offer *tehillah* to *ADONAI*? Over and over He invites, instructs and even commands all people everywhere to minister this beautiful form of praise to Him. Individually and corporately, intimately and publicly, our God delights in our *tehillim!* In both Old and New Covenants *tehillah* is to be manifested as a glorious symphony of praise.

Tehillah ~ As a Mantle

Tehillah is defined as "renown, fame, glory, renown as a mantle, a splendid garment."[78] Isaiah penned a beautiful revelation in Chapter 61:

> "The Spirit of *ADONAI ELOHIM* is upon me, because *ADONAI* has anointed me … to comfort all who mourn, yes, provide for those in Tziyon who mourn, giving them garlands instead of ashes, the oil of gladness instead of mourning, and a **cloak of** *tehillah* instead of a heavy spirit, so that they will be called oaks of righteousness planted by *ADONAI*, in which He takes pride.[79]

We know from Luke 4:18-20 that Y'shua publicly declared He is this Anointed One and that the works of transformation from grief to joy are His works. He is the One who garments our lives with *tehillah*.

God gives this cloak of *tehillah* **to His people as His creation and the works of His hands!** In Zephaniah we read that the LORD will one day bestow *tehillah* as a mantle of renown, honor, fame and praise **to the lame** and **to those of the nation of Israel who were driven out** in every land where they have been put to shame![80] He will give the *tehillah* mantle to re-gathered Israel in their own land when He brings them back home from the nations, restoring their fortunes before their very eyes.[81] *ADONAI* declares in Deuteronomy that He will set **Israel** in *tehillah* – in honor, renown and praise – high above all the nations He has made.[82] The word of the LORD to Jeremiah confirms that after He judges Israel for their sin, He will "bring health and healing;" He will "heal them and reveal to them the abundance of peace and Truth." The LORD continues,

"And I will cause the captives of Judah and the captives of Israel to return, and will rebuild those places as at the first. I will cleanse them from all their iniquity by which they have sinned against Me, and I will pardon all their iniquities by which they have sinned and by which they have transgressed against Me. Then it shall be to Me a name of joy, a praise (*tehillah*) , and an honor before all nations of the earth, who shall hear all the good that I do to them; they shall fear and tremble for all the goodness and all the prosperity that I provide for it."[83]

Here the picture of Judah and Israel is one of preeminence: God's *tehillah* will clothe His people Israel with rank, dignity and great honor. Oh! The mercy and love of God!

Not only will Messiah mantle Israel, but He will especially distinguish the **city of Jerusalem** with His mantle of *tehillah*. Isaiah prophesies:

"I have set watchmen on your walls, O Jerusalem; they shall never hold their peace day or night. You who make mention of the LORD, do not keep silent, and give Him no rest till He establishes and till He makes Jerusalem a *tehillah* in the earth."[84]

Jerusalem will be a city of honor and renown, her *tehillah* bestowed on her by her Creator and Bridegroom.

Our God will have His way which He purposed from the foundation of the earth! Who will stand on the LORD's side? Who will receive His great salvation? Who will take up *tehillah* for Jerusalem?

*O LORD, establish and make Jerusalem a **tehillah** in the earth!*[85]

Tehillah ~ **Psalm of the Day**

Peter wrote that "with the Lord one day is as a thousand years, and a thousand years as one day."[86] From antiquity Hebrew sages have seen a parallel and prophetic connection between God's works on each of the first days of creation and each millennium of time. These first works set the prophetic plan for God's future works on each millennial day. For instance, ancient Rabbis believed that Messiah, the "Sun of Righteousness" who would "arise with healing in His wings,"[87] would appear in the fourth millennium (the fourth thousand-year day) because God created the sun on the fourth day of the first week. In fact, Y'shua **was** born near the end of this fourth millennial day, probably on the first day of the Feast of Tabernacles when he "tabernacled" or "dwelt with men."[88]

In keeping with this prophetic view, psalms were chosen to be ministered in Solomon's Temple each day which mirrored the works of each corresponding day of creation. Each of these was called the "Psalm of the day." On the first day of the week, the psalm corresponding to the first day of creation was sung. On the second day, the psalm ministered corresponded to the second day of creation and so on. The psalm for the seventh, being a special day – a day when the Creator rested from all His works – was chosen because it honors the Creator, praising and delighting in Him for all He has made. The seventh day of rest foreshadows the Sabbath rest of the millennial kingdom which will occur on the seventh Day, or the seventh period of one thousand years. In Leviticus 23:2 the Sabbath is described as our weekly feast*** or "appointment" with God to celebrate as a holy convocation or "rehearsal".††† In essence we, as the Bride, have been called to set apart each seventh day as a "date" with our King to give Him our love and praise without distraction and rehearse our coming wedding day.

*** Feast – Strong's Hebrew #4150 - *moed (mo-ade')* – an appointment, a fixed time or season, an assembly, a festival.
††† Convocation - Hebrew #4744 – *miqra (mik-rah')* – from #7121 – something called out, i.e. a public meeting. Also a **rehearsal**. Assembly, calling, convocation, reading.

Taking up David's throne and ministry, "...Solomon appointed the Levites to praise (*hallel*) and minister (serve) before the priests as the duty of every day required," as a regular part of the ministry at the Temple.[89] According to Alfred Edersheim in his book *The Temple and Its Services:*

> "The Psalm of the day was always sung in three sections. At the close of each the priests drew three blasts from their silver trumpets, and the people bowed down and worshipped."[90] "The following was the order of the Psalms in the daily service of the Temple. On the first day of the week they sang Psalm 24, 'The earth is the Lord's,' etc., in commemoration of the first day of creation, when 'God possessed the world, and ruled in it.' On the second day they sang Psalm 48, 'Great is the Lord, and greatly to be praised,' etc., because on the second day of creation 'the Lord divided His works, and reigned over them.' On the third day they sang Psalm 82, 'God standeth in the congregation of the mighty,' etc., because on that day the earth appeared, on which are the Judge and the judged.' On the fourth day Psalm 94 was sung, 'O Lord God, to whom vengeance belongeth,' etc., 'because on the fourth day God made the sun, moon, and stars, and will be avenged on those that worship them.' On the fifth day they sang Psalm 81, 'Sing aloud unto God our strength,' etc., because of the variety of creatures made that day to praise His name. On the sixth day Psalm 93 was sung, 'The Lord reigneth,' etc., 'because on that day God finished His works and made man, and the Lord ruled over all His works.' Lastly, on the Sabbath day they sang Psalm 92, 'It is a good thing to give thanks unto the Lord,' etc., 'because the Sabbath was symbolical of the millennial kingdom at the end of the six thousand years' dispensation, when the Lord would reign over all, and His glory and service fill the earth with thanksgiving.'[91]

Messiah delights in this *tehillah* ministry! After all, He gave the pattern. As we sing and decree these *tehillim*, we are calling the earth and its inhabitants into alignment with Yahweh's creative plans and purposes. Try beginning each new day by ministering one of the psalms to the LORD. First read or sing the psalm as if Y'shua is the psalmist, the "I" of each psalm. Then read or sing the psalm as if you are the psalmist, the "I" of the psalm. Ask the Holy Spirit to reveal the pronoun references as you sing. Praise the Father and prophesy to the lost, the nations and the saints of the LORD.

We will go into eternity forever basking in the glories of *tehillah*. *ADONAI* is awesome in *tehillah*. He is the God of our *tehillah*. He alone is the author, subject and object of our praise.

Tehillah and *Tefillah* ~ Partners in Our Mouths

David psalms, "I will bless the LORD at all times; His praise (*tehillah*) *shall* continually *be* in my mouth.[92] In his first letter to the Thessalonians, the Apostle Paul instructs us to "pray without ceasing."[93] Again in his letter to the Philippians he exhorts:

> "Be anxious for nothing, but in everything by prayer and supplication, with thanksgiving, let your requests be made known to God; and the peace of God, which surpasses all understanding, will guard your hearts and minds through Christ Jesus."[94]

Tehillah can also be a *tefillah*![‡‡‡]

David psalmed, "By day Yahweh commands His kindness, and by night His song is with me, a prayer (*tefillah*) to the El[§§§] of my life."[95] In the Hebrew language the word for prayer is *tefillah*. The Israelites sang their prayers. So we sing our praises and our prayers. **Praise and prayer are to be continual partners in our mouths.** The harp

---

[‡‡‡] Hebrew *Tefillah* (pronounced *tef-il-lah'*) meaning "intercession, supplication; by implication a hymn, prayer." (Strong's Concordance, Hebrew and Chaldee Dictionary #8605, p.126)

[§§§] *El* is a Hebrew word for God.

and bowl ministry in Revelation 5:8-9 is another example for us to look at:

> "Now when He (the Lion of the tribe of Judah) had taken the scroll, the four living creatures and the twenty-four elders fell down before the Lamb, each having a **harp**, and **golden bowls full of incense**, which are the prayers of the saints. And they sang a new song, saying:
>
> > 'You are worthy to take the scroll,
> > And to open its seals;
> > For You were slain,
> > And have redeemed us to God by your blood
> > Out of every tribe and tongue and people and nation,
> > And have made us kings and priests to our God,
> > And we shall reign on the earth.'"

When both *tehillah* and *tefillah* reside within us, they are a double armament against doubt, fear, unbelief, anger, bitterness, unforgiveness, jealousy, murmuring, and every other evil thing which tries to attach itself to us. This two-pronged weapon of praise and prayer thwarts the enemy's attempts to invade either our thoughts or our words. Therefore, praise and prayer are powerful weapons of warfare for us to wield against the enemy.

> "For although we do live in the world, we do not wage war in a worldly way: because the weapons we use to wage war are not worldly. On the contrary, they have God's power for demolishing strongholds. We demolish arguments and every arrogance that raises itself up against the knowledge of God; we take every thought captive and make it obey the Messiah."[96]

As we psalm to the LORD, we focus not on this world and its problems that surround us but upon our God and His Son and the Kingdom of God which is ours. Thus *psalming and intercession are mighty weapons of power in the hands of every saint.*

Tehillah ~ A Throne

Our *tehillim* builds a throne for the LORD to inhabit. David sings to the LORD, "…You are holy, enthroned on the *tehillim* of Israel!"[97] Nehemiah describes *tehillim* as a throne for the name of the LORD. "Blessed be Your glorious name, exalted (enthroned) above all blessing and *tehillah!*"[98]

"Build It and He Will Come"

Let us consider three significant passages that use the word *tehillah:*

In a vision, the prophet Habakkuk saw the coming of the LORD and wrote: "His glory covered the heavens and the earth was full of His *tehillim*. And His brightness was like the sunlight; rays streamed from His hand, and there [in the sun-like splendor] was the hiding place of His power."[99] When our *tehillim* fill the earth, the glory of the LORD covering the heavens will inhabit the throne that *tehillim* has built. Heaven will then kiss earth. We will actually see the manifestation of *tehillim:* the glory of the LORD covering the earth as the waters cover the sea, revealing the hiding place of His power!

Psalm 22:3 states: "…You are holy, enthroned on the **praises** of Israel."[100] The word for **"praises"** here is **"tehillim,"** the Hebrew word for Psalms. *Tehillim* are spontaneous, spirit-breathed songs sung from the very heart of God to His Beloved. They are the new songs we are commanded to sing. Considering the definition of *hallel* "to give in marriage" and remembering that *tehillim* are our *sung hallels*, then *tehillim* are the songs of the bride! When we sing our love songs to our heavenly Bridegroom, we are building a throne for His praise, a place for Him to dwell and inhabit!

Isaiah informs us that God will give a garment of *"tehillim"* instead of the spirit of heaviness to those who mourn over sin.[101] When we receive this beautiful robe, commanding our souls to put on this Garment of *Tehillim*, the result will be spontaneous love songs to Y'shua from His Bride. Transformed by the power of the

Holy Spirit, *tehillim* will pour forth from the One who dwells within her. These songs will garment the Bride and "in His presence her joy will be full!"[102] The Bride comes arrayed in *tehillim!*

Build *Tehillim*

Let us follow the direction of the Levites who said in Nehemiah,

> "Stand up, and bless *ADONAI* your God from everlasting to everlasting; let them say: 'Blessed be Your glorious name, exalted (enthroned) above all blessing and *praise (tehillah)!'*"[103]

Ask the LORD to give you a psalm or scripture to sing spontaneously to Him and begin to let the new "*tehillim*" come forth from you by the Holy Spirit. Build a throne for the LORD upon your heart and then over cities and nations. It is my prayer that your song, the "Song of the Bride," will cover the earth and make the way for the glory of Yahweh!

The Spirit and the Bride say, "Come!" Let anyone who hears say, "Come!" And let anyone who is thirsty come – let anyone who wishes, take the water of life free of charge."[104]

We Enthrone You!

We enthrone You in glory,

We enthrone You in majesty,

We enthrone You in victory

Upon the praises of our hearts!¶¶¶

We crown You King of Glory,

We crown You King of Majesty,

We crown You King of Victory

Upon the praises of our hearts!

We bring You glory and honor,

Glory and honor and power,

Glory and honor and power,

Upon the praises of our hearts!

Take up Your royal scepter,

Put on Your Kingly garments,

Rule and reign in righteousness

Upon the praises of our hearts!

¶¶¶   We enthrone You upon the *tehillim* of our hearts!

Fill All the Earth!

Fill all the earth with Your glory, O LORD,

Fill all the earth with the knowledge of Your Word,

Fill all the earth with Your **Tehillim**,

As the waters cover the sea,

As the waters cover the sea.

You are the God who healeth me,

You are the One who sets His people free,

You gave Your life to atone for our sin,

Your Salvation covers the earth.

Your Salvation covers the earth.

You feed the hungry, fill the empty within,

You save Your people and forgive their sin,

You clothe the meek with salvation,

As the waters cover the sea,

As the waters cover the sea.

Fill all our hearts with Your glory, O LORD,

Fill all our hearts with the knowledge of Your Word,

Fill all our hearts with Your **Tehillim**,

As the waters cover the sea,

As the waters cover the sea.

NOTES

1   Francis Brown, D.D., D.Litt. with the cooperation of S.R. Driver, D.D., Litt.D. and Charles A. Briggs, D.D., D.Litt., *The New Brown-Driver-Briggs-Gesenius Hebrew and English Lexicon* (Peabody, Massachusetts: Hendrickson Publishers, 1979), #8416, p. 239b.

2   Isaiah 43:21

3   *Yatsar (pronounced yah-tsar')* – press, squeeze into shape, mold into a form, fashion, form, frame, make, potter, purpose. Strong, *Hebrew and Chaldee Dictionary* #3335, p. 51.

4   *Caphar (pronounced sah-far')* – to score with a mark as a tally or record, to inscribe, and also to enumerate. To celebrate, commune, account, count, recount, declare, number, reckon, show forth, speak, talk, tell out, writer. Strong, *Hebrew and Chaldee Dictionary* #5608, p. 84.

5   Revelation 4:11b KJV

6   *Bara (pronounced bah-rah')* – create, creator, select, choose, feed (as formative processes). Strong, *Hebrew and Chaldee Dictionary* #1254, p. 23.

7   Psalm 66:2

8   Psalm 51:15

9   Psalm 34:1-2

10   Nusach Ashkenaz, *The Artscroll Tehillim*, Trans. Rabbi Hillel Danziger (Brooklyn, New York: Mesorah Publications, Ltd., 1988), p. vii.

11   Isaiah 53:3

12   Hebrews 4:15 (*Complete Jewish Bible* and *The Scriptures*)

13   II Corinthians 5:21

14   Isaiah 42:8

15   Isaiah 60:6

16   Genesis 17:4

17   *Unger's Bible Dictionary*, 851-852.

18   *Easton's Bible Dictionary*, "Ephah," http://www.eastonsbibledictionary.com

19   *Wikipedia*, the Free Encyclopedia, "Sheba," http://www.wikipedia.org

20   Psalm 106:2

21   Psalm 106:3

22   Psalm 24:3-5

23   Psalm 34:1

24   I Corinthians 14:26

25   Psalm 111:10

26   Psalm 9:13-14

27   Psalm 65:1

28   Isaiah 61:11

29   Psalm 149:6-9a

30   Ephesians 5:19

31   Psalm 149:9b

32   Psalm 22:22

33   Revelation 14:3

34   Isaiah 63:7
35   Psalm 33:1 NIV
36   Psalm 135:3
37   Romans 15:9
38   Ephesians 5:19; Colossians 3:16
39   I Peter 2:9
40   Revelation 5:9-10
41   James 5:13
42   Psalm 51:15
43   Psalm 106:47
44   Jeremiah 17:14
45   Psalm 145:21
46   Psalm 40:2-3
47   II Chronicles 20:22 NIV
48   Psalm 149:1
49   Psalm 149:3
50   Psalm 149:6
51   Psalm 149:7-9a
52   Brown, *The New Brown-Driver-Briggs-Gesenius Hebrew and English Lexicon* #7318, p. 928;
     Strong, *Hebrew and Chaldee Dictionary* #7319, p. 107 **and**
     George V. Wigram, *The Englishman's Hebrew Concordance of the Old Testament* (Peabody, Massachusetts: Hendrickson Publishers, 2001) Reprinted from the third edition originally published by Samuel Bagster and Sons, London, 1874, with Strong's numbering added by Hendrickson Publishers: #'s 7318-7319, p. 1164.
53   Psalm 148:14
54   Isaiah 48:9-11
55   Psalm 96:1-3
56   Isaiah 42:10a
57   Ibid.
58   "New" - Brown, *The New Brown-Driver-Briggs-Gesenius Hebrew and English Lexicon* #2318-2319, p. 294-295.
59   Psalm 97:1a *The Scriptures*
60   Colossians 3:10,16 CJB
61   Psalm 98:1
62   Psalm 40:3 CJB
63   Isaiah 42:10a
64   Psalm 108:3
65   Psalm 22:22-24
66   Psalm 22:25 NIV
67   Hebrews 2:10-13
68   Acts 2:46-47
69   "Praises" - Strong, *Greek Dictionary of the New Testament* #703, p. 73a.
70   I Peter 2:9 KJV

71 Isaiah 43:21 KJV
72 Ps 79:13
73 Psalm 24:7
74 I Thessalonians 4:15-18
75 Ephesians 5:18b-19 CJB

PSALMS (Hebrew=Tehillim):

Psalmos – Strong, *Greek Dictionary of the New Testament #5568,* p. 78.
A set piece of music, a Hebrew Cantillation, the "Book of Psalms."
From #5567 – to twitch or twang, to play on a stringed instrument, to celebrate the divine worship with music and accompanying odes, make melody, sing, sing psalms.
A Psalm is a spontaneous song of praise set to music without meter, to be sung in a free style. The psalms originated as spontaneous, spiritual songs, but when they were recorded they became the Hebrew canon of cantillations or songs of praise.

HYMNS:

Humnos – Strong, *Greek Dictionary of the New Testament #5215,* p. 73.
A religious metrical composition, *from "hudeo"* – to celebrate, a hymn or religious ode.
Also #5214, p.73 – *humneo* – to hymn, sing a religious ode, to celebrate (God) in song; one of the psalms, hymns.
A hymn set to music and meter (rhythm) which is recorded in some way and is to be sung over and over.

SPIRITUAL SONGS:

"Spiritual" - *pneumatikos* – supernatural, regenerate, spirit-breathed.
Strong, *Greek Dictionary of the New Testament #4152,* p. 59.
"Songs" – *hode* - a chant or ode, any words sung.
Strong, *Greek Dictionary of the New Testament #5603,* p. 79.
A spiritual song is a spontaneous, spirit-breathed ode or song of praise to the LORD.

76 Colossians 3:16 CJB – See note above
77 James 5:13 KJV, "Psalms" - Strong, *Greek Dictionary of the New Testament #5567,* p. 78.
78 *Tehillah* - Strong, *Hebrew and Chaldee Dictionary #8416,* p. 123.
79 Isaiah 61:1a, 2b- 3 CJB
80 Zephaniah 3:19
81 Zephaniah 3:20 CJB
82 Deut 26:19
83 Jeremiah 33:7-9
84 Isaiah 62:6-7
85 Ibid.
86 II Peter 3:8b
87 Malachi 4:2

88   John 1:14
89   II Chronicles 8:14 KJV
90   Alfred Edersheim, *The Temple: its Ministry and Services as they were at the time of Christ* (Grand Rapids, Michigan: Wm. B. Eerdmans Publishing Company, 1987), p. 172, quoted from *Tamid*, sect. vii, and Maimonides in *Tamid*.
91   Ibid., p. 173.
92   Psalm 34:1
93   I Thessalonians 5:17
94   Philippians 4:6-7
95   Psalm 42:8 *The Scriptures*
96   II Corinthians 10:3-5 CJB
97   Psalm 22:4 CJB
98   Nehemiah 9:5b CJB
99   Habakkuk 3:3b-4 *The Amplified Bible*
100   Psalm 22:3 CJB
101   Isaiah 61:3b
102   Psalm 16:11
103   Nehemiah 9:5b CJB
104   Revelation 22:17 CJB

Yadah

Cast Your Praises with Open Hand

Yadah ~ The Definition

It is significant that the first occurrence of the word translated "praise" in the scriptures is *yadah*. *Yadah* is variously translated as "praise, give thanks, confess, cast, shoot and throw." This expression of worship is very powerful. According to the Strong's Concordance "*yadah*" (pronounced *yah-dah'*) means "to use, that is, hold out, the hand; to throw a stone or an arrow at or away, to revere or worship with extended hands, cast, cast out, confess, make confession, praise, shoot, thank, give thanks, thankful, thanksgiving."[1]

Contained within *yadah* is the word *yad* (pronounced *yahd*) which denotes "a hand, the open one – indicating power, means, direction, power to deliver, strength, display of strength, give into the possession of, deliver over to, entrust to, pledge, submit, to establish dominion, fill the hand with, stretch out the hand to, one's hand bringing deliverance to, in the possession of, out of the hand."[2]

Expanding our understanding even further, the Hebrew Lexicon defines *yadah* as "to throw, cast on or in, give thanks, confess, shoot (arrows) at, to cast down, acknowledge, laud, praise." The word "is commonly derived, perhaps, from gestures accompanying the act."[3]

As stated before, each Hebrew word for praise is accompanied by a physical action or gesture. From the definition above let us recap the action of *yadah*. **Filling our hands with praise, thanksgiving or confession, we stretch out our hands and throw, cast or shoot our message to the LORD*, releasing it to Him by opening our hands and giving it into His possession.** This would look much like the

---

*   When LORD is spelled with all capital letters in the King James Version and New King James Version, it translates the holy name of God. Called the Tetragrammaton, it is formed with the four Hebrew letters *Yud, Heh, Vav, Heh (YHVH or YHWH)* and is sometimes translated Jehovah, Yehovah, Yahweh or Yahveh. The Complete Jewish Bible translates this name as *ADONAI,* a title meaning "LORD."

acts of throwing a ball, casting a stone, shooting a flaming arrow or an arrow armed with a message.

Jeremiah

Arrows are weapons of war and judgment. The prophet Jeremiah commanded,

> "Put yourselves in array against Babylon round about; all you that bend the bow, shoot (*yadah*) at her, spare no arrows; for she has sinned against the LORD."[4]

These arrows unleash judgment on the enemy and praise and thanksgiving to the victorious King of kings and Lord of lords.

Casting stones is another scenario of the same principle. Jeremiah found himself in a dungeon, the victim of the enemy's stones. He lamented, "They forced me alive in a pit, and threw (*yadah*-ed)[†] stones on me."[5]

Jeremiah called on the name of the LORD from the bottom of the pit and testified that the LORD heard his voice and came near when he called. Comforting him, the LORD said, "Do not be afraid." Jeremiah was under assault from the enemy; however, God comforted and kept him. Praise the LORD! There is no pit too deep, no attack too strong that God is not there to comfort and deliver!

David

David the Shepherd-King demonstrated *yadah* with his sling and smooth stones. On one hand these stones carried swift judgment against the enemy and on the other hand they carried praise to the Father. The testimony of God's power over Goliath and faithfulness to His people is an eternal memorial of praise heralded by every

---

†   I have occasionally used the English endings -ed, -ing, and –s on the end of the Hebrew word *yadah* for easier reading. Also I have used the form of the Hebrew word recorded in the Strong's Concordance and not the appropriate Hebrew form which changes according to usage in Modern Hebrew.

succeeding generation. With both Jeremiah and David, *yadah* brought God's deliverance as well as an everlasting memorial of praise to Him.

These examples give a clear picture of the physical gestures of ministering *yadah*. Since praise is one of our most powerful weapons of warfare, we can see how these Biblical examples teach us to *yadah* our praises to Yahweh. I am reminded of the psalmist's words,

> "Blessed be the LORD my Rock, who trains my hands for war, and my fingers for battle – my lovingkindness and my fortress, my high tower and my deliverer, my shield and the One in whom I take refuge, Who subdues my people under me."[6]

The word for hands in Psalm 144 is *yad* which is contained in the word *yadah*. It is interesting to note that this word means "power, means, direction and the power to deliver." Whether warring on the battlefield or on the musical instruments he made, David understood the power of *yadah* and through it established God's dominion while destroying the enemy.

When we extend our hands in *yadah* to the LORD, we unite our soul and body with our spirit in this act of praise.[‡] There are some contemporary gestures made with the hand that illustrate *yadah*. For example, wedding guests throw rice on newly weds as they leave for their honeymoons as an expression of their joyful hope and wishes for the newly married couple. Cheering crowds throw confetti at parade floats in exuberant celebration. Families and friends throw kisses and wave goodbyes to their loved ones wishing them God-speed. Soldiers raise their hands as they salute their commanding officers.

---

‡   Psalm 86:11

Leah

As I have already noted, the first mention of the English word "praise" in scripture is the translation of *yadah*. We first encounter *yadah* in Genesis 29:33:

> "She (Leah) conceived again and bore a son, and said, 'Now I will praise **(yadah)** the LORD.'"[7] So she named him Judah – meaning "celebrated, praised," taken from the root word **"yadah."**[8]

Leah, Jacob's wife, brought forth her fourth son Judah, her *praise*, to the God of all the earth. She *cast* him in birth upon the heavenly Father and named him for the very act of *yadah*.[§] Leah was saying, "This time, instead of looking for the praise of my husband, I will **cast in birth** my praise and thanksgiving, my son, to the Yahweh. My son will be celebrated and praised. He will receive *yadah*." Not only did Judah receive praise but because of Leah's praise-act, Judah **became** praise. Oh, the power of *yadah*!

Judah

The second mention of the English word "praise" in scripture is also *yadah*. Jacob blessed his sons and prophesied over each one by inspiration of the Spirit of the LORD. Confirming Leah's prophetic naming of her son he said,

> "Judah, your brothers will **praise (yadah) you**; your hand will be on the neck of your enemies; your father's sons will bow down to you. You are a lion's cub, O Judah; you return from the prey, my son. Like a lion he crouches and lies down, like a lioness – who dares to rouse him? The scepter will not depart from Judah, nor the ruler's staff from between his feet, until He

---

§   *Yadah* is the word used for "casting," "throwing" stones and "shooting" arrows. The very act of giving birth is a type of casting. Birthing is accompanied by energy, force and forward motion. "*Yud*," the first Hebrew letter of *yadah* which means "hand," is associated with the revelation of birth.

(Shiloh) comes to whom it belongs and the obedience
of the nations is His."[9]

Obviously this prophecy goes beyond Judah and his descendants
and extends through time to the "Lion of the Tribe of Judah," Jesus,
our Messiah. He is the Lion of the "Celebrated and Praised" tribe
who rules all nations with His scepter forever. He is the one to be
celebrated and praised (*yadah*-ed) by His brothers – all of Israel and
all who believe on His name. He is the One to whom all the earth will
cast forth their praises with open hands in surrender and honor, the
One to whom all obedience belongs! While the hands of the people
will be extended to Messiah in *yadah*, **His** hand will be on the neck of
His enemies! *Yadah's* two-fold ministry again expresses both praise
and judgment. The Lion is both conqueror and king!

Y'shua

Y'shua testifies of His own birth in His Psalm 22:9-10:

"Yet You are He who brought me forth from the womb;
You made me trust when upon my mother's breasts.
Upon You I was cast from birth; You have been my
God from my mother's womb."

His birth accompanied by the act of praise (*yadah*),[¶] Himself the offering
of praise (*yadah*), named "Praise"[**] (*yadah*) and destined to receive
the highest praise (*yadah*) of all the earth, Y'shua will reign forever
as King of kings and Lord of lords. Every knee will bow and every
tongue *yadah* (confess) that Jesus Christ, *Y'shua HaMashiach*, is LORD!

¶   Psalm 22:9-10 – Y'shua as the Living Word authored the psalms.
**   Y'shua was named "Praise" as Lion of the Tribe of **Judah** (meaning "praised
and celebrated").

Who Gives *Yadah*? ††

- All men of all positions and generations
- Every people group, good and evil
- Y'shua's brothers
- All the kings of the earth
- Prophets
- Priests
- Levites
- Psalmists
- The people of Israel
- The tribes of Israel in Jerusalem
- The builders of the Temple
- The trumpeters, singers, priests, Levites and the congregation at the dedication of Solomon's Temple
- All peoples and nations
- The living
- Every tongue
- The wrath of men
- All the works of the LORD
- The heavens
- Y'shua-To His Father as LORD of heaven and earth
- Y'shua - *Yadah*-s the names of overcomers before His Father and the angels

To Whom Is *Yadah* Addressed?‡‡

- The LORD God of Israel
- God's glorious name
- God's wonderful works
- The LORD our God
- The LORD God of our fathers
- The God of gods
- The Lord of lords
- The God of heaven
- The Help of our countenance
- God's faithfulness

†† These lists are taken from the scriptures in the *Yadah* Concordance in the "Created to Praise Study Guide."

‡‡ Same as previous footnote.

- All God's wonders
- God's name as Father *Yadah*-ed by Y'shua

When Is *Yadah* Offered?[§§]

- Every morning
- Every evening
- At midnight
- At every presentation of a burnt offering
- On Sabbaths, New Moons and the set feasts
- At the remembrance of Yahweh's holy name
- Upon hearing the Words of His mouth
- At the Tabernacle of David worship
- At the dedication of Yahweh's Temple
- At the time of battle
- At the revelation of the wisdom of God
- At the restoration of Jerusalem
- Forever and ever throughout eternity

Where Is *Yadah* Offered?[¶¶]

- In the great congregation
- In the assembly of the saints
- In the assembly of the upright
- At the altar of God
- In Jerusalem
- On the battlefield before God's army
- To the Gentile nations and all peoples
- Among the Gentiles
- Before the Father and the angels, *Y'shua* will *yadah* the names of the overcomers
- In restored Jerusalem

[§§] These lists are taken from the scriptures in the *Yadah* Concordance in the "Created to Praise Study Guide."

[¶¶] Same as previous footnote.

What Are the Messages of *Yadah*?***

- Thanksgiving
- Praise
- Confession of God's name and works
- Confession of our sins, faults and weaknesses
- Confession of the sins of our fathers and nation

How Is *Yadah* Offered?†††

- With our souls
- With our glory
- With our mouths
- With our hearts
- With our songs
- With musical instruments
- In wholeness and righteousness
- In harmonious sound

Why should we *yadah* the LORD?‡‡‡ Below are some reasons for *yadah*-praise. We can each individualize the *yadah* presented in the Word. The following are examples of *yadah* in Scripture. Let us practice offering *yadah* now:

Why Is *Yadah* Offered?

- Because You are good and Your mercy endures forever, I *yadah* You!
- Because Your Truth endures forever, I *yadah* You!
- According to Your great righteousness, I *yadah* You!
- For all Your wonderful works to the children of men, I *yadah* You!
- Because it is good to praise You, I *yadah* You!
- For the help of Your countenance that brings health to my countenance, I *yadah* You!
- Because You satisfy the thirsty and fill the hungry with good things, I *yadah* You!

*** Same as previous footnote.

††† Same as previous footnote.

‡‡‡ Same as previous footnote.

- Because You break down gates of bronze and cut through bars of iron making my path straight, opening doors before me that no man can shut and closing doors behind me that no man can open, I *yadah* You!
- Because You have heard me and have become my Salvation, I *yadah* You!
- For Your loving-kindness and Your Truth, I *yadah* You!
- Because You are worthy of all my praise, I *yadah* You!
- Because of Your righteous judgments, I *yadah* You!
- Because Your loving-kindness is better than life, I *yadah* You!
- For Your unfailing love, I *yadah* You!
- Because I am fearfully and wonderfully made by You, I *yadah* You!
- I *yadah* You because though You were angry with me, Your anger is turned away and You comfort me!
- I *yadah* You because You brought my soul out of prison!
- I *yadah* You because You have done wonderful things!
- I *yadah* You because You have given me wisdom and might and have made known to me what I have asked of You!
- I *yadah* you for Your faithfulness to Your people Israel and for Your promise to restore the blessings of that land as before!
- Your faithfulness to Israel through all these generations and Your forgiveness for all her sins confirms my faith in Your faithfulness and I *yadah* You!
- I *yadah* Your name as my LORD before the sons of men.
- In restored Jerusalem I will lift my hands in *yadah* to You and greatly praise You for Your wonderful works!

Daniel *Yadah*-ed the LORD!

In Response to Answered Prayer

It is important to know when it is appropriate to use one praise word or another when ministering to the LORD. Of course we must ask the Holy Spirit to guide us, but it *is* interesting and helpful to see how the saints of the Bible used the various words. Daniel, prophet to the Gentiles, *yadah*-ed Yahweh at very strategic times. In chapter two we find him giving praise and thanksgiving to the LORD in response to the revelation and interpretation of King Nebuchadnezzar's dream. Not only had the king asked for the interpretation, he had forgotten the dream and needed to be reminded of his visions in the night that had so troubled him. Daniel called a prayer meeting. Joining together with his friends in intercessory prayer, God showed him both the dream and its interpretation. With this word of knowledge and wisdom Daniel was able to unlock the mystery. His first act, however, was not to run to the king with the answer. Instead, he bowed before his Father in heaven and blessed and *yadah*-ed Him. Looking to Yahweh, Daniel said,

> "Blessed be the name of God forever and ever, for wisdom and might are His. And He changes the times and the seasons; He removes kings and raises up kings. He gives wisdom to the wise and knowledge to those who have understanding. He reveals deep and secret things, He knows what is in the darkness and light dwells with Him. I thank – *yadah* – You and praise[§§§] You, O God of my fathers; You have given me wisdom and might, and have now made known to me what we asked of You. For You have made known to us the king's demand."[10]

In the Face of Persecution

Later, during the reign of Darius the Mede, Daniel found himself the object of an evil plot. Out of jealousy the other leaders in the kingdom decided to trap Daniel so they could overthrow him. Because they could find no fault in him, they decided to use Daniel's faith and loyalty to the God of Israel to accuse him of treason. They persuaded King Darius to make a decree that "whoever petitions any god or man for thirty days, except the king, should be cast into the den of lions." Daniel's reaction amazes me. The Scripture reads,

---

§§§ Strong's Hebrew Concordance #7624 - the Chaldean word for *shabach*.

"Now when Daniel knew that the writing was signed, he went home. And in his upper room, with his windows open toward Jerusalem, he knelt down on his knees three times that day, and prayed and gave thanks – *yadah*-ed[11] – before his God, as was his custom since early days."[12]

Of course we know the rest of the story. Daniel was thrown into the lion's den, but God sent an angel and delivered him from the lions' mouths. What a mighty testimony to the God we serve! And what a mighty faith Daniel had in his God. It is also important to notice that *yadah*-praise was not new to Daniel in this situation. *As was his custom* since his early days in Babylon, he continued kneeling three times every day praying and *yadah*-ing toward Jerusalem. As he knelt in front of his open window, any passerby could look up and see him. His practice of prayer and praise had prepared him for "such a time!"

In Identificational Repentance

While reading the scroll of Jeremiah, Daniel received revelation of a powerful truth. His response to this prophetic unveiling is a lesson for all of us. When he realized that Jeremiah's prophecy specified 70 years for the Babylonian captivity and that those years would soon be completed, he set his

"...face toward the Lord God to make request by prayer and supplications, with fasting, sackcloth and ashes. He said, "And I prayed to the LORD my God, and made confession – *yadah*[13], and said, 'O Lord, great and awesome God, who keeps His covenant and mercy with those who love Him, and with those who keep His commandments, we have sinned and committed iniquity, we have done wickedly and rebelled, even by departing from Your precepts and Your judgments.'"[14]

Interestingly, Daniel did not sit and simply believe God would do what He said. He perceived that he was to play a part in God's prophetic timing. Knowing this, he began to fast and pray. He understood that earth must come into agreement with heaven. Identifying himself with the sins of his nation, he interceded for God's mercy. His confession of *yadah* was two-fold. First Daniel confessed who God is:

> "O Lord, great and awesome God, who keeps His covenant and mercy with those who love Him and keep His commandments."

In order to fulfill her destiny Israel had to repent. Confessing his own sin first, Daniel then stood in the gap and confessed the sins of Israel. Daniel, who understood *yadah,* was an intercessory bridge for the restoration of his nation.

Yadah resulted in Angelic Visitation and Prophetic Vision

Look at what happened as a result of Daniel's *yadah*-ing the LORD. He wrote,

> "Now while I was speaking, praying, and confessing – *yadah*-ing[15] -- my sin and the sin of my people Israel, and presenting my supplication before the LORD my God for the holy mountain of my God, yes, while I was speaking in prayer, the man Gabriel, whom I had seen in the vision at the beginning, being caused to fly swiftly, reached me about the time of the evening offering. And he informed me, and talked with me, and said, 'O Daniel, I have now come forth to give you skill to understand.'"[16]

The angel went on to reveal one of the most powerful prophetic timetables ever given to man. The understanding of this revelation continues to unfold even to this day.

Yadah in the New Covenant

Using our "key"¶¶¶ to unlock the secrets of *yadah* in the New Covenant, we find that the Greek word *exomologeo* (pronounced *ex-om-ol-og-eh'-o*) is used for *yadah* and is variously translated as "confess" and "thank." The Septuagint (Greek translation of the Old Covenant) confirms our key by its usage of *exomologeo* to translate *yadah* in several passages in the Psalms.[17]

Thayer's Greek Lexicon states that *exomologeo* is defined as "to confess forth from the heart – freely, publicly, openly; to profess – that is, to acknowledge openly and joyfully, to profess to one's honor, to celebrate, give praise to; to profess that one will do something, to promise, agree, engage.[18]

Yadah ~ Translated "Confess"

Our search for *yadah* in the New Covenant scriptures begins with several examples of "confessing" (*yadah*-ing) the name of God. In the book of Acts, miracles worked by the hand of Paul brought the fear of God on all who saw them "*and many who had believed came confessing (yadah-ing) and telling their deeds.*"[19] Another example of *yadah*-confession is when Paul quotes Isaiah 45:23 in his letter to the Romans:

> "For it is written: 'As I live, says the LORD, every knee shall bow to Me, and every tongue shall confess (*yadah*) to God.'"[20]

Then, in his letter to the Philippians, Paul unveils the mystery of this verse in Isaiah by filling in the details and defining the content of the confession. Through the power of the Holy Spirit, Paul presents one of the most powerful and yet simple professions of faith in Y'shua:

¶¶¶ As noted in the chapter on *Hallel*, the "key" to finding the seven Hebrew words for praise in the New Covenant is in Old Covenant praise scriptures quoted there. The Greek word used to translate each praise word reveals other related New Covenant scriptures.

"...that at the name of Jesus every knee should bow, of those in heaven, and of those on earth, and of those under the earth, and that every tongue should confess (*yadah*) that Jesus Christ is Lord, to the glory of God the Father."[21]

Another intriguing example of *yadah* is found in Romans. Paul states that the purpose of Y'shua's ministry to the Gentiles is to give them reason to "glorify God for His mercy."[22] To validate his point, in Romans 15:9 he quotes Y'shua's promise to the Father from Psalm 18:49.

"For this cause I [Y'shua] <u>will</u> **confess (*yadah*)** to You [Father] among the Gentiles, and sing to Your name."

Here in Psalm 18 Jesus prophesied His coming to earth to fulfill this mission. By *yadah*-ing the Father among the Gentiles and singing to His name, Y'shua invites Gentiles to believe on Him and to glorify and praise the Father for His mercy.

Y'shua *yadah*-s praise to the name of the Father. Believers *yadah* praise to the name of the Father and of the Son. However, to the overcomers in the book of Revelation Y'shua makes an astounding promise:

"He who overcomes, shall be clothed in white garments; and I will not blot out his name from the book of life, but I will confess – *yadah* – his name before My Father, and before His angels."[23]

Not only will the LORD clothe the overcomer with garments of salvation and *not* erase his name from the Book of Life, but He declared that He will *yadah* (cast or shoot forth) their names before the Father and the angels! Picture and relate this to a graduation ceremony where each student's name is announced to the Head Master or Dean in the hearing of the whole assembly as having met the requirements for their degree. What a day that will be!

Yadah is also a vehicle of confessing sin. The Greek word *exomologeo* is not only used to describe confessing God's name and wonderful attributes, it is also used to describe the casting forth of faults, misdeeds and sins as propelled messages of *yadah*. Like missiles that are aimed and launched to their target, our faults, misdeeds and sins are sent forth and released to God in *yadah*-confession! What a burden-lifter! What liberty comes when we confess our sins of omission and commission! We not only acknowledge our sins and weaknesses, we throw them off and are released from them. Y'shua in the Book of James exhorts us:

> "Confess *(yadah)* ...*your* sins one to another, and pray
> one for another, that ...(you) may be healed,"[24] adding
> that "the effective, fervent prayer of a righteous man
> avails much"[25] to the receiving of forgiveness, release
> **and** healing of our souls.

John preached in the wilderness, "Repent, for the kingdom of heaven is at hand."[26] "Then Jerusalem, all Judea, and all the region around the Jordan went out to him in the Jordan, confessing – *yadah*-ing – their sins."[27] Our God desires for us to be set free and healed and He works in us to will and to do the works of God.[28] He has made every provision for us and continues to draw and deliver us by **His outstretched hand**. Micah the prophet comforts us with these words:

> "Who is a God like You, pardoning iniquity and
> passing over the transgression of the remnant of His
> heritage? He does not retain His anger forever, because
> He delights in mercy. He will again have compassion
> on us and will subdue our iniquities; You will **cast all
> our sins** into the depths of the sea."[29]

What does God do with the sins we cast upon Him? Amazingly, when we confess our sins to God by casting and releasing them to Him, He in turn takes those sins and casts them into the depths of the sea! It is much like a ball game! We cast our sins to God; He catches them and throws them into the sea. In turn, He "hurls back"**** mercy and grace, cleansing and healing. What an exchange!

Until I did this study, I never understood the relationship of the confession of sin to praise. When you think about it, we must believe God for who He is and what He says to even be willing to acknowledge and confess our sins to Him. In turn, we can trust Him to cast our sins into the sea's depths. We must know that God's responses to our confession are waves of mercy and grace. *Yadah*-confession becomes then an act of faith and praise!

Yadah ~ Translated "Thank"

Y'shua *yadah*-ed the Father in thanksgiving. When the seventy disciples came back to Him with their glowing report that demons were subject to them in His name, Y'shua *yadah*-ed His Father for His great wisdom and perfect plan for man. Luke wrote,

> "At that moment he [Y'shua] was filled with joy by the *Ruach HaKodesh* and said, 'Father, Lord of heaven and earth, I thank (***yadah***) You, because You concealed these things from the sophisticated and educated, yet revealed them to ordinary people. Yes, Father, I ***yadah*** You that it pleased You to do this.'[30]

Judas *Yadah*-ed!

On the negative side, Judas threw out his open hand and vowed to betray Y'shua.

> "So he [Judas] went his way and conferred with the chief priests and captains, how he might betray Him to them. And they were glad, and agreed to give him money. So he promised (***yadah*-ed,** cast forth his promise)[31] and sought opportunity to betray Him to them in the absence of the multitude."[32]

**** "Hurl" is a synonym for "cast," one of the definitions of *yadah*.

God forbid that we *yadah* any other than our Lord and Savior. The Scriptures tell us that Judas did not find repentance. Let us be careful to give all our praise to the LORD and not to make any false oath.

From these illustrations, you see how *yadah* is the vehicle that carries praise, thanksgiving, confession and promise. *Yadah* can deliver our deepest utterances. Understanding this, let us be like Daniel and even Y'shua Himself. Let our *yadah* always be to Him (Yahweh) who delivers, forgives and blesses.

Yadah ~ The Hebrew Letters

The Hebrew letters that spell *yadah* are the *Yud*, meaning "hand;" *Dalet*, meaning "door' and *Hey* meaning "to reveal" or "what comes from." The letter *Yud* is a picture of the closed hand but when joined to the *Dalet* becomes the word for "the open hand." So "to give thanks," "to praise" and "to confess" define what comes from or is revealed by the open hand. Remembering that *hey* also means breath or spirit, we can picture the wind (breath) of the Holy Spirit carrying our *yadah* messages up to the LORD. It is amazing to me that these letters were chosen as the written representation of our offerings of confession, thanks and praise. In practice, the gestures accompanied by the word *yadah* are casting, throwing, hurling, thrusting and shooting. Bill Cloud states in his "The Wisdom of Hebrew" series:

> "From the term 'to thrust' the word for 'give thanks' is derived. We thrust out our hands to receive; we should then use our hands to 'give thanks.' The Modern Hebrew form for "give thanks" is *hodu*. This in turn is related to *hod*, 'glory, majesty.' So the hand – 'to thrust' – is connected to giving thanks (*hodu*) and glory and majesty (Hebrew *hod*)."[33]

Hodu l'Adonai ki tov! Give thanks to the LORD for He is good!

What is in your hand? Will the LORD find there the treasures of praise, thanksgiving and confession? Will you now release *yadah*, whether in confession, thanksgiving or praise to Him as an act of obedience and love?

"Song of the Ages"

Yadah ~ The Sacrifice of Praise and Thanksgiving

Over the years as I have read the Old Covenant, I began to notice a recurrent song. As I studied the Word, I found this song sung at every major event in the history of Israel:

1. **At the Tabernacle of David**[34]
   (It was committed to Asaph and his worship team)
2. **At the Tabernacle of Moses in Gibeon**[35]
   (It was committed to Jeduthan and Heman and their worship teams)
3. **At the Dedication of Solomon's Temple**[36]
   ("When the trumpeters and singers were as one, to make one sound to be heard in praising and thanking the LORD and when they lifted up their voice with the trumpets and cymbals and instruments of music, and praised the LORD...")
4. **After Solomon's famous Prayer of Dedication**[37]
   (Heavenly fire consumed the sacrifices and the people fell on their faces in worship and sang this song.)
5. **After the second set of sacrifices were offered at the Dedication of Solomon's Temple**[38]
6. **At all the Feasts of the LORD**
   (*Pesach*-Passover, *Shavuot*-Pentecost, and *Sukkot*-Tabernacles - Sung in the Great *Hallel* and the Egyptian *Hallel*)
7. **At the Head of Jehoshaphat's Army**[39]
8. **At the Dedication of Zerubbabel's Temple**[40]
9. **In the future in Restored Jerusalem**[41]

Notice the power of this song, how it is used and how it is ministered:

1. **Ministers before the Ark of the LORD, His very presence**
2. **Sung in worship at the Tabernacle and Temple of the LORD**
3. **Brought down the** *Shekinah* **glory**
4. **Brought down heavenly fire to consume sacrifices**
5. **Sets our enemies to flight**
6. **Dedicates the LORD's house ~ former and latter**
7. **Celebrates the LORD at every Feast Day**
8. **Sung by Y'shua & His Disciples at the Last Passover**
9. **Penned by the Living Word ~ Y'shua, Jesus**
10. **Acted out by Y'shua on the Cross**
11. **Sung in the streets of restored Jerusalem**

What Is this Song?

The priests, Levites, psalmists and prophets all chanted and proclaimed this song to the children of Israel. Are you sitting on the edge of your seat, wondering what this amazing song could be? It is simple but very powerful. Let us sing it now: *"O give thanks (yadah) to the LORD, for He is good; for His mercy endures forever!"* Just think of it! David sang this song when celebrating the bringing up of the Ark of the Covenant to Zion. He then instructed Asaph and his worship team to minister *yadah* and *hallel* to the LORD before the Ark and to remind[42] Yahweh and His people of the covenant and promises made to the seed of Abraham.[43] This song is also recorded in I Chronicles, "**That day** David first committed to Asaph and his associates this "Psalm of Thanks" (Psalm of *Yadah*) to the LORD."[44] This "Psalm of Thanks" is a medley of verses taken from Psalms 105,[45] 96[46] and 106.[47] This "Song of the Ages" was sung at the dedication of Solomon's Temple:

> "...when the trumpeters and singers were as one, to make one sound to be heard in praising (*hallel*-ing) and thanking (*yadah*-ing) the LORD; and when they lifted up their voice with the trumpets and cymbals

and instruments of music, and praised (*yadah*-ed) the LORD, saying: *'For He is good; for His mercy endures forever'* – that the house, the house of the LORD, was filled with a cloud, so that the priests could not continue ministering because of the cloud; for the glory of the LORD filled the house of God."[48]

How awesome! This is the song that brought down the glory – the *Shekinah* glory – of the LORD. God honored this offering of praise and obedience with His splendor and glorious presence. Further on, we read that after Solomon had finished His prayer of dedication, fire fell from heaven and consumed the sacrifice. The glory of the LORD filled the house for a second time so that the priests could not enter the house because of the cloud. The people fell on their knees in worship, bowed their faces to the ground and sang an encore! What song do you think they sang? The "Song of the Ages:"

> *"For He is good; for His mercy endures forever."*[49]

What a song! It flowed straight from the Father's heart through the voice of the Living Word to us so that we can please Him with our praise. If we spent eternity trying, we could never write lyrics more perfect than His.

Where again do we find this song? Jehoshaphat and the people of Judah faced a vast enemy army. Jehoshaphat prayed the same prayer Solomon had offered at the Temple dedication. Again, God answered as mightily as He did when the children of Israel were at the Red Sea. II Chronicles records the faith of Jehoshaphat and the impact of this song:

> "...Jehoshaphat appointed men to sing to the LORD and to praise Him for the splendor of His holiness as they went out at the head of the army, saying: *'Give thanks (yadah) to the LORD, for His love endures forever.'* As they began to sing and praise, the LORD set ambushes against the men ... who were invading Judah, and they were defeated."[50]

At the dedication of the foundation of the second temple built by Zerubbabel, this song was sung again. Zerubbabel and those who returned from Babylon

> "...sang together by course in praising and *giving thanks (yadah-ing) to the LORD, because He is good; for His mercy endures forever toward Israel.*[51] And all the people gave a great shout of praise to the LORD; because the foundation of the house of the LORD was laid . . . No one could distinguish the sound of the shouts of joy from the sound of weeping, because the people made so much noise. And the sound was heard far away."[52]

Once more *yadah* is used when Jeremiah prophesied the future restoration of Jerusalem. Jeremiah tells of a time when the sounds of joy and gladness will again be heard in the towns of Judah and the streets of Jerusalem. This sound will include the voices of the bride and the bridegroom, and the voices of those who bring thank offerings to the house of the LORD:

> *Give thanks (yadah) to the LORD Almighty, for the LORD is good; His love endures forever."*[53]

We sing this song of thanks (*yadah*) before the ark of the LORD – His very presence. It is the song that invites the *Shekinah* glory. It is this same song that sets our enemies to flight. Not only was this song used to dedicate the house of the LORD but it will be sung again in the millennium. This is the song that touches the heart of God. It is a song written by Him to be sung throughout eternity.

In Psalm 100 we find a similar instance of the same song of *yadah.*

> "Enter into His gates with thanksgiving and into His courts with praise. *Yadah* Him and bless His name, *for the LORD is good, His mercy is everlasting and His Truth endures to all generations!"*[54]

Yadah, then, is the expression of praise that carries the thanksgiving message. Every work of God deserves thanksgiving. Psalm 136 is recognized as the "Great *Hallel*." This psalm is sung at three festivals each year: Passover (*Pesach*), Pentecost (*Shavuot*) and Tabernacles (*Succot*). Here are the first three verses of Psalm 136:

> *"Oh, give thanks to the LORD for He is good! For His mercy endures forever. Oh, give thanks to the God of gods! For His mercy endures forever. Oh, give thanks to the Lord of lords! For His mercy endures forever!"*

Here the psalmist offers thanks for each blessing and work of God. In the Passover service there is a place where each act of God toward Israel listed in this psalm is read and the people respond with the word *"Dayenu"* (a Hebrew word meaning "it would have been enough.") Because we are undeserving, it would have been enough if God had performed only one mighty act, one deed of valor. Instead, because His mercy endures forever, He continues to act on behalf of His people throughout every generation. The psalm ends with *"Oh, give thanks to the God of heaven. For His mercy endures forever."*

Even though Psalm 136 is called the "Great *Hallel*," the Hebrew word *"hallel"* never appears in this psalm. However, *"yadah"* is used over and over. Conclusion: *"Yadah"* is an expression of *"hallel."*

Y'shua crowns His forthcoming suffering with the ending verses from Psalm 118. This psalm is the last hymn of the Egyptian *Hallel* sung at Passover. It offers an astounding picture of the praise of Y'shua facing the cross. This is the most vivid and complete portrait of praise that we find.

> *You are my God, and I will praise (yadah) You;*
> *You are my God, I will exalt You.*
> *O give thanks (yadah) to the LORD, for He is good;*
> *For His mercy endures forever.*[55]

The first word for "praise" in this passage is the Hebrew word, *yadah*. If we remember that it means "to use the hand, to throw out the open hand forcefully and victoriously, to revere or worship the LORD with extended open hands," we see a powerful scenario.

Y'shua, the Psalmist, sings to His Father:†††

"You are My God, and I will **yadah** You. I will stretch forth My hands to You in victorious praise yielding My open hands to the nails of Calvary as I submit to Your highest will, revering and adoring You in humble obedience and worship. I will submit My whole spirit, soul and body to Your perfect will. As I hang on the cross, I will give You the highest praise – the ultimate sacrifice. I spread My hands in *yadah* to You, casting Myself upon You as 'The Sacrifice of Praise.' You love Me because I lay down My life, trusting You to take it up again. My worship of You is never separated from my devotion and sacrifice to Your divine will – all that You have made Me to be and asked Me to do.

'You are My God and I will exalt You!' I will lift You up to the highest place by humbling Myself - by lowering Myself and bowing before You. I will always serve You, for You are My Father. My ultimate expression of praise to You is to drink the cup of suffering You have offered Me and to do Your will, O Father.

'I give thanks (*yadah*) to You, Father, because You are good, and Your mercy endures forever!' My sacrifice now completely fulfills the 'Song of the Ages.' As Your great mercy flows through the blood of My sacrifice, spilling from My hands and feet to the ground of the earth, it becomes the purifying, cleansing stream by which man's sin is forgiven, washed, and cast as far away from Him as the east is from the west. Man will be reconciled to You by its power! And Your mercy endures forever because My sacrifice is offered once for all and it is eternal. It will never have to be

---

†††† This is my concept of what was in Y'shua's heart.

repeated. I die once for the sins of the people and I sit down at Your right hand forevermore. By My eternal sacrifice I have purchased Your salvation for all those who will receive it. Out of the goodness of Your own Being You have ordained and accomplished it!"

Yielding His open hands to the nails of Calvary was only the beginning of Y'shua's act of *yadah* to the Father. (The conclusion of His *yadah* culminated in the most extraordinary event that changed the world.) After Y'shua committed His Spirit into the Father's hands, He then visited the saints in prison (*She'ol* - hell), retrieved the keys to "death and hell" and led captivity captive. By the *Ruach HaKodesh* Y'shua catapulted[‡‡‡‡] – *yadah*-ed – Himself from earth back to heaven as the ultimate sacrifice of praise!

Let me share a vision I had a few years ago. I was at the side of the Father in heaven. I looked down upon the earth far away in the distance and saw a sight beyond imagination. I was taken back in time just before the Resurrection. I could see only the top of Y'shua's head, His hair as black as a raven's. Suddenly, defying natural law, "in the twinkling of an eye"[56] He reached the throne of the Father. The Father then said to me, "The same Spirit which raised Y'shua from the dead lives in you and He will also give life to your body."[57] I now know that Resurrection was the very act of *yadah*-praise!

Who is the "You" of *Yadah*?

The understood subject of "*Yadah* the LORD, for He is good, and His mercy endures forever!" is "You." The "you" in Psalm 118:29 can be understood at three levels: "You" as Messiah (Divine); "You" as His people (corporate) and "You" as you and me (individual).

"You" as Messiah

Yadah is a huge part of the divine praise Y'shua ministers to His Father throughout eternity and for a brief time from the earth. From

---

‡‡‡‡ "Catapulted" is a synonym for "cast," one of the definitions of *yadah*.

the very first time this "Song of the Ages" was sung, it pictured the work of Messiah on the cross for the reconciliation of man to God. These words were penned many years before the cross. As the children of Israel sang it, they **Proclaimed** His coming, they **Prayed** for His coming, and they **Praised** – gave *yadah* to – the God of Israel for the promised coming of the Messiah. Without even realizing it, they were addressing Messiah and asking Him to come and *yadah* the Father. They were saying, "You, Messiah, come and do Your perfect work! For in Your shed blood the mercy of the LORD *will* endure forever." In this "Song of the Ages," Y'shua and His people were singing of the Cross and the Resurrection!

"You" as His people

The psalmists, priests and Levites instructed the people of Israel on many occasions to corporately "*Yadah* the LORD, for He is good and His mercy endures forever!" I have listed nine of these special occasions earlier in this chapter. Knowing that singing *yadah*-thanks is also a part of the daily Temple services adds quite a few more to the list.

"You" as you and me

As Y'shua, the author of the Psalms, sang the last verse of Psalm 118:29 on the night of the last supper, the last verse He would have sung before going to Gethsemane, He turned and spoke to His disciples and all who would follow Him throughout the generations:

"Yadah the LORD, for He is good, for His mercy endures forever."

"You, My people, *yadah* the LORD. You take up your cross and follow Me. You stretch forth your hands in submission and praise."

> "…if anyone desires to come after Me, let him deny himself and take up his cross and follow Me. For whoever desires to save his life will lose it, but whoever loses his life for My sake will find it. For what profit is

it to a man if he gains the whole world, and loses his own soul? Or what will a man give in exchange for his soul? For the Son of man will come in the glory of His Father with His angels; then He will reward each person according to his works. Assuredly, I say to you, there are some standing here who shall not taste death until they see the Son of Man coming in His kingdom."[58]

Let **us** now *"Give thanks – yadah – to the LORD for He is good, for His mercy endures forever."* Let us lay down our lives in worship before the King of kings and Lord of lords. Let us praise – *hallel* – His holy name and all His wonderful works.

As we move into eternity with him – **walking with Him from earth to heaven** – we will continue to sing this "Song of the Ages" as prophesied in Jeremiah:

"…again there shall be heard in this place…in the cities of Judah, in the streets of Jerusalem…the voice of joy and the voice of gladness, the voice of the bridegroom and the voice of the bride, the voice of those who will say:

'Yadah the LORD of Hosts, for the LORD is good; His mercy endures forever.'

And of those who will bring the sacrifice of praise (*todah*) into the house of the LORD. For I will cause the captives of the land to return as at the first,' says the LORD." [59]

In Y'shua's own earthly language of Hebrew using the appropriate form of *yadah*, we say,

"Hodu[§§§§] l'adonai ki tov, ki le-olam chasdo."

---

§§§§ Correct form of *yadah* used in modern Hebrew.

"Give thanks to the LORD, for He is good,
for His mercy endures forever."

Not only does Y'shua sing the "Song of the Ages," He acted out – lived and dramatized – the "Song." He Himself is the "Song of Songs." He was *born to praise;* we are *created to praise.* He continues to sing to His Father from the earth through us. He is the Song we sing. We are the instruments He plays. Together we become a symphony of melody and harmony forever living and singing the "Song of the Ages."

My prayer is that of King David, "Bring my soul out of prison that I may praise (*yadah*) Your name."[60] A soul in prison cannot *yadah* the LORD because it is bound and cannot "cast itself" in total surrender or freely praise Him.

"LORD, we long to walk in the complete liberty
and full expression of **yadah***!*

Our story does not end here. For we see Y'shua,

> "…manifest in the flesh, justified in the Spirit, seen of angels, preached unto the nations, believed on in the world, received up into glory."[61]

When Y'shua left the earth, casting (*yadah*-ing) Himself by the power of the Holy Spirit as "The Sacrifice of Praise" into Resurrection glory, He took off His garment of flesh and donned His robe of light. Hebrews tells us,

> "But now … (God) has spoken to us through His Son, to whom He has given ownership of everything and through whom He created the universe. This Son is the *radiance of the Sh'khinah, the very expression of God's essence,* upholding all that exists by His powerful word."[62]

Habakkuk describes his vision of Y'shua at His second coming:

> "His glory covered the heavens and the earth was full of His praise. And His brightness was like the sunlight; rays streamed from His hand, and there [in the sunlike splendor] was the hiding place of His power." [63]

Today and forever He shines forth the glory and *hallel* of the Father's image. He is the shining essence of *hallel* and the expression of *yadah*.

> Y'shua …Born in *yadah*.
>> Y'shua …born as *yadah*.
>>> Y'shua …born to give *yadah*.
>>>> Y'shua …born to receive *yadah*.
>>>>> Y'shua …resurrected in *yadah*.
>>>>> **Y'shua…"born to praise!"**

Only the *"yadah"* of the cross gives place to the *"hallel"* – the shining forth – of resurrection glory!

Open the Gates!

O give thanks unto the LORD for He is good,
For His mercy endureth forever!
O give thanks unto the LORD for He is good,
For His mercy endureth forever!

I will praise You for You have heard me,
You are become my salvation,
I will praise You for You have heard me,
I will lift my hands and praise the LORD!

O give thanks unto the LORD for He is good,
For His mercy endureth forever!
O give thanks unto the LORD for He is good,
For His mercy endureth forever!

Open the gates of righteousness and I will go through them,
Open the gates of righteousness and I will go through them
And praise the LORD!

O give thanks unto the LORD for He is good,
For His mercy endureth forever!
O give thanks unto the LORD for He is good,
For His mercy endureth forever![64]

Copyright 1998 Nancy E. Morgan

NOTES

1   James Strong, S.T.D., L.L.D., *Strong's Exhaustive Concordance of the Bible* (Madison, N.J.: James Strong, 1973), *Hebrew and Chaldee Dictionary* #3034, p. 47. *Yadah* (pronounced *yah-dah'*)

2   Strong, *Hebrew and Chaldee Dictionary* #3027, p. 47. *Yad* (pronounced *yahd*)

3   Francis Brown, D.D., D.Litt. with the cooperation of S.R. Driver, D.D., Litt.D. and Charles A. Briggs, D.D., D.Litt., *The New Brown-Driver-Briggs-Gesenius Hebrew and English Lexicon* (Peabody, Massachusetts: Hendrickson Publishers, 1979), #3034, p. 392a. *Yadah* (pronounced *yah-dah'*)

4   Jeremiah 50:14

5   Lamentations 3:53 CJB

6   Psalm 144:1-2

7   Genesis 29:35

8   Strong, *Hebrew and Chaldee Dictionary* #3063, p. 47.

9   Gen 49:8-10 NIV

10   Daniel 2:20b-23

11   Strong, *Hebrew and Chaldee Dictionary* #3029, p. 47. Chaldean form of *yadah* corresponding to #3034 Hebrew

12   Daniel 6:10

13   Strong, *Hebrew and Chaldee Dictionary* #3029, p. 47. Chaldean form of *yadah* corresponding to #3034 Hebrew

14   Daniel 9:3-5

15   Strong, *Hebrew and Chaldee Dictionary* #3029, p. 47. Chaldean form of *yadah* corresponding to #3034 Hebrew

16   Dan 9:20-22

17   According to Thayer's *The New Thayer's Greek-English Lexicon*, the Septuagint Old Testament uses the Greek word *exomologeo* to translate "*yadah*" in Psalm 30:4, Psalm 106:47, Psalm 122:4, and Psalm 18:49 - Joseph Henry Thayer, D.D., *The New Thayer's Greek-English Lexicon of the New Testament* (Peabody, Massachusetts: Hendrickson Publishers, 1981), #1843, p. 11.

18   Thayer, *The New Thayer's Greek-English Lexicon of the New Testament* #1843 p. 11.

19   Acts 19:18

20   Romans 14:11

21   Phil 2:10,11

22   Romans 15:9 – "…and that the Gentiles might glorify God for His mercy; as it is written, 'For this cause I will *confess* (*exomologeo* #1843 Greek - *yadah*) to You among the Gentiles, and sing to Your name.'" (quoting Psalm 18:49)

23   Revelation 3:5

24   James 5:16a KJV

25   James 5:16b

26   Matt 3:5

27   Mark 1:5

28   Philippians 2:13

29 Micah 7:18-19
30 Luke 10:21 CJB
31 Luke 22:4-6
32 Mark 14:10-11
33 Bill Cloud, "The Wisdom of Hebrew," Session 8 on *Yud*, Shoreshim Resources, 114 Stewart Rd, PMB 431, Cleveland, TN 37312, http://www. billcloud.org.
34 I Chronicles 16:7, 34
35 I Chronicles 16:39-41
36 II Chronicles 5:13
37 II Chronicles 7:3
38 II Chronicles 7:6
39 II Chronicles 20:21
40 Ezra 3:10-11
41 Jeremiah 33:10-11
42 I Chronicles 16:15
43 I Chronicles 16:4
44 I Chronicles 16:7, 34
45 Psalm 105:1-15
46 Psalm 96:1-13
47 Psalm 106:1, 47-48
48 II Chronicles 5:13-14
49 II Chronicles 7:3
50 II Chronicles 20:21-22 NIV
51 Ezra 3:10-11a KJV
52 Ezra 3:13 NIV
53 Jeremiah 33:10-11 NIV
54 Psalm 100:4-5
55 Psalm 118:28-29
56 I Corinthians 15:52
57 Romans 8:11
58 Matthew 16:24-28
59 Jeremiah 33:10-11
60 Psalm 142:7
61 I Timothy 3:16 KJV
62 Hebrews 1:2, 3 CJB
63 Habakkuk 3:3b, 4 Amplified Version
64 Psalm 118:1, 19, 21 KJV

Barak

Kneel in Adoration and Adore with Bended Knees

Barak ~ The Definition

The Hebrew word sometimes translated "praise" but most often translated "bless" is *barak* (pronounced *bah-rak'*). The Hebrew Lexicon defines it as: "kneel, bless, praise, kneel down, bless God, adore with bended knees, salute, greet, to be blessed, adored, prospered by God."[1]

Barak, as with the other Hebrew words for praise, is communicated by both a physical posture and a message of the soul. Carried to the LORD by the sound waves of the human voice, it is accompanied by the thoughts and emotions of the human heart. Here we see an expression of the whole person – spirit, soul and body. We kneel down before the LORD with our body, acknowledging Him as the Creator and giver of all good gifts. By this act of humbling ourselves, we exalt Him to the highest place, giving Him glory, honor, praise and adoration from the deepest places of our souls and spirits.

An interesting ancient Hebrew custom was to "pay homage." The greeter or worshiper got down on one knee and touched his forehead to the ground at the feet of someone of royal rank. Jesus was often greeted in this way.[2] It was the appropriate way to enter the presence of the King.

In his book *Bless You! Restoring the Power of Biblical Blessing,* Dr. John Garr gives us a beautiful insight on blessing from God's perspective:

> "*Berakhah** paints a wonderful portrait of God in his infinite tender mercy kneeling in order to reach down to his weak, suffering children and to lavish his loving kindness upon them. God is king, but he is also father, and, as father, he is intent upon reaching down to his children and showering them with his infinite

---

*   *Berakhah* is the Hebrew word for "blessing" from the root word *barak*.

blessings. God Himself, then, has set the example of blessing's posture by reaching down to humanity and lifting them up.... The bent knee is the root of the blessing."[3]

Barak ~ Cycle of Blessing

Blessing begins and ends with God. Having created the world and all that is in it, He then blessed it and called it "good."[4] In blessing man He enabled him to be a blessing both to Himself and to others. Like a snowball rolling down a mountain gathering more and more snow and more and more momentum, blessing begets blessing and a circle of blessing is set in motion by God – Him to us, us to Him, us to others, others to Him.

There are 361 occurrences of blessing in the *Tanakh*[†] and 70 in the *B'rit Hadashah*.[‡] Obviously the subject of blessing is infinite. However, in line with the purpose of this book, we will only consider blessing as *praise* to God. Since God is the source of all blessing, man can only bless God for who He is and what He has done for us in the form of praise, worship and service. We can never be a source of blessing to God in any way except by giving back to Him what He has given us. We can only love Him with the love He has shed abroad in our hearts; we can only give offerings to Him of all He has first given to us and we can only praise and bless Him with the revelation and life He has breathed into our spirits. How very precious He is to pour out His own love to bless us and bring us into relationship with Him, the Creator of heaven and earth! Bless the LORD that He chooses to take pleasure in our love and praises!

Barak ~ The Hebrew Letters

Barak is made of the Hebrew letters *Bet* ("B"), *Reysh* ("R") and *Kaf* (K or Ch). (There are no vowel letters in Hebrew.) The letter *Bet*

---

†   **Tanakh** – Hebrew acronym from the first letters of the words *Torah* (Teaching), *Nevi'im* (Prophets), and *K'tuvim* (Writings); i.e., the Hebrew Scriptures (see Luke 24:44). (Also known as "The Old Testament")

‡   **B'rit Hadashah** – Hebrew for New Covenant.

is a picture of a tent or house and means "house."[5] *Reysh* ("R") is a picture of the head of a man and means "a head" and is also used to mean a "man, a person, the highest, the supreme, the first, or the sum."[6] When *Bet* and *Reysh* are put together it spells the word for "son (*bar*)."[7] The son is the "house man" or the "man from within the house."[8] *Kaf* is a picture of the palm (open hand) or wing and means "to cover, to open, allow."[9] Related to the Hebrew word for "knee (*berek*)," *barak* speaks of kneeling, and thus blessing, as a son to a father, or a father to a son. The word picture is of a son kneeling before his father covered by the father's open hand. The father's outstretched hand denotes protection and the fact that it is open means that good things are given and allowed.[10] The word *bar* also means "mature."[11] *Reysh* and *Kaf* put together spell the Hebrew word "*rak*," meaning "tenderness." Putting *rak* together with *bar*, *barak* is the "son of tenderness, to treat as a mature son, with tenderness."[12] This speaks to me of intimate relationship between a father and his mature son, one who receives his father's wisdom and stays in relationship with him. It is from this intimacy that first our Father God blesses us and we in turn bless Him for who He is and what He does, both universally and personally.

Who Should Receive *Barak*?[§]

Blessing in scripture is addressed to the "**LORD**[13] (**Yahweh**)[¶]," "**the LORD our Maker**,"[14] "**God**[15] (**EL**)**,**" the "**God of Israel**,"[16] "**God, my Rock**,"[17] the "**God of heaven**,"[18] "**LORD God**[19]**,**" "**LORD God of Israel**,"[20] "**the name of the LORD**,"[21] "**His holy name**,"[22] "**His glorious name**,"[23] the "**Creator**,"[24] "**He who comes in the name of the LORD**,"[25] the "**name of Jesus (Y'shua)**,"[26] "**Christ**" or "**Messiah**,"[27] and the "**God and Father of our Lord Jesus Christ**."[28] From this we

---

§   The responses to the questions Who? When? Where? Why? and How? are given in bold.

¶   When LORD is spelled with all capital letters in the King James Version and New King James Version, it translates the holy name of God. Called the Tetragrammaton, it is formed with the four Hebrew letters *Yud, Hey, Vav, Hey* (*YHWH or YHVH*) and is sometimes translated Jehovah, Yehovah, Yahweh or Yahveh. The Complete Jewish Bible translates this name as *ADONAI*, a title meaning "Lord."

see that blessing is addressed to God the Father and the Son, His name and His attributes.

Who Should Give *Barak*?

All nations[29] and **all peoples**[30] are called to bless the LORD. This includes geographical nations as well as people of every race and ethnic background. The letter to the Philippians promises that one day *every knee will bow* before *ADONAI.* Kneeling is the ultimate expression of blessing God.[31] As the Author of all scripture and the Psalmist and Messiah of Israel, **Jesus - Y'shua** - blessed the Father while He was on the earth as an example for all who would follow Him. Y'shua lives eternally to continually bless His Father forever and ever. Psalm 95:6 gives **all who read it** the invitation to "Come, let *us* worship and bow down, let *us* kneel (*barak*) before the LORD our Maker." As a worshipper, **my soul** and **all that is within me** is called to bless the LORD. **All His angels** who excel in strength and do His Word, **all His hosts** in heaven and in earth, **all ministers of the LORD** who do His pleasure, **all the servants of the LORD** who stand by day and by night in the house of the LORD and **all the works of the LORD** are instructed to bless Him. **The house of Israel, the house of Aaron, the house of Levi, all those who fear the LORD, all His saints and all flesh** are called to be instruments of blessing to the LORD and His name.[32]

When Should We *Barak*?

Forever[33] and **eternally**[34] our Creator and His Son shall be blessed. We bless God **at mealtimes** for His provision of food. It is interesting that Jewish families bless the LORD and not the food, assuming that all God has created is good, and so they bless Him **before and after the meal**. "Grace after the Meal" is in obedience to the Word of the LORD in Deuteronomy: "**When you have eaten and are full**, then you shall **bless** (*barak*) the LORD your God for the good land which He has given you."[35]

Even though there are special times for special blessings, our LORD desires us to bless Him **every day** in everything. The psalmist taught, "Sing to the LORD, bless (*barak*) His name; proclaim the good news of His salvation **from day to day**."[36] Y'shua, the Living Word, asks us to bless God and sing psalms which proclaim His good news of His great salvation, the gospel, every day. Notice that blessing, thanking and singing psalms are often partnered together in the scriptures. The very act of singing about Messiah and His work of redemption brings blessing to our King.

In "The Song of Deborah" the first lines give further instruction on when to bless:

> **"When leaders lead in Israel,**
> **When the people willingly offer themselves,**
> Bless (*barak*) the LORD!"[37]

Deborah continues in verse 9:

> "My heart is with the rulers of Israel
> Who offered themselves willingly with the people.
> Bless (*barak*) the LORD!"

When the leaders and people of Israel submitted wholly to God in order to fight the enemy, the directive, "Bless the LORD!" rang forth. Psalm 110 prophesies of a future time when Messiah's people will offer themselves willingly: "*ADONAI* will send Your powerful scepter out from Tzion, so that You will rule over your enemies around you. **On the day your forces mobilize**, your people **willingly offer themselves** in holy splendors from the womb of the dawn; the dew of your youth is yours."[38] Here we see blessing connected to humility, submission and faith in the will and plan of God. In its very definition, *barak* means to "kneel," and to "salute." We kneel before our King and raise our salute. Trusting Him, we obey. *Barak* should be our first praise to God before any battle begins. Our humility, submission, faith and obedience *prepare the way* for God to avenge and conquer the enemy on our behalf!

Scripture asks us to bless God **daily** (from sunset to sunset** in the Biblical definition of day: "...so the evening and the morning were the first day"[39]),[40] **continually,**[41] **forever and ever,**[42] **at all times,**[43] **while I live,**[44] **from this time forth and forevermore,**[45] **every day**[46] and **eternally.**[47] Traditionally, blessings are lifted up **at the beginning of all the feasts including the weekly feast, the Sabbath.** We do not *have* to bless Him, we *get* to. Remember that nothing is a "have to" with God. Our free will is His gift to us. Religion, divorced from the heart of God, gives us rules of do's and don'ts, but relationship with Him gives us the privilege to acknowledge (intimately know) Him in all our ways and trust Him to direct our paths.[48] Just think, the God of all the earth, the Creator of all things, has made us and blessed us with His own life. He has invited us into relationship with Him – to be His friend, heir and Bride – and paid the price for our redemption. He has blessed us with **all** spiritual blessings in heavenly places. What else could be our response, but to return all blessing and praise and glory and honor to Him?

Where Should We *Barak*?

Psalm 95 tells us, "Let us kneel (*barak*) **before the LORD our Maker.**[49] Whatever physical location in which we find ourselves, in the Spirit we are **before Him!** Blessing to the LORD is appropriate **in the congregation,**[50] **in all places of His dominion,**[51] **in the house of the LORD,**[52] **out of Zion**[53] and **in His Holy Temple.**[54] We are the living Temple of Messiah and His blessing should dwell within us at all times. The psalmist sang, "I will bless (*barak*) the LORD **at all times**, His praise (*tehillah*) shall continually be **in my mouth.**[55] Since His dominion includes the entire universe, we are to bless and bow before the LORD, His Son and His name **in every place at all times.**

** On the Biblical lunar calendar set up by God in Genesis, the day begins and ends at sunset. "So the evening and the morning were the first day." Genesis 1:5.

Why We Should *Barak*

The reasons for blessing the LORD are as infinite as His being and works. Let us bless the LORD together with some of the blessings recorded in His Word and minister them to Him right now:

O LORD,
Because You daily load us with benefits, [56]*daily bear our*
burdens[57] *and because Your name will endure forever,*
continuing as long as the sun,[58] **We bless You.**

Because all men shall be blessed in You and all nations shall call
You blessed to the glory of God the Father,[59] **We bless You.**

Because You have given us counsel[60]*and because You have*
given David a wise son (Solomon and then Y'shua) over
Your people,[61] *for wisdom and might are Yours,*[62]
We bless You.

Because You change the times and seasons, remove
and raise up kings, give wisdom to the wise and
knowledge to those who have understanding,[63]
We bless You.

Because You reveal deep and secret things and know
what is in the darkness, because light dwells with You[64]
and You delight in Your people, **We bless You.**

Because You have loved Israel forever, You have blessed Your children
and You have visited and redeemed Your people,[65] **We bless You.**

Because You have raised up a horn of salvation for us in the house of
Your servant David,[66] *even Y'shua our Messiah,* **We bless You.**

Because our eyes have seen Your salvation which You have prepared
before the face of all peoples, a light to bring revelation to all the
Gentiles and the glory of Your people Israel,[67] **We bless You.**

*Because according to Your abundant mercy, You have
begotten us again to a living hope through the resurrection
of Jesus Christ from the dead,*[68] **We bless You.**

*Because You have given us an inheritance incorruptible and undefiled
that does not fade away, reserved in heaven for us,*[69] **We bless You.**

*Because we are kept by the power of God through faith for salvation
ready to be revealed in the last time,*[70] **We bless You.**

*Because You have blessed us with every spiritual
blessing in heavenly places,*[71]
We bless You.

Blessed *are You Y'shua who comes in the name of the LORD.*[72]

Special Blessings (*Barak-s*) to YHWH

Eliezer, Abraham's servant, upon completing his journey to find a bride for Isaac, cried out, "Blessed be *ADONAI*, God of my master Abraham, who has not abandoned his faithful love for my master."[73]

Jethro, Moses' father-in-law, greeted Moses after the deliverance from Egypt and said, "Blessed be *ADONAI*, who has rescued you from the Egyptians and from Pharaoh."[74]

At the birth of Ruth's son, the women rejoiced with Naomi and said, "Blessed be *ADONAI*, who today has provided you a redeemer!"[75]

David blessed the LORD after Abigail met him with appeasement saying, "Blessed be *ADONAI* the God of Israel, who sent you today to meet me."[76]

David blessed the LORD for His faithfulness, saying, "Blessed be *ADONAI*, for He heard my voice as I prayed for mercy."[77]

So you see, we bless God by humbling ourselves before Him and exalting Him in response to each act of His goodness, each answered prayer as well as each revelation of Himself, His name and His kingdom in the earth and in our lives. Far from just the spoken words, "I bless You," the blessings which delight and minister to the LORD are lives laid down before Him, hearts which exalt and enthrone Him, ready obedience to His every command and mouths continually filled with praise and gratitude.[††]

How Should We *Barak*?

On **bended knee**, with **uplifted hands**, by the act of **standing** and **with the tongue** we bless *(barak)* the LORD. According to the patterns in Scripture, we bless God as King Solomon did by **kneeling** and **spreading our hands** toward heaven[78] and as the psalmist by **lifting up our hands** in the sanctuary.[79] The psalmist declared, "Thus (This is how) I will bless You while I live, I will **lift up my hands in Your name**."[80] James noted that New Testament believers bless our God and Father **with their tongues**.[81] This tells us that blessing the LORD is not just silent prayer within our hearts but spoken words. In fact, he speaks of our tongues having the power to bless or curse. The Levites commanded the people to **stand up and bless the LORD Your God** forever and ever.[82] When King David said to all the congregation, "Now *bless (barak)* the LORD your God," "...all the assembly *barak*-ed (**knelt before**) the LORD God of their fathers, and **bowed their heads** and **prostrated themselves** before the LORD and the king.[83] The postures of **bowing** and **lying prostrate** before the LORD are expressions of deep worship flowing from the act of blessing God. **In the holy presence of Yahweh "Who shall stand?"**[84]

The Jewish Practice of Blessing God

In order to complete our section on "How should we *barak*?" we must examine the Jewish concept of blessing. We have received a rich heritage of Biblical blessing from the God of Israel as revealed to the

[††] The point is that we should always bless the LORD, especially at important benchmarks in our walk with Him.

nation of Israel. In his book *Bless You! Restoring the Power of Biblical Blessing*, Dr. John Garr gives us great insight into the historical and modern-day practice of Jews in blessing God. He informs us,

> "The central prayer in Jewish life is called simply *ha-Tefillah* (the Prayer) ... composed of eighteen benedictions [blessings], not mere petitions! ...this prayer originated in the second century before the time of Jesus. ... It is certain that Jesus and the apostles prayed some form of this prayer of blessings in their faithful attendance in Israel's synagogues. This prayer of blessings has remained so important to the Jewish people that it is always prayed with each worshiper standing facing Jerusalem (hence, its alternate name *Amidah*, meaning 'standing'). The act of praying while standing is an indication of the worshipers' readiness to receive and obey God's instructions."[85]

Upon reading this last sentence by Dr. Garr, the LORD focused my attention on the definition of *barak* as "salute." I could picture a soldier standing at attention, poised to receive his orders for the coming battle. He stood out of respect and obedience with a readiness to go quickly and complete the task as soon as it was assigned.

Dr. Garr continues,

> "In each of the [eighteen] blessings, God is blessed first for one or more of his qualities or the elements of his character and his provision for his people. The first three define God's innermost being: lovingkindness (*chesed*), power (*gevurah*) and holiness (*kedushah*). The final three benedictions express the themes of gratitude, the hope of restoration, and abundant peace. The twelve intermediate blessings deal with understanding, repentance, forgiveness, freedom, bodily health, abundance of the earth, reunification of the scattered, justice, punishment of enemies, reward

for the just, the new Jerusalem, the Messiah, and hearing of prayers."[86]

These eighteen blessings make up what is titled "Tractate Berakhot."[‡‡] This tractate is the first section of the Mishnah (the oral law) and also of the Talmud (the written oral law). Because the Blessings are given first place, this leads us to conclude that they are also the most important. Jewish blessing is a thanksgiving and praise response to both natural and spiritual life.

In Jewish practice "every *berakhah* (blessing singular) begins with the words, "*Barukh atah Adonai Eloheynu Melekh ha'olam*" ("Blessed are You, O LORD our God, King of the universe") and continues with the specific blessing such as "who has created the fruit of the vine."[87] "We bless the LORD, mentioning His name and His kingship."[88] It is interesting that the one who offers the blessing first addresses God in the second person – "Blessed are You" – and ends by referring to Him in the third person – "who has." Sages throughout the ages have commented on this seeming inconsistency. Irene Lipson in her "Blessing the King of the Universe" quotes the explanation of one of these sages, Benyamin Forst:

> "Significantly, every *b'rakhah* begins in the second person, addressing God by name and title: "Blessed are you, O LORD our God." Having thus acknowledged not only who he is but also our relationship to Him, we then move into the third person, describing His will and His commands. It is as if we begin by perceiving His immediate, personal presence. We then move on to describing His essence, at which point we become conscious of His "otherness." The God with whom we are intimately related is yet far beyond our comprehension."[89]

---

‡‡ *Berakhot* is the Hebrew plural for blessing.

As a child and young adult, I learned about the God of heaven who is worshiped and served with awe and reverence – a holy God who lives in heaven but seemed far away and almost unreachable. I was taught that He is the judge and I associated Him with punishment when I failed to obey. I often knelt at the altar of my church to pray and kept myself very reserved and quiet. Later in life, from the desperation of my circumstances, I sought for more of God because what I had was not enough to get me through the various situations I faced. In my search, I learned the intimacy of relationship with Jesus my Savior, Lord, Shepherd, friend and bridegroom - the Son of man. He was more approachable as His Spirit dwelled within me and I walked with Him. I delighted in His tenderness and love as my Father, Brother and Teacher. However, in this place in my life the reverence and awe of Him was not emphasized. Although my intimate relationship with Him was wonderful, I missed the reverential worship of the exalted King of kings and Lord of lords. Now I understand that Y'shua is the Son of God **and** the Son of Man and that both relationships are appropriate and accurate. My discovery is validated and affirmed in the traditional Jewish blessing as we first address Him in the second person as our intimate friend and then refer to Him in the third person describing His kingship and majesty, power and might.

Barak ~ At All Times

After David *hallel*-ed God (pretended madness[§§]) before his enemy, Abimelech called him a madman and drove him away. David's response was to pen Psalm 34. Delivered through the power of praise, his first words were, "I will bless (*barak*) the LORD at all times, His praise (*tehillah*) shall continually be in my mouth. My soul shall make its boast (*hallel*) in the LORD; the humble shall hear of it and be glad."[90] Narrowly escaping death yet miraculously saved by God, David's first utterance was to vow to *barak* the Father at all times and let perpetual praise reside in his mouth! Not only did he praise God for this one act of deliverance but he promised to praise God continually forevermore. He had just experienced the saving,

§§ The definition of *hallel* used in this passage is "to feign madness, act like a madman." See the chapter on *Hallel*.

delivering power of the weapon of praise. David was thankful to God for His faithfulness. Not only did David rejoice at God's faithfulness, but that his testimony of God's deliverance would produce joy and faith in others, thereby magnifying God's praise. Paul stated it this way in II Corinthians 4:15:

> "…that grace, having spread through the many, may cause thanksgiving to abound to the glory of God."

Instead of responding in fear, David chose to praise God when his life was threatened. We can do the same. If we practice a lifestyle of blessing God, we will know Him more intimately and be able to trust Him in the most difficult situation – even unto death.

Job *Barak*-ed

Job was confronted with a series of disasters. First his oxen and donkeys and his servants, except for one, were killed. This remaining servant ran to Job with the tragic news. Before this servant finished telling Job the news, another came to say that the fire of God had fallen from heaven and had burned up Job's sheep and servants, leaving only him to report the event. Before this servant finished speaking, another servant ran in to say that Job's camels had been stolen and all the servants tending them, except for him, had been killed. Before this servant finished speaking another came with the news that strong winds had collapsed the house where his sons and daughters were dining together; they were all dead. Now Job had a very close relationship with God. Rising up, Job tore off his robe and shaved his head. Then he fell to the ground and worshiped. "And he said: 'Naked I came from my mother's womb, and naked shall I return there. The LORD gave, and the LORD has taken away; Blessed (*barak*-ed) be the name of the LORD.'"[91] Scripture records, "In all this Job did not sin nor charge God with wrong."[92]

I wonder how many of us would react as faithful Job did. Notice, Job did not blame the devil, even though these attacks were from Satan. God had permitted the attack. Job understood this. Then, as though this were not enough, Satan received further permission from God to strike Job's body. Even though Job's body was covered with boils, Job did not curse God. This was surely a disappointment to the devil!

Temptation then came from Job's wife, "Curse God and die!" Job's answer should inspire us, "Shall we indeed accept good from God, and shall we not accept adversity?" In all these tests Job did not sin with his lips.[93] Finally Satan used Job's best friends to accuse, condemn and provoke him. In their misguided religious mindsets, they were sure all this must be Job's fault. In their religious pride, they were sure they had the answer.

Make note that in the first test, God limited Satan from touching Job's person. After Job did not sin by cursing God, Satan got further permission to hurt Job's body but God put another limit: "Spare his life."[94] We need to be mindful that Satan has no power except what is given him by God. He is like a dog on a leash, but God is holding the leash! The LORD will allow us to be tested and chastened as sons and daughters so that He can bring us from one level of glory to another. As our understanding and intimacy with Him deepens, we are formed into His image. We can learn from God's dealings with His people as we read and study the Scriptures and we will find that God is not only good but has the power to restore. Although hard things may come to us, God ultimately uses it for our good.[95] The benefits of our victories are eternal.

The important lesson of Job is that if we learn to trust God, and understand Him and His ways, we will not be shocked when we are "beset" about. Instead we will count Him faithful and continue to bless Him even when we do not understand. We will come to know that in these trying times we need to turn to Him even more. Repeatedly, the lives recorded in the Scriptures teach us these lessons.

There are two important points to note about Job's victory in blessing God. First Job received back double from God of all that he had lost. If you compare the first and the last chapter, you will find this to be true: twice as many sheep, oxen, camels, etc. There is one puzzling thing in the list, however. In the beginning Job had seven sons and three daughters and in the end God gave him seven sons and three daughters more, not fourteen sons and six daughters as you would expect. The thrilling conclusion we draw is that Job's first children were still alive -- in the arms of the blessed LORD in the heavenly realm! Secondly, the crowning gift: Job said, "**I have heard of You by the hearing of the ear, but now my eye sees You.**"[96] Though humbled by his troubles, Job was lifted to a higher level of glory and gained a deeper revelation of God.

Daniel *Barak*-ed

Daniel asked *El Elyon*, the Most High God, to reveal the secret of Nebuchadnezzar's dream. In a night vision the LORD answered Daniel and gave the forgotten dream and its interpretation. Daniel's first response was *barak*.[¶¶] I like the way it is recorded in the Book of Daniel. It says, "Daniel answered and said." Notice, God spoke to Daniel in a vision and Daniel "answered." Here we have an indication of the close communion between YHWH and Daniel. Daniel's response to God's wisdom was to offer God this beautiful blessing:

> "Blessed (*barak*-ed) be the name of God forever and ever, for wisdom and might are His, and He changes the times and the seasons; He removes kings and raises up kings; He gives wisdom to the wise and knowledge to those who have understanding. He reveals deep and secret things. He knows what is in the darkness, and light dwells with Him."[97]

Daniel realized that God Himself had raised up Nebuchadnezzar for His own purposes and that God had imparted the dream. He also had the confidence to ask *ADONAI* for the interpretation. Paul, in his letter to the Corinthians, admonishes us to pray that we may interpret and covet to prophesy.

¶¶ The Chaldean form of *barak* is used in the book of Daniel. It is Strong's Hebrew #1289.

Nebuchadnezzar *Barak*-ed

Blessing begets blessing. Daniel's faithfulness to bless the Most High God bore the fruit of multiplication. His testimony influenced the Gentile king Nebuchadnezzar to bless the God of the universe. Scripture records two occasions on which King Nebuchadnezzar offered *barak* to the Most High God. Do you remember the story in Daniel of the fiery furnace? The enemy had devised an evil plot to kill three young Israelite men, but God had other plans: to turn what the enemy meant for evil into a powerful, miraculous testimony. Nebuchadnezzar had increased the furnace's fire seven times its usual intensity. In fact, the men who threw the Hebrew young men into the furnace were immediately consumed by its flames. Drawing near to this intended holocaust, Nebuchadnezzar was amazed by what he saw. Scripture records his exclamation:

> "Look!" He answered, "I see four men loose, walking in the midst of the fire; and they are not hurt, and the form of the fourth is like the Son of God."[98]

Witnessing God's mighty intervention on behalf of His servants, Nebuchadnezzar said:

> "Blessed (*barak*-ed) be the God of Shadrach, Meshach and Abed-Nego, who sent His Angel and delivered His servants who trusted in Him, and they have frustrated the king's word, and yielded their bodies, that they should not serve nor worship any god except their own God!"[99]

Nebuchadnezzar then decreed:

> "Therefore I make a decree that any people, nation or language which speaks anything amiss against the God of Shadrach, Meshach, and Abed-Nego shall be cut in pieces, and their houses shall be made an ash heap; because there is no other God who can deliver like this."[100]

This decree reflected a revelation to the heart of Nebuchadnezzar. Even though his understanding was limited, God's patience was unlimited. The king saw God's works, but still did not understand that Yahweh was the only God – God Most High. Although Nebuchadnezzar knew no other "god" as powerful as Yahweh, he still did not understand that there was no god but the God of Israel.***

God gave Nebuchadnezzar a second dream. Again, this dream needed Daniel's interpretation. This dream was a warning from God to King Nebuchadnezzar that it is not a man who rules the "kingdom of men," but it is He, the Most High God.[101] If you remember the story, within a year Nebuchadnezzar walked through the royal palaces of Babylon and exalted the works of his own hands. God's response was immediate: Nebuchadnezzar was driven from among men and, like a wild beast, he ate the grass of the field. In short, he lost his sanity. At the end of seven years Nebuchadnezzar's mind was restored. What was Nebuchadnezzar's response to his restoration and what was his understanding now of the God of Israel and the universe? Daniel 4:34 records the *barak* of Nebuchadnezzar. A heathen king now blesses the King of kings:

> "And at the end of the time I, Nebuchadnezzar, lifted my eyes to heaven, and my understanding returned to me; and I blessed (*barak*-ed) the Most High and praised and honored Him who lives forever: For His dominion is an everlasting dominion and His kingdom is from generation to generation."[102]

What do we learn from these accounts? We learn that God does intervene in the affairs of men: sometimes to save us from our enemies and at other times, to save us from ourselves. No matter the circumstance, we need to understand that God's acts are acts of love: that He is for us and not against us. And, at the end of the day, when understanding and revelation are ours, our hearts and mouths will want to bless (*barak*) an all-loving and all-knowing God.

*** I use the term "god" here simply as a literary reference. It is understood that demons are not gods.

Daniel's Warfare Praise in Babylon ~ Our Example

Daniel's praise[†††] in Babylon is also a spiritual weapon. Daniel lived his life under a government who opposed Godly rule and justice; however, his faith-walk brought stunning victories, on-time miracles and breath-taking deliverances. The God of Daniel is the same God of believers today. What He did for Daniel, He will do for us. "He is the same today, yesterday and forever."[103] God loves to show Himself in might and power to every generation.

The important key to Daniel's success was a three-fold cord of *barak-yadah-shabach* praise. Daniel was known for his wisdom and his unswerving faithfulness to Yahweh. Interestingly enough, Daniel's life spanned the rule of three kings. Remembering that Daniel was in his 80's when he faced the lion's den, we see a man who walked in his time with integrity and without fear. When we examine his *barak-yadah-shabach* praise, we gain insights into the power of Daniel's life.

Daniel always first positioned himself in *barak*-praise, whether in daily worship or in crisis. On his knees, Daniel's prayers in Hebrew often began with, "*Baruch ata Adonai Eloheynu* – Blessed be the LORD our God…" *Barak* is a word-picture of a *mature* son in relationship with his father, a son of tenderness, kneeling underneath the outstretched right hand or wing of the father.[104] In Scripture, the right hand is the hand that imparts the father's blessing and protection. *Barak*-praise, when combined with humility and worship, releases God's hand to move in our personal lives and in nations.

Yadah-praise is a threefold expression of thanksgiving, confession and praise. *Yadah* is unique in that it is accomplished by the physical act of lifting and opening the hand to release its message. Picture your thanksgiving, confession and praise as a dove. Holding the dove in your hands, you lift it toward the Father. Then, opening your hands, you release this dove (thanksgiving, confession and praise)

---

††† See the chapters on *Shabach* and *Yadah* for reference.

to fly to the Father. *Yadah* is a spiritual act with a physical expression. Daniel's praise included all three expressions of *yadah*-praise.

Shabach is the culmination of *barak* and *yadah* in the shout. When Daniel offered *shabach*-praise, he shouted. Like Jesus Himself, or Joshua of old, when praise messages are lifted in *shabach*, they trumpet the shout of power and pull down the enemy's fortresses, bringing forth life.

What is the testimony of Daniel's persevering three-fold praise? We witness a man walking in the power of Isaiah 30:15b, "...in quietness and confidence shall be your strength." Daniel's focus is not on the lion's den; it is on the power and might of the God of Israel. Remembering that a three-fold cord is not easily broken, we see revelation-praise (*barak-yadah-shabach*) move through identificational repentance, confession and intercession. In Daniel 9:6, Daniel confronts a government, a kingdom and spiritual wickedness in high places. His response is not one of panic. In fact, upon hearing Darius' decree that whoever petitions any god or man for thirty days except the king will face the lion's den, Daniel immediately goes home. Heavenly warfare had begun and would be won in Daniel's prayer closet. (His response is a lesson we can all learn.)

Daniel went home, opened his window toward Jerusalem, knelt down and prayed (*barak*-ed). Since his early youth, Daniel had prayed and given thanks to God three times a day. Holding praise, thanksgiving and confession in his hands, he cast *yadah* to El Elyon, the Most High God and Maker of heaven and earth. In an act of loud (*shabach*-ed) prophetic demonstration, Daniel opened his hands toward God and released a *barak-yadah-shabach* praise.

This praise would change history. Thanking God for His Word and His promises, Daniel used the three-fold cord of *barak-yadah-shabach* praise. Moving into a three-fold confession, he confessed who God is, his sin and the sin of his nation. His identificational repentance, confession and intercession would bring heaven's promise to earth and impact generations to come. Daniel's three-fold praise magnified God and lifted the people of God above and beyond their circumstances. Again, we learn the Word is true: a three-fold cord is not easily broken.[105]

Daniel's prayer and worship were not hidden. His window was open and his prayers were heard, both by his friends and his enemies. The knowledge that there were evil onlookers did not daunt his devotion or change his heart's conviction: God was to be praised. This conviction and understanding is the wisdom that under-girds and sustains praise. Unmoved by opposition, censure and opinion, the prayers of Daniel changed the direction of the enemy's plans for God's people in history. Daniel's *barak-yadah-shabach* praise catapulted the people of God toward the end of their 70-year captivity in Babylon. Thus, fulfilling the prophecy by Jeremiah:[106]

> "...these nations shall serve the king of Babylon seventy years. Then it will come to pass, when seventy years are completed, that I will punish the king of Babylon and that nation, the land of the Chaldeans, for their iniquity, says the LORD...."

A case can be made that the *barak-yadah-shabach* praise-warfare of Daniel and his friends, together with their lives of obedience to Yahweh, laid a foundation for and was an influencing factor in the following:[107]

Daniel:
- Received supernatural revelation and interpretation of Nebuchadnezzar's two dreams and saved the lives of the wise men of Babylon
- Received interpretation of the writing on the wall
- Delivered in the Lions' Den
- Received interpretation and understanding of Jeremiah's prophecy
- Received the 70 weeks prophecy and the time-table of Messiah's coming
- Released archangels to war in the second heaven

- Received revelation of nations and kingdoms in the last days
- Prayed in the restoration of the nation of Israel

Nebuchadnezzar:
- Received revelation of God and salvation through the testimony of Daniel and his friends, signs and wonders, God's judgment and deliverance
- Offered *barak-yadah-shabach* praise to the Most High God

Three Hebrew young men:
- Delivered in the fiery furnace
- Saw the fourth man in the furnace – Y'shua
- Promoted in the province of Babylon

Darius:
- Made decree to the nations that Yahweh is the eternal living God whose kingdom will not be destroyed

It is interesting to note that Daniel's tenure in Babylon brought impartation of God's wisdom to others. This revelation would come to Israel in an auspicious time of visitation and hidden glory. Daniel's revelation would reach down through time and history. His gifts to the Messiah would come through the wise men from the East who would lay Daniel's wealth at the feet of Mary and Joseph on the eve of their escape to Egypt. In essence, it was not only the wise men who worshiped at the feet of the Christ-child; it was also Daniel. This is the mystery and power of *barak-yadah-shabach* praise.

Barak in the New Covenant

Using our "key" of comparing the New Covenant Greek translations of Old Covenant scripture quotes, we find that the Greek word which translates *barak* is *eulogeo*, the root of our modern word "eulogy." It means "to speak well of, to bless, to thank or invoke a benediction upon, bless, praise."[108] Remember that no two languages are completely interchangeable and this Greek word does not include the root meaning of "kneel" which is the foundation and picture-word for *barak*.

Y'shua *Barak*-ed His Father

Why are these Hebrew concepts and practices important to New Covenant believers? Jesus studied and memorized the Torah (Five books of Moses), the Prophets and the Writings (including the Psalms) as all young Hebrew children. It only follows that Y'shua grew up learning and speaking many *berakhot* (blessings) commonly used in His day. On one occasion He burst forth in spontaneous praise upon hearing the joyful reports of the seventy disciples. These disciples had gone out at His command and "returned with joy, saying, 'Lord, even the demons are subject to us in Your name.'"[109] The Scripture tells us,

> "In that hour Jesus rejoiced in the Spirit and said, "I thank You (bless You, *barak* You), Father, Lord of heaven and earth, that You have hidden these things from *the* wise and prudent and revealed them to babes. Even so, Father, for so it seemed good in Your sight."[110]

However, His first and most prominent blessing was to His Father. This blessing was His submission and obedience to the Father's will. Y'shua's mission was to reveal His Father's name and heart to His people. As the Living Word and author of all the Psalms, Y'shua both sang His blessings to the Father and instructed and commanded the people to bless the LORD. In keeping with the traditions of the Passover Seder He spoke the blessings over the four cups of wine and over the bread (*matzah*‡‡‡). Both Matthew and Mark record this account:

---

‡‡‡ *Matzah* is the Hebrew word for unleavened bread eaten in the Passover service. Because leaven represents evil or wickedness in the scriptures, *matzah* represents the pure sinless righteousness of the Bread of Life, Messiah. The *matzah* is also striped, pierced and unleavened (pure) as was Y'shua's body.

"And as they were *about to* eat, Jesus, after He took bread praised (*barak*-ed) God, broke it and when He gave *it* to the disciples He said, 'You must take *this and* you must *now* eat, this is My body.' Then having taken a cup after He gave thanks (*barak*-ed) He gave *the cup* to them saying, 'You must all drink from this, for this is My blood of the covenant, which is being poured out on behalf of many for forgiveness of sins.'"[111]

In keeping with the Biblical tradition of blessing God and not the food, Messiah blessed God before He fed the multitudes.

"And having taken the five loaves and the two fish, after He looked up into the sky He praised (*barak*-ed) *God* and broke the loaves and was giving *them* to His disciples so that they could set *the food* before them, and He divided the two fish to all."[112]

The specific prayer of blessing that Y'shua would have spoken to the Father at the Passover table, at every meal and at the feeding of the multitude before breaking the bread was: "Blessed are You, O LORD our God, King of the Universe, who brings forth bread from the earth." The prayer He would have spoken after the pouring of the wine was: "Blessed are You, O LORD our God, King of the Universe, who creates the fruit of the vine."

He is our example, but much of His example has been lost or misinterpreted throughout the centuries. In our day He is restoring His Truth. The heavens must retain Him until the restitution of all things.[113] Blessed are You, O LORD, King of the Universe, who restores Your Truth to Your people! Blessed are You who comes in the name of the LORD!

Y'shua *Barak*-ed His Disciples

As He ascended from the Mount of Olives Y'shua lifted up His hands and blessed (*barak*-ed) them.[114] What blessing did Jesus speak over His disciples? Since He was then operating in the priestly office of Melchizadek, the only blessing (*barak*) a priest could offer with uplifted hands was the Aaronic blessing.[115] Messiah lifted up His hands and with great love and compassion spoke to his betrothed Bride:

"The LORD bless and keep you,
The LORD make His face shine upon you, and be gracious to you,
The LORD lift up His countenance upon you, and give you peace."[116]

This is the blessing given to Aaron. With it he blessed the people of Israel.

According to Dr. John Garr in his book *Bless You! Restoring the Power of Biblical Blessing*, the first line of the (Aaronic) blessing is made of three Hebrew words expressing divine perfection and is the blessing of the Father. The second line is made of five Hebrew words and represents the blessing given by Y'shua, five symbolizing grace. The third line comprised of seven Hebrew words is the blessing of the Ruach Ha-Kodesh, representing the seven-fold spirit of God.[117] "So they shall put My name on the children of Israel and I will bless them."[118] As the priest pronounced the blessing, he raised his hands to impart God's name and formed the Hebrew letter *shin* with his fingers. This letter represents God's name El Shaddai, the double-breasted One, the Almighty. The understanding was that the *Shekinah* glory of God hovered over the priest's head and the rays of the *Shekinah* gleamed through the priest's open fingers, thus placing God's name El Shaddai on the hearts of His people.[119] This blessing would nurture, strengthen and prosper the children of God.§§§

As Y'shua ascended to the Father, He looked down upon His worshiping disciples and pronounced this priestly blessing upon them. In blessing them, He gave them His name. This fulfilled part

---

§§§ In his book *Bless You! Restoring the Power of Biblical Blessing*, Dr. John Garr includes a picture of an echocardiogram of a human heart. The caption reads, "Echocardiogram of human heart clearly reveals the Hebrew letter *shin,* the first letter of one of the most ancient of God's names, *El Shaddai* (Page 39). The letter *shin* can also be seen in the topography of Jerusalem.

of the marriage covenant where the groom gives His name to the bride. Then His disciples, filled with overwhelming joy, thankfulness and love, bowed down and worshiped Him. Returning to Jerusalem, they celebrated in the temple **continually *hallel*-ing and *barak*-ing God**.[120]

The Disciples and New Covenant Multitudes *Barak*-ed

The disciples blessed (*barak*-ed) God in response to Jesus' crucifixion, resurrection, ascension and promise of return. In response to the miracles performed by Jesus, the multitudes blessed (*barak*-ed) God. In Matthew we read the story of the paralytic whom Y'shua healed and then extended forgiveness of sin. "Now when the multitudes saw *it*, they marveled and glorified (blessed) God, who had given such power to men."[121] Again after many miracles "the multitude marveled when they saw *the* mute speaking, *the* maimed made whole, *the* lame walking and *the* blind seeing; and they glorified the God of Israel."[122]

Barak ~ A Blessing Bouquet for Our Beloved!

I must include this quote from Irene Lipson's book, "Blessing the King of the Universe." A Hasidic rabbi expressed his view of prayer:

> "'Every word of your prayer is like a rose which you pick from its bush. You continue until you have formed a bouquet, a complete blessing. From them you form new bouquets of blessings, until you have [plaited] a wreath of glory unto the Lord.'[123] Imagine that every time you make a *b'rakhah* (blessing) you are offering a beautiful, fragrant bouquet to your beloved! Hence, the *b'rakhah* is an expression of the way we see ourselves in relation to God. He is divine, and we approach him not only with gratitude and love but also with awe and reverence."[124]

Y'shua Will Return to the Words of a Special *Berakhah!*

In Psalm 118:26 we find this Messianic Greeting: *Barukh ha-ba' be-Shem ADONAI* – "Blessed is He who comes in the name of the LORD." These words were traditionally recognized as the greeting that would acknowledge and welcome Messiah. In Matthew when the crowds shouted, "Hosanna to the Son of David, Blessed is He who comes in the name of the LORD...,"[125] they were consciously acclaiming Y'shua as Messiah and King. Looking for a political leader, they did not understand His mission. Sadly, we remember that days later Jesus would weep over Jerusalem:

> "O Jerusalem, Jerusalem, the one who kills the prophets and stones those who are sent to her! How often I wanted to gather your children together, as a hen *gathers* her brood under *her* wings, but you were not willing! See! Your house is left to you desolate; and assuredly, I say to you, you shall not see Me until *the time* comes when you say, 'Blessed is He who comes in the name of the LORD!'"[126]

Praise the LORD for a second chance! Let us pray fervently for the nation of Israel to recognize their Messiah. With this powerful blessing that they alone can utter, they will usher in Messiah and He will hear the invitation that He so longs to hear.

Barak ~ A Conscious Choice

Psalms 103 and 104 give us a powerful key to the practice of *barak*. We can choose to *barak* regardless of our feelings or our circumstances. David wrote, "Bless *(barak)* the LORD, O my soul; and all that is within me, bless *(barak)* His holy name. Bless *(barak)* the LORD, O my soul, and forget not all His benefits.[127]

David learned there were times he had to take charge of his own soul and command it to praise the LORD. Using the present continuing tense, he recalls all the good things God had done and continues to do. He reminds his soul what God had done for him personally:

> God "forgives (and continues to forgive) all your iniquities, heals (and continues to heal) all your diseases, redeems your life from destruction, crowns you with lovingkindness and tender mercies and satisfies your mouth with good *things*, so that your youth is renewed like the eagle's."[128]

In the verses that follow, David recounts all the good things the LORD does (and continues to do) for the nation of Israel and for all who fear and serve Him.[129] Next David commands the angels, the heavenly hosts, all of Yahweh's ministers who do His pleasure and all the works of the LORD to *barak* the LORD![130] It is as if David becomes the conductor of a beautiful symphony of *barak*. First, his own soul begins playing as a solo instrument and then as he points the baton, first the angelic hosts and finally all of creation add their voices to the rapturous chorus of blessing.

In Psalm 104 God's *barak*-blessing extends to all physical creation. After reviewing all the blessings of God, any soul would be recharged and bursting with love and faith. Remembering God's faithfulness in the past builds faith for the present and the future. Understanding that God's ways never change gives comfort and hope. Will you join David in encouraging your soul to bless the LORD and see what God does?

Barak ~ Before the Throne of God Forever

Blessing is a form of praise to be continued before the throne of God forever. Before the throne, blessings are sung continually to God and to the Lamb. Let us join our voices with the heavenly choir of angels, the living creatures and the elders rendering the blessings due Him:

"Worthy is the Lamb who was slain to receive power and riches and wisdom, and strength and honor and glory and blessing!"[131]

Next we can join the chorus of every creature which is in heaven and on the earth and under the earth and such as are in the sea, and all that are in them, saying:

"Blessing and honor and glory and power be to Him who sits on the throne, and to the Lamb, forever and ever!"[132]

Now, falling on our faces before the LORD as do all the angels, the elders and the four living creatures, let us worship God, saying:

"Amen! Blessing and glory and wisdom, thanksgiving and honor and power and might, be to our God forever and ever. Amen."[133]

Barak ~ David's Last Words

We all know the stories of King David's life, how he loved and followed God as a shepherd boy, slew the giant Goliath, became King of Israel and was called the Sweet Psalmist of Israel. Through his psalms he has given us vast understanding about the nature of God, our love relationship with Him and living a life in praise. It is interesting that his last recorded words are a blessing to God and an instruction to the people of Israel to continue to bless Him:

> "Blessed are You, LORD God of Israel, our Father, forever and ever. Yours, O LORD, is the greatness, the power and the glory, the victory and the majesty; for all that is in heaven and in earth *is Yours*, Yours *is* the kingdom, O LORD, and You are exalted as head over *all*. Both riches and honor *come* from You, and You reign over all. In Your hand *is* power and might; in Your hand *it is* to make great and to give strength to all. Now therefore, our God, we thank You and praise Your glorious name."[134]

David concluded his exhortation to the people of God with this charge, "'Now bless the LORD your God.' So, all the assembly blessed (*barak*-ed) the LORD God of their fathers, and bowed their heads and prostrated themselves before the LORD and the king."[135]

Barak ~ In Practice

Blessing is a distinctive element of intimate communion. Through *barak*-blessing, we are brought closer to our God. The more our humility is expressed through *barak*, the closer our union with Him. And, the closer our union with Him, the more humility is expressed in our lives. It is truly a holy calling to bless the King of the Universe.

Studying and meditating on the subject of praising God through *barak* has intensely deepened His worthiness in my own heart. I now view situations and circumstances in my own life from a different perspective. In lifting up blessings to Him in every situation, we can expand and heighten our love for Him. Mountains that loom before us suddenly become flat plains; faith rises to new levels and we are transformed.

Y'shua said, "Seek first the kingdom of God and His righteousness, and all these things will be added unto you." God's blessings are not the focus -- simply the overflow. He is the focal point. All else pales in the light of His glory and love.

Tehillah (Psalm) 134

*Behold, bless **(barak)** Yahweh,*
All you servants of Yahweh,
Who by night stand in the house of Yahweh!

Lift up your hands in the sanctuary,
*And bless **(barak)** Yahweh.*

Yahweh who made heaven and earth
Bless (Barak) *you from Zion!*¶¶¶

Come Bless ADONAI!

Come bless ADONAI, All you servants of ADONAI,
Who stand by night in the house of ADONAI,
Lift up your hands in the sanctuary,
Come bless, Come bless ADONAI.

Come bless the King of the universe,
Come bless the Maker of heaven and earth,
Come bless the One who gives new birth,
Come bless, Come bless ADONAI.

ADONAI, You're the Holy One,
ADONAI, You're the Mighty One,
ADONAI, the Victorious One,
I lift my hands in praise!

¶¶¶   I have replaced LORD with Yahweh.

Come bless, kneel down before Him,
Come bless, love and adore Him,
Come bless, praise and exalt Him,
Come bless, Come bless ADONAI.
Come bless, Worship His holiness,
Come bless, Worship His loveliness,
Come bless, Worship His greatness,
Come bless, Come bless ADONAI.

I worship Your holiness,
I worship Your loveliness,
I worship Your greatness,
I bow before Your throne.

I bless You, I bless ADONAI,
I bless You, I bless ADONAI,
ADONAI, my King!

I love and adore You,
Bow down before You,
Praise and exalt ADONAI,
ADONAI, my King!
I worship ADONAI!

NOTES

1   Francis Brown, D.D., D.Litt. with the cooperation of S.R. Driver, D.D., Litt.D. and Charles A. Briggs, D.D., D.Litt., *The New Brown-Driver-Briggs-Gesenius Hebrew and English Lexicon* (Peabody, Massachusetts: Hendrickson Publishers, 1979), #1288, p.138b.

2   *The Power New Testament: Revealing Jewish Roots, Trans. William J. Morford* (Lexington, SC: Rev. William J. Morford, 2003), p. 388.

3   Dr. John Garr, *Bless You! Restoring the Power of Biblical Blessing* (Atlanta, Georgia: Restoration Foundation, 2005), p. 93-94.

4   Genesis 1:31

5   Dr. Frank T. Seekins, *Hebrew Word Pictures: How Does the Hebrew Alphabet Reveal Prophetic Truths?* (Phoenix, Arizona: Living Word Pictures, Inc., 1994, 2003) p. 19.

6   Ibid, p. 88

7   Ibid, p.18

8   Ibid, p.18

9   Ibid, p.52

10 Ibid, p.18

11 Ibid, p. 133, 147

12 Ibid, p. 133

13 I Kings 5:7

14 Psalm 95:6

15 Psalm 66:8

16 psalm 72:17-20

17 Psalm 18:46

18 Daniel 2:19

19 I Chronicles 29:20

20 Luke 1:68-75

21 Job 1:20-21

22 Psalm 103:1

23 Psalm 72:1-20

24 Romans 1:25

25 Psalm 118:26, Matthew 21:9

26 Philippians 2:10

27 Romans 9:5

28 I Peter 1:3-5

29 Psalm 72:17

30 Psalm 66:8

31 Philippians 2:9-11; Isaiah 45:23; Romans 14:11

32 Psalm 103, 115, 134, 135, 145

33 Romans 1:25

34 Romans 9:5

35 Deuteronomy 8:10

36 Psalm 96:2

37 Judges 5:2
38 Psalm 110:2-3 CJB
39 Genesis 1:5
40 Ps 72:15 (Daily – continually, perpetually, from sunset to sunset)
41 Psalm 34:1
42 I Chronicles 16:36 KJV
43 Ps 34:1
44 Ps 63:4
45 Psalm 113:2; 115:18
46 Psalm 145:2
47 Romans 9:5
48 Proverbs 3:6
49 Psalm 95:6
50 Psalm 26:12; Ps 68:26; II Chronicles 6:13
51 Psalm 103:22
52 Psalm 134:1
53 Psalm 135:21
54 Luke 24:53
55 Psalm 34:1
56 Psalm 68:19
57 Psalm 68:19 CJB
58 Psalm 72:17a
59 Psalm 72:17b
60 Psalm 16:7
61 I Kings 5:7
62 Daniel 2:20b
63 Daniel 2:21
64 Daniel 2:22
65 Luke 1:68
66 Luke 1:69
67 Luke 2:30-32
68 I Peter 1:3
69 I Peter 1:4
70 I Peter 1:5
71 Ephesians 1:3
72 Matthew 21:9;Matthew 23:39; Mark 11:9; Luke 13:35; John 12:13; Psalm 118:26
73 Genesis 24:26-27 CJB
74 Exodus 18:10 CJB
75 Ruth 4:14 CJB
76 I Samuel 25:32 CJB
77 Psalm 28:6 CJB
78 II Chronicles 6:13
79 Psalm 134:2
80 Psalm 63:4

81   James 3:8-10
82   Nehemiah 9:5
83   I Chronicles 29:20
84   Psalm 24:3
85   Garr, *Bless You! Restoring the Power of Biblical Blessing*, p. 82.
86   Ibid, p. 83
87   Irene Lipson, *Blessing the King of the Universe* (Baltimore, MD: Lederer Books, 2004), p. xiv.
88   Ibid, p. xiv.
89   Ibid, p. xiv. [Quote from Benyamin Forst , *The Laws of B'rachos* (New York: Mesorah, 1990), p. 29.]
90   Psalm 34:1-2
91   Job 1:20-21
92   Job 1:22
93   Job 2:9-10
94   Job 2:6
95   Romans 8:28
96   Job 42:5
97   Daniel 2:19-22
98   Daniel 3:25
99   Daniel 3:28
100   Daniel 3:29
101   Daniel 4:17
102   Daniel 4:34
103   Hebrews 13:8 CJB
104   Seekins, *Hebrew Word Pictures: How Does the Hebrew Alphabet Reveal Prophetic Truths?* p. 19
105   Ecclesiastes 4:12
106   Jeremiah 25:11b-12
107   See Psalm 149:6-9 which instructs us to "Let the high praises of God be in their mouth and a two-edged sword in their hand, to execute vengeance on the nations, and punishments on the peoples; to bind their kings with fetters of iron; to execute on them the written judgment – this honor have all His saints. Praise the LORD!"
108   Joseph Henry Thayer, D.D., *The New Thayer's Greek-English Lexicon of the New Testament*
      (Peabody, Massachusetts: Hendrickson Publishers, 1981), #2127, p. 259b.
109   Luke 10:17
110   Luke 10:21
111   Matthew 26:26-28, See also Mark 14:22-24 TPNT
112   Mark 6:41 TPNT See also Matthew 14:19
113   Acts 3:21
114   Luke 24:50
115   Numbers 6:24-26
116   Numbers 6:24-26

117 Garr, *Bless You! Restoring the Power of Biblical Blessing*, p. 39, 52-53.
118 Numbers 6:27
119 Garr, *Bless You! Restoring the Power of Biblical Blessing*, p. 54-55, 57-58.
120 Luke 24:53 Amplified Version
121 Matthew 9:8
122 Matthew 15:31
123 Lipson p 15, from *"The Hasidic Anthology"* by Louis I. Newman, p. 337.
124 Lipson p 15, from *"The Laws of B'rachos"* by Benyamin Forst, p. 26.
125 Matthew 21:9
126 Luke 13:34-35
127 Psalm 103:1-2
128 Psalm 103:3-5
129 Psalm 103:6-19
130 Psalm 103:20-22
131 Revelation 5:12b
132 Revelation 5:13b
133 Revelation 7:12b
134 I Chronicles 29:10b-13
135 I Chronicles 29:20

Zamar

Praise and Prophesy with Musical Instruments

Zamar ~ The Definition

Zamar (pronounced *zah-mar'*) is the playing of musical instruments, accompanied by the voice, in celebration and praise to God. The Hebrew Lexicon defines it as: "Make music in praise of God; pipe, play on a reed, make music, melody, instrumental accompaniment, of playing musical instruments."[1] Strong's Concordance states it this way: "to touch the strings or parts of a musical instrument and play on it."[2] *Zamar* is variously translated as "praise," "give praise," "make melody," "sing," "sing forth praises" and "sing psalms." Amazingly, none of the English words or phrases used to translate *zamar* in any way denotes the playing of musical instruments!

In both the Old and New Covenants the expression of *zamar* is varied. It can be defined as instrumental music ministered alone in praise to God. It can also be defined as instrumental music used to accompany the voice or instrumental music accompanied by the voice. The latter seems backward in our thinking today. When we think of singing with instruments, we consider the vocals the prominent part and instruments as the background or accompaniment. However, *zamar* is sometimes expressed when the instrument is the lead and the voice is the accompaniment. This lends itself to some very interesting scenarios. In I Chronicles 25 we read that David selected some of the sons of Asaph, Heman and Jeduthan (the three choir leaders at the Tabernacle of David) to "prophesy with harps, stringed instruments and cymbals."[3] The word "prophesy" here is *naba* (pronounced *nah-bah'*). This Hebrew word means "to prophesy, to speak or sing by inspiration – either in prediction or simple discourse."[4] So sometimes prophecy predicts the future and sometimes it simply voices whatever is on God's heart, whether encouragement, comfort, correction or reproof. Further, this scripture commands that these words be spoken or sung to the accompaniment of musical instruments.

Many prophets respond to the voice heard from instruments in praise and worship. This is *zamar*. The musical voice of instruments can be a catalyst for the moving of the Holy Spirit. Instrumental music coupled with the inspiration of the Holy Spirit oftentimes enables prophets to hear the word of the LORD more clearly. In ministering to the LORD, I have discovered that there are times when the sounds from instruments musically communicate God's message while the voice of the worshiper sings the interpretation. Occasionally I have heard sounds resembling music of other nations rising beneath my fingers. I call it "playing in tongues." At other times the sounds of instruments paint pictures. Some of the pictures these sounds may bring to mind are splashing waterfalls, flowing rivers, bubbling brooks, showering rain, roaring waves, rushing winds, gentle breezes, flaming fire, fluttering wings, or the pouring of oil. Love, peace, joy, delight, tenderness, light, power, comfort and strength are a few of the manifestations the Holy Spirit ministers through His music.

Zamar ~ Weapon of War

David prayed, "Teach my hands to war and my fingers to fight."[5] Even though he was a mighty warrior, having slain tens of thousands of God's earthly enemies, I believe David was speaking here of warring on the musical instruments God inspired him to make. David had great insight into Yahweh's heart and kingdom. He knew the battle was fought and won in the Spirit before it was played out in the natural.

In her Song of Victory after defeating Sisera, Deborah sang:

> "Hear, O kings! Give ear O princes! I, *even* I, will sing to the LORD;* I will **sing praise** (*zamar*) to the LORD God of Israel."[6]

---

* When LORD is spelled with all capital letters in the King James Version and New King James Version, it translates the holy name of God. Called the Tetragrammaton, it is formed with the four Hebrew letters *Yud, Heh, Vav, Heh (YHVH or YHWH)* and is sometimes translated Jehovah, Yehovah, Yahweh or Yaheh. The Complete Jewish Bible translates this name as *ADONAI,* a title meaning "LORD."

Instrumental "war sounds" bring up images of charging troops, blasting trumpets, stamping horses' hooves, racing chariot wheels and clashing swords. This conflict, voiced by musical instruments, often transitions praise and worship to sounds of victory and triumph. As we war in the Spirit, we can move from conflict and battle to peace and sovereignty. We sense the entry of the triumphant King of kings and Lord of lords. Understanding *zamar* helps us know that the weapons of our warfare not only include our vocal praise and worship but also the voice of our instruments. By this we enter new realms of glory, shatter the enemy's gates, cast down strongholds and thwart the enemy's plans.

Zamar ~ **Prophets of Israel**

In the life of Israel's prophets the playing of instruments went hand and hand with prophesying. After anointing Saul as King of Israel, Samuel prophesied to him:

> "...you will come to Giv'ah (the hill) of God, where the P'lishtim (Philistines) are garrisoned. On arrival at the city there, you will meet a group of prophets coming down from the high place, **preceded** by lutes, tambourines, flutes and lyres, and they will be prophesying. Then the Spirit of *ADONAI* will fall on you; you will prophesy with them and be turned into another man!"[7]

It happened just as Samuel had predicted. The spirit of prophecy fell on Saul and he prophesied with the others. Note that the musicians preceded or walked in front of the prophets. Their music set the atmosphere for the spirit of prophecy to flow.

Elisha illustrated this relationship between musical instruments and prophecy when he said to King Jehoram, "'But now bring me a musician.' Then it happened, when the musician played, that the hand of the LORD came upon him."[8] As the anointing flowed from the music, Elisha prophesied the Word of the LORD.

The playing of musical instruments brought the presence of the LORD and stilled the enemy. King Saul's servants counseled him,

> "…seek out a man who *is* a skillful player on a harp. And it shall be that he will play it with his hand when the distressing spirit from God is upon you, and you shall be well."[9]

Saul sent out his servants to find a minstrel and they returned with the young shepherd-boy David. In I Samuel we read,

> "And so it was, whenever the spirit from God was upon Saul, that David would take a harp and play it with his hand. Then Saul would become refreshed and well, and the distressing spirit would depart from him."[10]

What power resides in the ministry of the psalmist yielded to the LORD – power to revive, refresh, encourage, heal and deliver! Even the power to set the enemy to flight![11] It is no wonder that the enemy fights both the worship of the Creator and His worshipers.

Zamar ~ Honor His name!

Early in my walk with the LORD He gave me a prophetic word. He confirmed it several times in various ways. I knew it had to do with His call on my life. He spoke to my heart, "Sing forth the honor of (My) name and make (My) praise glorious!"[12] Years passed before I thought to look up the Hebrew words that compose this verse from Psalm 66. (Actually I did not even own a concordance or a lexicon for many years. That purchase turned out to be one of the best investments of my life and I encourage everyone to make it if you have not already.) When I researched the words and their meanings, I was astounded. "Sing forth" is the Hebrew "*zamar*." The piano is my main instrument and from the time I first experienced the fullness of the Holy Spirit, I would place my Bible on the piano and improvise melodies to the psalms. New songs from the LORD began to flow in my times of personal worship. I had never heard of a modern-day psalmist and did not realize what I was doing – psalming to the LORD while playing an instrument. Without being aware of it, I had been lifting *zamar* to the LORD as He instructs in His Word.

Interestingly, God calls us not only to sing and play our songs to Him, but also to sing forth, sending out His message **and** its sound. I am reminded of the modern word "broadcast." We are commissioned to publish the message of the good news, which when joined with *zamar*, produces a heavenly sound-byte. This message-sound brings His name honor, praise and glory. The Hebrew word for "glory" here is *kabod* (pronounced *kah-bode'*) and means "full of splendor, weighty in value, full of glory and honor."[13] Psalm 66:2 with the Hebrew praise words inserted reads,

> "*Zamar* the honor of His name and make His *tehillah*
> (psalm) glorious."

Y'shua is the speaker of this psalm and "you" is the understood subject. "You (everyone in His body) *zamar* the honor of His name. "His" name and "His" praise in verse two refers to the Father. And since Y'shua, the Living Word, composed the psalms and instructs us to *zamar* His name and make His *tehillah* glorious, we could paraphrase this verse as follows:

> [You] *Zamar* the honor of our Father's name and make
> His *tehillah* (psalm) glorious.

The call to *zamar* came to me thirty years ago. Because I was shy, introverted and insecure, I struggled with the LORD's command to "sing forth." The enemies of fear and timidity used intimidation to stop me from freely singing forth His praises; however, the LORD encouraged me and quietly adjusted **my** perspective. He said, "I am not calling you to sing to the people, I am calling you to sing to Me in front of the people." It was a statement I have never forgotten. Then the LORD made an amazing promise, "I'll deliver you from fear as you walk through the doors I open before you."

Delighting in His promise I thought that I would be completely delivered the very next time He opened a door of opportunity for me to minister in song. Little did I know that the LORD was going to take me through a process of deliverance over time. Refusing to give in to fear, each time I heard His voice, I obeyed. The LORD was true to His Word no matter how weak or unskilled I sounded. His anointing was strong on my sacrifice of obedience. You see, the power is from the LORD and not in our skill. Fear left. Gradually I began to realize that many different fears had strongholds in my life. It was the growing knowledge of my Creator and Savior and what He had done for me that loosened fear's grip. So, we must set our faces like flint toward the promises of God and obey even in the face of fear. David sang, "Whenever I am afraid, I will trust in You."[14] Praise the LORD! He has been and will continue to be faithful because His Word is true. I encourage you to step out in faith in whatever the LORD has called you to do and trust Him to "perfect that which concerns (you)."[15] He is pleased with our obedience and our skill, no matter how imperfect. He will bless and anoint and deliver. **God** has ordained maturing in Him to be a process.

Remember, we carry the treasure of His Being in our earthen vessels so that all the power and glory may be of Him.[16] It is the humble walk of the cross to lay down our lives and obey, trusting Him more than we fear man and desiring His favor above man's acceptance and praise.

Zamar[†] ~ **Summary of Scriptural Instructions**

As recorded in the scriptures, **all saints**, **all the earth** and **each individual soul** – which the psalmist refers to as "my glory" – are instructed to offer *zamar* to the **"LORD God of Israel," "LORD Most High," "Holy One of Israel," "God of Jacob"** and **His name** in all its expressions. That leaves no one out! We are all called to *zamar* a new song to the LORD, exalting His power and the honor of His name. Our songs, accompanied by harps, stringed instruments, psalteries, timbrels and other musical instruments, are to be sung

†   For Scripture references see the *Zamar* Concordance in the "Created to Praise Study Guide."

among the nations and **before the throne of God**. They are to be sung **in and from hearts fixed on Him**. We are called to sing and play **with understanding, in Spirit and in Truth**. Y'shua, the Psalmist of psalmists, vows to *zamar* praise to His Father "**as long as I live, while I have my being and forever.**"[17]

Why should we *zamar* the LORD?

- To declare His lovingkindness
- To declare His faithfulness
- Because it is a good thing
- Because the LORD has done excellent things
- Because His name is pleasant
- To daily perform my vows to Him
- To praise His name
- To declare His deeds
- To praise His power
- Because my head shall be lifted up above my enemies all around me
- Because You have turned my mourning into dancing
- Because You have put off my sackcloth & clothed me with gladness
- To awaken the dawn with praise
- Because God is my defense, my God of mercy
- Because You have redeemed my soul
- To make a joyful noise to the LORD
- To sing of the mercy and justice of the LORD
- To praise with my soul

Zamar-ing[‡] the LORD brings great joy! The psalmist exclaims, "My lips shall greatly rejoice when I *zamar* You; and my soul, which You have redeemed."[18] Not only my lips, but the deepest part of my being will *zamar* the LORD and rejoice with great joy. This is the reward of *zamar*!

---

‡   I have used the endings –s, -ed and –ing to facilitate the flow in English. These are not Hebrew forms. Also I have used the root forms of the Hebrew words for praise which are not the forms used in Modern Hebrew.

Zamar ~ A Serenade

When I think of *zamar*, I think of the word, "serenade." Can you picture a lover beneath the window of his beloved, playing his instrument and serenading the girl of his dreams? Melodious notes of his instrument and song find their way into the ears and heart of the sought-after girl, winning her undying love. Our Bridegroom Y'shua psalms His songs of love into the spiritual ears of His beloved Bride. Having penned an entire book of songs to be ministered to each soul in every generation, He woos us with unconditional love too great to comprehend. We are compelled, in the light of such great love, to return that love to Him. He calls His Bride to serenade Him each day with songs of love and praise, proclaiming His wonderful works.

Zamar ~ In Restored Jerusalem!

Zamar will resound in restored Jerusalem. Isaiah prophesied:

> "For the LORD will comfort Zion, He will comfort all her waste places; He will make her wilderness like Eden, and her desert like the garden of the LORD; joy and gladness will be found in it, thanksgiving and the voice of **melody**."

The word translated melody here is *zimrah* (pronounced *zim-rah'*), a derivative of the root word "*zamar*."[19] It means "a piece or song to be accompanied by a musical instrument; melody, psalm." Singing and the music of instruments will again resound in God's garden!

Zamar ~ Its Derivatives

Other scriptures featuring *zimrah* reinforce the use of instruments in worship. Psalm 81 says, "Raise a **song** (*zimrah*) and strike the timbrel, the pleasant harp with the lute.[20] Psalm 98 commands, "*Zamar* to the LORD with the harp, with the harp and the sound of a **psalm** (*zimrah*).[21]

We must take time here to heed a warning. Our praise must go forth out of sincere hearts given wholly to our King. The prophet Amos cried out against sin in Israel and spoke forth the hurt and anger of the LORD: "I hate, I despise your feast days, and I do not savor your sacred assemblies...Take away from Me the noise of your songs, for I will not hear the **melody** (*zimrah*) of your stringed instruments. But let justice run down like water, and righteousness like a mighty stream."[22] Here the LORD emphasizes the necessity of purity in worship. Without pure hearts and righteous ways our songs are like "sounding brass" or "clanging cymbals"[23] and are a stench in His nostrils.

Timbrels were used with the famous "Song of Deliverance" sung by Moses and the children of Israel after God's great and mighty miracle of parting the Red Sea. God brought His people safely to the other side and drowned the enemy army of Egypt in its depths. They sang, "The LORD is my strength and *song*. "Song" is translated from another derivative of *zamar* – *zimrath* (pronounced *zim-rahth'*). It is defined as "instrumental music; praise; song."[24] This timeless exclamation of victory and faith is repeated in Psalm 118 and Isaiah 12.[25] A powerful message emerges from its words: this "Song" is the LORD Himself. Y'shua not only sings songs and is the subject and object of our songs; He is the "Song." In fact, He is the "Song of songs."

Zamir (pronounced *zah-meer'*)[26] is another derivative of *zamar*, and means "a song to be accompanied with instrumental music, psalm, psalmist, singing, and song." Scriptures using *zamir* give us further insight into its meaning. Everything that has breath is an instrument of praise. In the Song of Solomon, the Bridegroom calls the Shulamite maiden to rise up and come away for… "The time has come for (the birds) to **sing** (*zamir*) and the cooing of doves can be heard in the land."[27] The birds pipe their songs announcing the arrival of spring. Even creation joins the musical symphony as instruments of His song.

The prophet Samuel called David "the sweet **psalmist** (*zamir*) of Israel."[28] By the direction of Y'shua, the Word of God, David made many instruments with which to *hallel, tehillah, yadah and zamar ADONAI.*

God composes and then gives us His songs. In the book of Job, Elihu attributes God the Creator with giving **songs** (*zamir*) in the night."[29] God's own living Word becomes the lyrics of our songs for instrumental accompaniment. David sang, "Your statutes have been my **songs** (*zamir*) in the house of my pilgrimage."[30]

Songs accompanied by instruments sound across the earth. Isaiah prophesies, "From the ends of the earth we have heard **songs** (*zamir*) (accompanied by instruments): "Glory to the righteous!"[31] The playing of musical instruments throughout the scriptures is vitally linked with praise, prophecy, intercession and warfare.

Zamar ~ In the New Testament

In the New Testament *zamar* is translated with the Greek word *psallo*, meaning "to rub or touch the surface of an instrument, play on a stringed instrument and celebrate the divine worship with music and accompanying odes, to make melody, sing a hymn, sing to the music of the harp and sing psalms. "[32] Notice the similarity of this definition to that of *zamar. Psallo* is translated into English as "sing," "sing psalms" and "making melody." Surprisingly, again in the New Covenant the English translation makes no mention of musical instruments.

However, the Hebrew tradition did not allow public performance of psalms without instrumental accompaniment. This practice continued in the Messianic church, though not explicitly stated in the English translation of the scriptures. The very definitions of the Hebrew word *zamar* and the Greek word *psallo* called for the use of musical instruments. This was understood and practiced by the early believers in Y'shua. As the verses in Revelation describing heavenly worship reveal, singing – accompanied by harps – is an integral part of worship before the throne, the Holy of Holies, throughout eternity.

Let us examine some New Covenant passages that teach us about the use of *psallo*. In Ephesians 5, Paul gives the key to walking in the fullness of God's presence. He instructs, "And be not drunk with wine, in which is excess;[33] but be filled (keep on being filled)[§] with the Spirit, speaking to one another in psalms (*psalmos-tehillim*) and hymns and spiritual songs, singing and **making melody** (*psallo-zamar*) in your heart to the Lord."[34] Here Paul instructs new believers how to be continually filled with the new wine of the Holy Spirit: keep singing psalms and hymns and spiritual songs to God and one another accompanied by the music of strings and pipes!

James counsels, "Is anyone among you suffering? Let him pray. Is anyone cheerful? Let him **sing psalms** (*psallo*)."[35] In other words, let him play a musical instrument and sing to the Lord or sing along with another musician. *Psallo* is the natural outflow of joyful hearts expressing praise to the Lord.

In I Corinthians 14:15 Paul gave instructions on the use of the gift of speaking in tongues. He said "I will pray with the spirit and I will also pray with the understanding." He continued "I will *psallo* with the spirit and I will also *psallo* with the understanding." This literally says that Paul sang in accompaniment to a musical instrument as he ministered to the Lord. His use of an instrument certainly would be in keeping with the tradition of Old Covenant prophets who prophesied to the playing of instruments in Israel. Could it also be that Paul was saying that he was the instrument upon which Y'shua played and through which He sang?

Y'shua ~ Born to *Zamar*

If there is still any question in our minds whether the Hebrew expressions of praise in the Old Covenant are for New Covenant believers, Romans 15 will put it to rest. Verses eight and nine of this chapter state that Messiah became a servant with a two-fold mission. His first purpose was "to **show God's truthfulness** by

---

§   Definition in parentheses is taken from verse 18 in the Complete Jewish Bible. The Amplified Bible says, "…but ever be filled and stimulated with the (Holy) Spirit."

making good His promises to the Patriarchs" – in other words to fulfill that which was promised to Abraham, Isaac, Jacob, Moses, David and other "fathers" in Israel's history. His second purpose was "to **show His mercy** by causing the Gentiles to glorify (*shabach*) God…." Paul continues, "…as it is written in the *Tanakh* (the Old Covenant), 'Because of this "I" will acknowledge (*yadah*) You among the Gentiles, and sing praises (*psallo - zamar* - play musical instruments accompanied by My voice singing psalms) to Your name.'"[36] More simply stated, 'Because of this "I", Messiah, will *yadah* You, My Father, among the Gentiles, and *zamar* Your name.' This is a quotation from Psalm 18:49 which reads as follows in the New King James Version of the Bible, "Therefore I will give thanks (*yadah*) unto you, O LORD, among the nations (Gentiles), and sing (*zamar*) to Your name." Notice that the writer of Romans refers to the speaker of Psalm 18 (the "I" of Romans 15:9) as being Messiah! (Go back and read that again. Most of the New Testament teachings simply interpret and expound upon what we have called the "Old.") Continuing to speak to New Covenant Gentile believers Paul quotes three other Old Covenant passages in Romans 15:10-11:

> "And again it says, 'Gentiles, **rejoice** (sing and shout aloud for joy) **with** His people.'[37] "And again, 'Praise (**Hallel**) *ADONAI*, all Gentiles! Let *all* peoples praise (*shabach*) Him.'[38] And again, (Isaiah) says, 'The root of (Jesse) will come, He who arises to rule Gentiles; Gentiles will put their hope in Him.'"[39, 40]

These verses tell us that the Messiah Himself, further identified as the "Root of Jesse," will *yadah* the Father among the Gentiles and *zamar* the Father's name. He will *shabach* the Father through the Gentiles ~ singing in and from their hearts and using their voices ~ as they join Him and the people of Israel in praising the Father. Here it clearly states that Y'shua will *shabach, zamar, yadah and hallel* the Father – in, through and together with both Jew and Gentile, individually, as well as in the congregation! It also affirms that Gentile believers in Him are commanded to *shabach, zamar, yadah and hallel* the Father. Understanding now the full import of these Hebrew words, take a moment and meditate on the awesome revelation that Messiah praises the Father with and through us!

Before He came to earth, Y'shua prophesied through the psalmist David that He would come and *zamar* to the Gentiles.[41] It was one of the ministries He would fulfill in the flesh. Y'shua was born to *zamar*! Notice also that Y'shua continues to *zamar* after His resurrection. When He came to earth, He came only to the lost sheep of the house of Israel. His ministry to the Gentiles, except for a few individuals, began **after** His resurrection!

How does Y'shua *zamar* – play upon the strings or pipes of an instrument? There is no reference of which I am aware that tells us that Y'shua played a musical instrument while He walked on the earth. However, since many things Messiah did while on earth were not recorded, it was certainly possible.[42] We do know that David made many instruments with which to praise by the "Word" or instruction of the LORD. That means that the "Living Word" Y'shua gave the instructions to David as to how to build each musical instrument. I believe that He, in His resurrected body seated at the right hand of the Father, plays upon us, His living instruments – born of Him and called by His name. As He sings to the Father in the midst of the congregation, He plays upon our strings (vocal chords) and our pipes (windpipes) by His Holy Spirit and *zamar(s)* (plays instruments and sings psalms) through us to the Father. We are His instruments to play upon, His voices to sing through — bondservants of love, devotion, service and praise!

What an awesome privilege to become His instrument of praise and have His life, love and praise flow through our beings to His throne. What a holy calling. Mere words cannot express our wonder that He is not only mindful of man as Psalm 8 declares, but loves us beyond our comprehension. I have experienced times when, as I sing in the Spirit, I am aware of the Holy Breath of the *Ruach Ha Kodesh* (the Holy Spirit) flowing in and out of my mouth, playing my vocal chords much like the strings of a violin. His words are like honey on my lips and His name like perfume poured out![43] In the

Spirit I have seen droplets of honey forming on my fingertips as I touched the strings of my harp. The LORD made me to know that the honey represents the ministry of the Word – Y'shua – carried by His Spirit on the wings of His music. Music that is birthed and borne by the Holy Spirit is a powerful vehicle to communicate not only the mind of God – His Word – but also the emotion of God – His heart! *Zamar* the LORD your God and make His *tehillah* glorious!

Zamar ~ Its Hebrew Letters

The Hebrew letters which spell *zamar* teach us an amazing lesson. The letter *zayin* (our "Z") was originally drawn as the picture of a weapon. "*Mar*" is the Hebrew word meaning "bitter." Thus *zamar* is a weapon to cut off bitterness. One definition of *zamar* is "to prune." Until I found this study of the letters, I could not reconcile the definition of "to prune" with the playing of instruments. Frank Seekins in his book *Hebrew Word Pictures: How Does the Hebrew Alphabet Reveal Prophetic Truths?* says, "The weapon or instrument of pruning cuts away the bitter part just as singing takes away bitterness."[44] No wonder David asked the LORD to teach his fingers to fight and his hands to war! His fingers became the "weapon" to pluck the strings which sent out the sound of music to cut off the bitterness and control of demonic strongholds. No evil thing can dwell in the atmosphere of *zamar*!

A perfect example of this *zamar*-weapon is the closing song found in the book of the prophet Habakkuk. Perhaps you have sung or heard this song put to music and it ministered to you in a time when you could see no promise of the goodness of God in the land of the living or on the horizon. However, as most of us know by experience, His promises are true. If we lean into *zamar* with our whole hearts, in God's time we will walk on new heights.

Habakkuk left instructions for his song: "To the Chief Musician. With my stringed instruments."[45] Singing the Word of God, especially to the accompaniment of instruments, has more power than simply reading it silently or aloud. It has been proven that words put to melody are more easily memorized and retained than spoken words. Habakkuk's song of testimony accompanied by stringed instruments is a powerful weapon of overcoming faith in times of trouble:

> "Though the fig tree may not blossom,
> Nor fruit be on the vines;
> Though the labor of the olive may fail,
> And the fields yield no food;
> Though the flock may be cut off from the fold,
> And there be no herd in the stalls –
> Yet I will rejoice in the LORD,
> I will joy in the God of my salvation.
> The LORD GOD is my strength;
> He will make my feet like deer's *feet*,
> And He will make me walk on my high hills."[46]

Zamar ~ Sign of His coming

Rabbis in Israel today have been looking for the restoration of David's musical instruments as a sign that Messiah is coming. Several years ago a young American Jewish couple, Micah and Shoshanna Harrari, made *aliyah*[¶] to Israel. While wandering through the caves of Megiddo, they noticed a carving of a harp on the cave wall. After being told that the carvings dated back to the time of King David, Shoshanna asked Micah to make her a harp like the one from David's time. After several unsuccessful attempts, Micah crafted a harp which was beautiful in appearance **and** sound. Today, he has a whole line of harps for sale. Micah has also designed the *nevel*, a harp with a soundboard, and the *kinnor* (much like a lyre) with ten strings. [47]

¶   *Aliyah* is the Hebrew word meaning "go up." It is not only the term used to depict the "going up" of celebrants to Jerusalem to celebrate the feasts of the LORD but is also used to describe the return of Israelites from the north, east, south and west to Israel, their homeland, which was promised to Abraham and prophesied to be restored to his seed in the last days. (See Isaiah 43:5-6; Jeremiah 16:14-16; Ezekiel 36:24-27.)

One day while working in the shop in Jerusalem, several rabbis came to the door and asked Shoshanna if they might come in. Without saying a word they looked at every harp on display. Suddenly they began to dance around the room with great joy. The Harrari's, in great suspense, wondered why they were so excited. When the rejoicing subsided, the rabbis told them that it had been prophesied that when the *kinnor* is again made in Jerusalem the *Mashiach* (Messiah) is near! Long ago David sang:

> "Rejoice in the LORD, O you righteous! For praise from the upright is beautiful. Praise the LORD with the harp; make melody to Him with an instrument of ten strings. Sing to Him a new song. Play skillfully with a shout of joy."[48]

These timeless words which rang from Y'shua's heart to David's are as timely now as they were when he penned them. The righteous of every generation are challenged to rejoice, sing a new song, praise the LORD on stringed instruments and shout for joy.

My Heart Is Fixed

My heart is fixed, O God,
My heart is fixed, O God,
I will sing and **zamar***!*
My heart is fixed, O God,
My heart is fixed, O God,
I will sing and **zamar***!*

Wake up, my glory,
Wake up, my glory,
Wake up, my psaltery and harp,
Wake up early,
Wake up early,
Wake up and **zamar** *our God.*

I will awaken the dawn with my song,
I will awaken the dawn with my song,
I will rise up early and **zamar** *my King,*
I will awaken the dawn with my song.

Wake up harp and lyre,
Wake up psaltery and flute,
Rise up early and **zamar** *our King,*
We will awaken the dawn with our song.

Love's Serenade
(Zamar ADONAI)

I will sing Your praises,
I will show my love for You,
I will bring my sacrifice
And worship at Your feet.
I'll sing of Your righteousness,
I'll sing of Your holiness,
I'll sing of Your loveliness,
Your faithfulness to me.

I'll bring my finest perfume
And pour sweet fragrance upon You,
With my tears of rejoicing
Anoint Your feet with my love.
Y'shua, I love You,
Y'shua, I bless You,
I praise and adore You,
You're my turtledove!

I will bow before You,
Pouring out my praises,
Worship as sweet incense
Ascending unto Your throne.
ADONAI, You're the Holy One,
ADONAI, You're the Mighty One,
ADONAI, the Victorious One,
I give myself in praise!

O sing to me Your love song,
Woo me by Your Spirit,
Serenading heaven's music,
Anointing me with fresh oil.

I worship at Your feet,
I worship at Your feet,
I worship ADONAI,
ADONAI, my King,

I bow down before You,
Love and adore You,
Praise and exalt ADONAI,
ADONAI, my King,
I worship ADONAI.

NOTES

1   Francis Brown, D.D., D.Litt. with the cooperation of S.R. Driver, D.D., Litt.D. and Charles A. Briggs, D.D., D.Litt., *The New Brown-Driver-Briggs-Gesenius Hebrew and English Lexicon* (Peabody, Massachusetts: Hendrickson Publishers, 1979), #2167, p. 263b. *Zamar* – make music in praise of God; pipe, play on a reed, make music, melody. Of singing to God, to His name. Sing to thee. Praise thee in song. Instrumental accompaniment. Of playing musical instruments.

2   James Strong, S.T.D., L.L.D., *Strong's Exhaustive Concordance of the Bible* (Madison, N.J.: James Strong, 1973), *Hebrew and Chaldee Dictionary* #2167, p. 35. *Zamar* – to touch the strings or parts of a musical instrument, i.e. play upon it; to make music, accompanied by the voice, hence to celebrate in song & music; give praise, sing forth praises, psalm.

3   I Chronicles 25:1-3

4   Strong, *Hebrew and Chaldee Dictionary* #5012, p. 75.

5   Psalm 144:1 — "teach my hands to **war** [Strong, *Hebrew and Chaldee Dictionary* #7128, p. 105. *Qerab (ker-ahb')* — hostile encounter, battle, war], and my fingers to **fight.**" [Strong, *Hebrew and Chaldee Dictionary* #4421, p. 67. *Milchamah (mil-khah-mah')* — a battle, the engagement, war, fight]."

6   Judges 5:3

7   I Samuel 10:5-6 CJB

8   II Kings 3:15

9   I Samuel 16:16

10 I Samuel 16:23

11 **Refreshed** - *ravach* – *(rah-vakh')*--breathe freely, revive, have ample room, be refreshed [Strong, *Hebrew and Chaldee Dictionary* #7304, p. 107.]; **Well**: #2895 - *towb* – *(tobe)* — be or do better, be or do good, be or do well. [Strong, *Hebrew and Chaldee Dictionary* #2895, p. 45.]

12 Psalm 66:2 KJV (paraphrased)

13 **glorious**: *kabod (kah-bode')* [Strong, *Hebrew and Chaldee Dictionary* #3519, p. 54]

14 Psalm 56:3

15 Psalm 138:8

16 II Corinthians 4:7

17 Psalm 61:8; 104:33; 146:2

18 Psalm 71:23

19 Isaiah 51:3 – **melody**: *zimrah* – *(zim-rah')* – a musical piece or song to be accompanied by an instrument – melody, psalm [Strong, *Hebrew and Chaldee Dictionary* #2172, p. 35. (From #2167 *zamar*)]

20 Psalm 81:2

21 Psalm 98:5

22 Amos 5:21, 23-24

23 I Corinthians 13:1

24 Exodus 15:2; Psalm 118:14; Isaiah 12:2 – **song** – zimrath – (zim-rahth') – instrumental music; praise; song. [Strong, *Hebrew and Chaldee Dictionary* #2176, p. 35. (From #2167 *zamar*)]

25 Psalm 118:14 and Isaiah 12:2b

26 zamir –(zah-meer)' –- fr 2167 – a song to be accompanied with instrumental music, psalm, psalmist, singing, song. [Strong, *Hebrew and Chaldee Dictionary* #2158, p. 35. (From #2167 *zamar*)]

27 Song of Solomon 2:12b CJB

28 II Samuel 23:1

29 Job 35:10

30 Psalm 119:54

31 Isaiah 24:16a

32 Thayer, *The New Thayer's Greek-English Lexicon of the New Testament* #5567, p. 31. *Psallo* – to rub, wipe; to handle, touch. A. to pluck off, pull out. B. to cause to vibrate by touching, to twang, to touch or strike the chord, to twang the strings of a musical instrument so that they gently vibrate; to play on a stringed instrument, to sing to the music of the harp; to sing a hymn, to celebrate the praises of God in song.

Strong, *Greek Dictionary of the New Testament* #5567, p. 78. *Psallo* – (psal'-lo) – prob. strengthened from *psao* (to rub or touch the surface; comp. #5597); to twitch or twang, i.e. to play on a stringed instrument (celebrate the divine worship with music and accompanying odes): Make melody, sing, sing psalms.

33 Ephesians 5:18 KJV

34 Ephesians 5:19 CJB

35 James 5:13

36 Psalm 18:49 CJB

37 Deuteronomy 32:43 CJB

38 Psalm 117:1 CJB

39 Isaiah 11:10 CJB

40 Romans 15:8-12 CJB

41 Psalm 18:49

42 John 21:25

43 Psalm 119:103; Song of Solomon 1:3 and 4:11

44 Dr. Frank T. Seekins, *Hebrew Word Pictures: How Does the Hebrew Alphabet Reveal Prophetic Truths?* (Phoenix, Arizona: Living Word Pictures, Inc., 1994, 2003), p.36, 38.

45 This instruction leads us to the conclusion that Habakkuk lived during the times when Temple worship was being practiced and that he gave this prophetic song to be ministered in the Temple.

46 Habakkuk 3:17-19

47 Website: House of Harrari, http://www.harrariharps.com

48 Psalm 33:1-3

Seven Expressions of the Bride

In summary, these seven praise expressions color and create a praise-picture that delights the Father's heart. Each of these expressions has a unique place in the procession of praise that brings us into His presence. In this psalm we find that

Hallel and *Shabach* lead us to the house of God.

Todah ministers to the LORD at the gates of the temple.

Tehillim and *Zamar* psalm to the LORD in the courts of the house of God.

Yadah and *Barak* position us for worship in the Holy of Holies.

Y'shua instructs people of every tribe, tongue and nation to offer all of the expressions of praise by the leading of the *Ruach HaKodesh*.[1] Placing the seven Hebrew words of praise in His psalm we sing:

> *[Hallel]* and *[shabach]** the LORD, all you lands!
> Serve the LORD with gladness;
> Come before His presence with singing.
> Know that the LORD, He is God;
> It is He who has made us,
> And not we ourselves;
> We are His people
> And the sheep of His pasture.
> Enter into His gates with ***todah***
> And into His courts with ***tehillah***.
> ***Yadah*** Him
> And ***barak*** His name.
> For the LORD is good;

---

*   I have placed *hallel* and *shabach* here by their definitions. The literal Hebrew word that begins Psalm 100 is *ruwa* (pronounced *roo-ah'*) meaning "Shout for joy to God in public worship with music and sacrifice, raise a shout, give a blast with clarion or horn, shout a war-cry or alarm of battle, sound a signal for war or march, shout in triumph, shout in applause." (*The New Brown-Driver-Briggs-Gesenius Hebrew-English Lexicon*, #7321, p. 929b.) These definitions are also descriptions of *hallel* and *shabach*. The triumphant shouted message of *shabach* here is the "Song of the Ages:" "The LORD is good; His mercy is everlasting, and His truth endures to all generations!" Remember that Psalm 136 in which this "song" is repeated over and over is called the "Great Hallel!" See the chapters titled "Hallel" and "Shabach.

His mercy is everlasting,
And His truth endures to all generations.
(Sung to the accompaniment of *zamar*)†

Psalm 100 ~ Call to Unified Praise

Y'shua composed this psalm from eternity and then sent it out inviting all nations to His throne. With the invitation He included the "Praise-Way" to His Presence. In this psalm we see His people, the sheep of His pasture, rejoicing in His never-ending goodness and mercy. This is a people who walk in perfected praise.

Can you imagine what perfected praise in all its expressions will look like? We see the Bride dressed in white, the redeemed, the image of the Son, entering the presence of Him who sits on the throne and the One Who died for all. Gladness fills every heart and there is unbroken joy. With uplifted hands,‡ nation after nation ascends the steps to the Temple. Singing songs and extolling Yahweh's mighty salvation, every knee bows and every tongue confesses that Y'shua is Lord. As the brilliantly-hued standards of the nations wave in the wind, the saved from every tribe, language, people and nation shout His praises. Accompanied by myriads of instruments,§ the sound of music rises with the crescendo of the nations' praise. With sacrifices of joy and thanksgiving they process to the throne of the King of kings. Kneeling in adoration, they bless His holy Name. Psalm 100, ordained by Y'shua, has become a reality – a rainbow of *Shekinah*.

Through the prophetic lens of time, we witness the nations *hallel*-ing Him with total abandonment in dancing, rejoicing and every form of exuberant celebration. The nations' loud messages of *shabach* and *hallel* are heard as the sound of many rushing waters, a roar of glorious praise to their God. Radiating from His people, we see the light of His presence, His resurrection glory, itself an offering of *hallel*.

---

† Traditionally, when performed publicly, the psalms were sung to the accompaniment of instruments.

‡ *Todah*

§ *Zamar*

The nations are in His holy Presence. Resting in the knowledge that Elohim is their Maker, they have become beautifully shaped vessels of *tehillah*. They are His finished work.

Breaking out in chorus, multitude upon multitude of saints *yadah* the Song of the Ages: **"For the LORD is good; His mercy is everlasting,"** a witness that **"His truth endures to all generations."** The salvation of those whose hope is in Him is now faith's reality. We see the *barak* of the nations; in awe and majesty they kneel to honor the LORD of glory and receive the blessing of eternal life. Psalm 100 has become a promise fulfilled, a dream come true. What our eyes now see and our ears now hear is the fulfillment of the longing of our hearts. We hear the beginning of the eternal song of the nations, the forever songs of Y'shua.

This is the time of the culmination of all things. Like John, we glimpse into eternity. We see and experience the new heavens and earth.[2] Gazing in wonder and holy delight, we behold the city of our God, the New Jerusalem. We are there. The bride is prepared and adorned.

> "…I saw a new heaven and a new earth; for the first heaven and the first earth had passed away. Also there was no more sea. And I, John, saw the holy city, New Jerusalem, coming down out of heaven from God, prepared as a bride adorned for her husband. And I heard a loud voice from heaven saying, 'Behold, the tabernacle of God is with men, and He will dwell with them, and they shall be His people….'"[3]

> Oh come, let us worship and bow down!
> Let us kneel before the LORD our Maker.[4]

The Garden Restored

Life in the garden is restored; the garden is now a city. The Lamb reigns. The river of life flows from the throne of God. Sparkling like liquid diamonds, it dances to the voice of praise. The tree of life, standing as a holy sentinel, yields its new and diverse fruit each month. Its healing leaves dance and rejoice in heaven's wind, beckoning every nation, "Come." Like garments, righteousness, peace and joy clothe the servants of the LORD. Light rules. Righteousness has kissed peace.[5] It is unending day. Darkness is broken and is no more. We see His face and His name is on our foreheads. We reign with Him.[6]

Hallel YAH! Praise His holy name forever and ever!

NOTES

1   *Ruach HaKodesh* – Hebrew for the Holy Spirit, the breath of God.

2   Isaiah 66:1-2 tells us that in the time of the new heavens and the new earth, all flesh will go up before the LORD and keep the weekly feast of Shabbat and the monthly feast of Rosh Kodesh (the new moon).

"'For as the new heavens and the new earth which I will make shall remain before Me,' says the LORD, 'So shall your descendants and your name remain. And it shall come to pass that from one New Moon to another, and from one Sabbath to another, all flesh shall come to worship before Me,' says the LORD."

These divine appointments (feasts) of the LORD have been holy rehearsals (convocations) since the Torah was given to Moses on Mount Sinai. Now what has been rehearsed for thousands of years is a present reality. Throughout eternity we will sing the psalms of Y'shua – including the Psalms of Ascent, the Great Hallel and the Psalms of Hallel, the Song of Moses and the Song of the Lamb - to the King of kings, Lord of lords and God of gods, to Yahweh Elohim, Creator and Lord of heaven and earth.

3   Rev 21:1-3a

4   Psalm 95:6a

5   Psalm 85:10

6   Revelation 22:1-5

EPILOGUE

Who Wrote Psalm 100?

Shortly before this manuscript was due to go to press, some fascinating information came into my hands. I believe these final tidbits are the crowning jewels of confirmation on the revelation and unveiling of Psalm 100 in this work – the finishing touch of the Master's hand. It seems that the human writer of this psalm, along with other interesting facts, **is** known by the people of "The Book," Israel, although none of this appears in any of the English Bibles I own. First, from Rabbi Avrohom Chaim Feuer, I learned the name of the Israelite who penned this psalm:

> "The fourth book of the Psalms begins with eleven consecutive works composed by **Moses** (Psalms 90-100). Rashi[1] explains that these correspond to the eleven blessings which Moses bestowed upon eleven of the tribes as enumerated in Deuteronomy 33. The tribe of Simeon was excluded from Moses' blessings because the Simeonites had led the orgy that resulted in the death of thousands of Jews (see Numbers 24:1-15)."[2]

Next, *The ArtScroll Tehillim* reveals the use of Psalm 100 in the Temple:

> "During Temple times, a person would bring a *todah, a thanksgiving-offering,* whenever he survived a life-threatening situation. This psalm was chanted during the service. Indeed, every human being goes through any number of potential dangers in the course of his life, dangers of which he most often is not even aware; for all of these he is duty-bound to render homage to God."[3]

I want to emphasize here that the "Thanksgiving Offering" or *Todah* was a voluntary or freewill offering brought by an individual who had endured great danger or distress and emerged safe and victorious.

Finally, Rabbi Feuer quotes Rabbi Hirsch as he delineates the prophetic nature of Psalm 100:

> "Rabbi Hirsch explains that this song of thanksgiving deals with the gratitude that will be due to God in the Messianic Age, when the world has reached perfection. Psalm 100 serves as a finale to the previous psalms concerning the approach of the Messianic Era."[4]

We can see that the individual's triumphant thanksgiving offering sets the pattern for corporate *todah*. For example, the nations who have victoriously endured and emerged from the great tribulation which precedes the Messianic Era will hear the call of the Psalmist of psalmists. Then, ringing out ecstatic, joyful shouts to the King of kings, they will enter His gates with the ultimate sacrifice of *todah* and partake of kingdom joy, rest and blessing. Psalm 100 is truly the Song of the Kingdom!

Rabbi Feuer also notes that Psalm 100 (written by Moses) is dedicated by Moses to the tribe of Asher whose name means "blessed, happy." This psalm is one of great joy and thanksgiving. No mention of judgment or anything negative clouds its message. The psalm's concluding verses ring out the "Song of the Ages" testifying that "the LORD is good; His mercy is everlasting; and His truth *endures* to all generations."[5]

Could it be that Psalm 100, the crowning twelfth stanza of the Song of Moses,[6] will be sung by the saints who have survived the great tribulation? And is it also possible that the Song of Moses (Y'shua's song given to Moses) is one and the same as the Song of the Lamb sung in Revelation 15?[7]

> "And I saw *something* like a sea of glass mingled with fire, and those who have the victory over the beast, over his image and over his mark *and* over the number

of his name, standing on the sea of glass, having harps of God. They sing the **song of Moses**, the servant of God, and the **song of the Lamb**...."

NOTES

1   Rabbi Shlomo Yitzhaki, better known by the acronym Rashi (February 22, 1040 – July 13, 1105), was a rabbi from France, famed as the author of the first comprehensive commentaries on the Talmud, Torah and Tanakh (Hebrew Bible). (Wikipedia, the free encyclopedia, http://en.wikipedia.org/wiki/ Rashi)

2   Rabbi Avrohom Chaim Feuer, *Tehillim,* Psalms – A New Translation with a Commentary Anthologized from Talmudic, Midrashic and Rabbinic sources, (Brooklyn, NY: Mesorah Publications, Ltd., 1985), p. 1121.

3   *The Artscroll Tehillim,* Trans. Rabbi Hillel Danziger, (Brooklyn, New York: Mesorah Publications, Ltd., 1988), p. 214.

4   Feuer, p. 1215.

5   Psalm 100:5

6   Moses' song includes Exodus 15, Deuteronomy 32 and Psalms 90-100.

7   Revelation 15:2-3

GLOSSARY

Abba – an affectionate way to say "father," hence, "Dear father," "Dad," or even "Daddy."

ADONAI – literally, "my Lord," a word the Hebrew Bible uses to refer to God. When in large and small capital letters, it represents the tetragrammaton, the Hebrew name of God consisting of the four letters, Yud-Heh-Vav-Heh (YHWH), sometimes rendered in English as Jehovah, Yehovah, Yahweh or Yahveh, but usually as LORD.

Amidah – Hebrew for "standing." It refers to the "Standing Prayer," the eighteen blessings recited regularly in public and private worship. Also known as the *Shemoneh Esreh* ((Eighteen Blessings).

Barukh – Hebrew for "blessed." The name given to the first part of a *b'rakhah* (blessing).

B'rakhah, b'rakhot (plural) – Hebrew for "blessing." *B'rakhot* is also the name of the first tractate of the Talmud.

B'rit – Hebrew for "covenant."

B'rit Hadashah – Hebrew for New Covenant, New Testament.

Elohim – Hebrew for "God." Actually it is plural in form and means both "gods" and "judges." "In the beginning *Elohim* created the heavens and the earth." Genesis 1:1

Hanukkah – Hebrew for "dedication." The Feast of Dedication is the festival honoring the Temple rededication by the Maccabees (164 B.C.E.) after its profanation under Seleucid king Antiochus IV. It is celebrated by lighting candles or lamps on eight succeeding days by means of a "servant" light, until on the eighth day all eight are lit.

K'tuvim – The Writings: the third of the three sections of the *Tanakh* (the Old Testament), consisting of Psalms, Proverbs, Job, the Five

Scrolls (Song of Songs, Ruth, Esther, Lamentations, Ecclesiastes), Daniel, Ezra, Nehemiah and Chronicles.

Mashiach – Hebrew for "Messiah," "anointed," "anointed one."

Mitzvah, mitzvot (plural) – Hebrew for "commandment" given by God. A good deed.

Nevi'im – The Prophets. The second of the three parts of the *Tanakh* including the Early Prophets (the historical books), namely, Joshua, Judges, Samuel and Kings; and the Later Prophets, namely, Isaiah, Jeremiah, Ezekiel, and the Twelve "minor prophets."

Pesach – Passover. The feast which celebrates the Exodus of the Jewish nation from Egypt under the leadership of *Moshe* (Moses). It is, along with *Shavu'ot and Sukkot,* one of the three pilgrim festivals when Jews were to come to *Yerushalayim* (Jerusalem).

Rosh HaShanah – Hebrew for "Head of the Year." The traditional Jewish New Year, which is the beginning of a ten-day period of repentance leading up to *Yom Kippur.* It is also called the *Feast of Trumpets* or *Yom Teruah,* a Day of Blowing.

Ruach HaKodesh – Hebrew for "The Holy Spirit."

Sh'khinah – The indwelling presence of God associated with His glory. It went before the people as a cloud by day and fire by night. It came upon the Tabernacle at its completion and the Temple at its dedication. It is said to be present with God's people when they pray and study *Torah.*

Shabbat – Hebrew for "[day of] rest; Sabbath." *Shabbat* is the seventh day of the week (from Friday sunset to Saturday sunset). God commanded Israel to cease from work on this day and to assemble for worship (Exodus 20:8-11; Leviticus 23:3).

Shalom – Hebrew for "peace, tranquility, safety, well-being, welfare, health, contentment, success, comfort, wholeness and integrity."

"Shalom!" is a common greeting.

Shavu'ot – The Feast of Weeks, since it comes seven weeks after Passover. It is also called Pentecost (from the Greek) since one counts 50 days after Passover. It is one of the three "Pilgrim Festivals" when Jews were expected to celebrate before God in *Yerushalayim* (Jerusalem). The other two are *Pesach* and *Sukkot*.

Sh'ol – (Sheol, Hades, hell) Afterlife; the netherworld. The place of the dead.

Sukkot – The Feast of Booths, or Tabernacles, commemorating Israel's forty years in the desert dwelling in *sukkot* (booths) before entering the Promised Land (Leviticus 23:33-43; Deut. 8). It is one of the three pilgrim festivals when Jews were expected to go up to *Yerushalayim* (Jerusalem).

Tanakh – Hebrew acronym from the first letters of the words *Torah* (Teaching), *Nevi'im* (Prophets), and *K'tuvim* (Writings); ie., the Hebrew Scriptures (see Luke 24:44). (Also known as "The Old Testament")

Tefillah – Hebrew for "prayer."

Tefillin – Hebrew for "prayers." Also, small leather boxes containing Scripture on parchments that are bound to the forehead and upper right arm of a Jew during morning prayers (except on *Shabbat* and festivals). The purpose of *tefillin* is devotional (Deut. 6:8).

Tehillim – Psalms.

Tetragrammaton – The ineffable Name of God, composed of four letters (*Yud-Heh-Vav-Heh*) – (YHWH or YHVH). It is variously translated LORD, Yahweh, Yahveh, Jehovah, Yehovah and as the title *ADONAI* (in the Complete Jewish Bible).

Torah – Hebrew for "Teaching." Torah refers to the five books of Moses (Genesis, Exodus, Leviticus, Numbers, Deuteronomy). It is translated by the Greek word *nomos* meaning "Law" in English.

Y'shua –(Yeshua) Variant of "Y'hoshua" (Joshua). It means "Y-H-V-H saves," "Yah" or "Yahweh" saves." *Y'shua* is Jesus' Hebrew name. It is also the masculine form of *yeshu'ah* meaning "salvation." *Yeshu'ah* is used in a word play on Yeshua's name at Luke 2:30.

Yerushalayim - the Hebrew word for Jerusalem, capital of Israel (*Eretz-Yisra'el*).

BIBLIOGRAPHY

Ashkenaz, Nusach. *The Complete ArtScroll Siddur.* Trans. Rabbi Nosson Scherman. Brooklyn, NY: Mesorah Publications ltd., 1988.

Brown, Francis, D.D., D.Litt. - Driver, S. R., D.D., Litt.D.- Briggs, Charles A., D.D., D.Litt. *The New Brown-Driver-Briggs-Gesenius Hebrew and English Lexicon.* Peabody,Massachusetts: Hendrickson Publishers, 1979.

Cloud, Bill. *The Wisdom of Hebrew,* Session 8 on *Yud.* Shoreshim Resources, 114 Stewart Rd, PMB 431, Cleveland, TN 37312, www. billcloud.org.

Complete Jewish Bible. Trans. David H. Stern. Clarksville, Maryland USA, Jerusalem, Israel: Jewish New Testament Publications, Inc., 1998.

Easton's Bible Dictionary, "Ephah," http://www.eastonsbible dictionary.com.

Edersheim, Alfred. *The Temple and Its Services.* Grand Rapids, MI: Wm. B. Eerdmans Publishing Company, Reprinted August 1987.

Forst, Rabbi Benyamin. *The Laws of B'rachos.* New York: Mesorah, 1990.

Garr, John D., Ph.D. *Bless You! Restoring the Power of Biblical Blessing.* Atlanta, Georgia: Restoration Foundation, 2005.

Hebrew-Greek Key Word Study Bible: King James Version. Chattanooga, TN: AMG Publishers, 1991

House of Harrari, http://www.harrariharps.com.

Lipson, Irene. *Blessing the King of the Universe*. Baltimore, MD: Lederer Books, 2004.

Newman, Louis I. *The Hasidic Anthology*. New York and London: Scribner's Sons, 1934.

Seekins, Dr. Frank T. *Hebrew Word Pictures: How Does the Hebrew Alphabet Reveal Prophetic Truths?* Phoenix, Arizona: Living Word Pictures, Inc., 1994, 2003.

Strong, James, S.T.D., L.L.D. *Strong's Exhaustive Concordance of the Bible*. Madison, N.J.: James Strong, 1973.

Tehillim, Psalms – A New Translation with a Commentary Anthologized from Talmudic, Midrashic and Rabbinic Sources. Trans. Rabbi Avrohom Chaim Feuer. Brooklyn, NY: Mesorah Publications, Ltd., 1985.

Thayer, Joseph Henry, D.D. *The New Thayer's Greek-English Lexicon of the New Testament*. Peabody, Massachusetts: Hendrickson Publishers, 1981.

The Amplified Bible. Grand Rapids, Michigan: Zondervan Bible Publishers, 1987.

The ArtScroll Tehillim. Trans. Rabbi Hillel Danziger. Brooklyn, NY: Mesorah Publications, Ltd., 1988

The Holy Bible: New International Version. London, Sydney, Auckland: Hodder & Stoughton, 1973.

The Holy Bible: The New King James Version. Nashville, TN: Thomas Nelson Publishers, 1999.

The New Inductive Study Bible: Updated New American Standard Bible. Eugene, Oregon: Harvest House Publishers, 2000.

The Power New Testament: Revealing Jewish Roots. Trans. William J. Morford. Lexington, SC: Rev. William J. Morford, 2003.

The Scriptures. Northriding, South Africa: Institute for Scripture Research (PTY) Ltd, 1998.

Unger, Merrill F. *The New Unger's Bible Dictionary.* Chicago, Illinois: Moody Press, 1998.

Wigram, George V. *The Englishman's Hebrew Concordance of the Old Testament.* Peabody, Massachusetts: Hendrickson Publishers, 2001. (Reprinted from the third edition originally published by Samuel Bagster and Sons, London, 1874, with *Strong's* numbering added by Hendrickson Publishers)

Wikipedia, the free encyclopedia, "Sheba" and "Rashi." http://www.wikipedia.org.

Nancy E. Morgan is the founder and director of Daystar Ministry International.

A gifted teacher, Nancy has ministered in many nations, including the United States. Her teaching emphasizes the foundational roots of biblical praise and offers deep insights into the Messiah's heart for His bride.

An anointed psalmist, Nancy has written many songs expressing the heights and depths of worship. She holds a BA degree in Music with a concentration in piano from Armstrong Atlantic State University, Savannah, GA. She also has a Bachelor of Religious Arts in Biblical Studies and received her ordination from Jacksonville Theological Seminary.

Nancy has spent many years studying and searching the scriptures, especially the Psalms. Her writing and music is her response to Y'shua's anointing on her life. In 2003 Nancy published Lift Up Your Eyes, a teaching/songbook, on the Psalms of Ascent. That same year she released her first CD, "Daystar Arise!" with an accompanying songbook. This volume, Created to Praise: Seven Expressions of the Bride which is her most recent work, further explores the multi-dimensional power of praise.

Nancy resides in Savannah, Georgia.

For speaking engagements or seminars you may contact Nancy Morgan at any of the following:

Daystar Ministry International
PO Box 15115
Savannah, GA 31416
Office: 912-354-3175
Fax: 912-354-8075
E-mail: bookings@daystararise.com

Daystar Ministry International
www.daystararise.com

For Volume Discounts, Please Contact Daystar Ministry At The Above Numbers.